W9-AVR-849

# THE ESSENTIALS OF CALIFORNIA MENTAL HEALTH LAW

A STRAIGHTFORWARD GUIDE FOR CLINICIANS OF ALL DISCIPLINES

Other Books in This Series

*The Essentials of Massachusetts Mental Health Law*
Stephen H. Behnke, James T. Hilliard

A NORTON PROFESSIONAL BOOK

# THE ESSENTIALS OF CALIFORNIA MENTAL HEALTH LAW

## A STRAIGHTFORWARD GUIDE FOR CLINICIANS OF ALL DISCIPLINES

STEPHEN H. BEHNKE, J.D., PH.D.
JAMES PREIS, J.D.
R. TODD BATES, J.D.

W. W. NORTON & COMPANY • NEW YORK • LONDON

Cases involving law and mental health can be exceedingly complex, highly specific, and require legal expertise that no book, pamphlet, or review will provide. In addition, laws change over time. You should therefore not use this book as a substitute for consultation with an attorney knowledgable in mental health law.

Copyright © 1998 by Stephen Behnke

All rights reserved

Printed in the United States of America

First Edition

For information about permission to reproduce selections
from this book, write to
Permissions, W. W. Norton & Company, Inc., 500 Fifth Avenue,
New York, NY 10110.

**Library of Congress Cataloging-in-Publication Data**

Behnke, Stephen H., 1958–
The essentials of California mental health law : a straightforward guide for
clinicians of all disciplines / Stephen H. Behnke, James Preis & R. Todd Bates.
p.  cm.
"A Norton professional book."
Includes bibliographical references and index.
**ISBN 0-393-70250-2**
1. Mental health laws—California. I. Preis, James. II. Bates, R. Todd. III. Title
KFC620.B44   1998
344.794′044—dc21   98-26013
CIP

W. W. Norton & Company, Inc., 500 Fifth Avenue, New York, N.Y. 10110
http://www.wwnorton.com

W. W. Norton & Company Ltd., 10 Coptic Street, London WC1A 1PU

1 2 3 4 5 6 7 8 9 0

To my dedicated colleagues and friends on Team 1 of the Massachusetts Mental Health Center Day Hospital.

*—S.H.B.*

To my wife, Debbie, and children, Annie and Johnny, for their love and support; and to the memory of Rob Peters, a friend and colleague at Mental Health Advocacy Services with whom I had worked for many years.

*—J.P.*

To my wife, Marianne, for her patience and support.

*—R.T.B.*

# CONTENTS

# ACKNOWLEDGMENTS

We would like to thank the many people who provided their encouragement and support as we wrote *The Essentials of California Mental Health Law*. A number of friends and colleagues read and commented upon drafts of the manuscript. We would like to thank William Arroyo, M.D., Richard N. Bates, J.D., Carole Bender, M.S.W., J.D., Paul Bong, M.D., Dan Pone, J.D., and Nancy Shea, J.D., for their thoughtful suggestions.

We would like to thank the *Massachusetts Psychological Association Quarterly* for allowing us to use material from Stephen H. Behnke's legal column.

We would also like to thank the staff of Mental Health Advocacy Services, Inc. for their support and assistance on this project.

Elyn Saks has been a friend and colleague to all of us. We would like to thank her for her invaluable assistance in writing this book.

James T. Hilliard, who coauthored the Massachusetts volume and is an enormously gifted mental health law attorney, has given the *Essentials of Mental Health Law* series a direction and focus. We are all indebted to him for his insight into mental health law, his clarity in thinking about these challenging questions, and his wisdom in knowing what it means to do the right thing.

Finally, we would like to thank our families for their love, encouragement, and understanding.

# INTRODUCTION

The idea for this book arose from our teaching mental health professionals about how best to address problems in risk management. The most
frequent comment from trainees and experienced clinicians alike—that
it is enormously helpful to have laws relevant to clinical practice explained in a simple and straightforward way—suggested the need for a
book to orient mental health professionals to their legal rights and responsibilities.

The purpose of this book is to set forth, in a clear and concise manner,
the laws most relevant to mental health practice in California. The book
is also designed to explain and demonstrate how these laws apply to the
many problems mental health professionals encounter on a day-to-day
basis. The format will be useful both to the student trainee and to the
more senior clinician; indeed, the majority of treaters find it difficult to
keep up to date on how the California legislature and courts have changed
the legal landscape of clinical practice. Lawyers, as well, may find the
explanations of state laws governing mental health practice useful to their
understanding of this interesting and ever-changing field.

*The Essentials of California Mental Health Law* is divided into two
parts. The three chapters of part I serve as a general introduction to the
law. The first chapter, A Brief Introduction to the Law, explains where the
different laws affecting clinical practice come from and, should a treater
feel particularly bold, how she would go about finding an actual statute,
court decision, or regulation.

The second chapter, *Tarasoff* and its California Progeny, takes an actual statute and illustrates how a law "works." This chapter sets forth the
philosophy of the California *Tarasoff* law, explains what the law requires,

and demonstrates how different parts of the law fit together like building blocks to form a coherent whole. *Tarasoff* and its California Progeny explains *why* the law was written, *what* the law says, and *how* the law goes about saying it. Any law can be analyzed in this manner, as we hope will become clear throughout the book.

The third and final chapter in part I discusses the set of laws and regulations perhaps most central to actual practice, those that pertain to privacy, confidentiality, and testimonial privilege. *Privacy* is an individual's right to make important life decisions without unreasonable interference from others, most especially the government. Part of the right to privacy is the right to decide with whom to share—and not to share—personal information. *Confidentiality* is the right to have communications with a therapist kept between the therapist and client. *Testimonial privilege*, often referred to simply as *privilege*, is the patient's right to prevent a therapist from divulging confidential information in a legal proceeding. Chapter 3 includes a discussion of mandatory reporting laws; these laws require a mental health professional to break confidentiality when certain circumstances are present. The actual texts of the confidentiality, privilege, and mandatory reporting laws most central to clinical practice are contained in appendix A. By the end of part I the clinician should have a good sense of how a law can be read, understood, and applied in her work.

Part II consists of 175 questions clinicians often ask about California mental health law. We have divided the questions into ten topic headings. Topics range from the standard for placing an individual in a psychiatric hospital against his will, to the rules of confidentiality that govern consultations, to the legal implications of serving as a non-MD therapist's med-backup, to the wisdom of meeting with a family after a patient commits suicide. Answers to these questions describe in a clear, direct manner how the law affects clinical practice.

Appendix B contains several examples of written materials that clinicians may find helpful in their practice. These materials include an informed consent letter to begin a psychotherapy, a letter terminating a therapy with a difficult patient, and a reply to a licensing board letter of complaint. A sample subpoena is also included.

At the heart of this book is our belief that good patient care and knowledge of the law go hand in hand. Our experience is that, far from restricting or inhibiting clinical practice, knowing the essentials of California mental health law will free treaters from much undue—and unwarranted—anxiety about their legal rights and responsibilities. We hope that such freedom will allow clinicians to concentrate on what they do best and enjoy most—treat patients.*

*A brief word about terminology. Solely for ease of reading, "client" and "patient" are used interchangeably, as are "clinician," "treater," "therapist," and "mental health professional." By "client" and "patient" we mean any individual who seeks services from a mental health professional. By the latter four terms we mean any individual who provides such services.

# Part I

## *An Introduction to the Law*

# 1

# A Brief Introduction to the Law

The American system of law is divided into two layers: federal and state. Federal laws affect the United States as a whole, while state laws are specific to a particular state or commonwealth. As a citizen of California, you are also a citizen of the United States. You are thus accorded the rights and privileges, as well as the responsibilities, afforded by both federal and state law. While our discussion will focus primarily on laws made in California, we will also mention important federal laws that affect California citizens.

California laws may be similar to laws found in other states, but always keep in mind that any state law is binding only for that state. Because each state is its own sovereignty, each is free to decide for itself what laws to enact, which means that things can get a bit confusing, since the 50 states may have 50 different laws governing the same topic. Thus, always note whether a law is a *state* law; if so, then, should you reside in that same state, the law applies to you and you are bound to follow it. If the law belongs to another state, then it is not binding on you, although you will want to know what your state says about the particular topic.

Our discussion will address, and explain how to cite, four types of laws: (1) the Constitution; (2) statutes enacted by the legislature; (3) regulations promulgated by administrative agencies; and (4) decisions made by courts. Although the hierarchical relationships between the Constitution, statutes, regulations, and court decisions can become quite complicated, each of these four is nevertheless considered part of the law.

*An outline of the discussion on how to cite California laws can be found on page 8.*

The first and most important law in the state and in the federal government is the Constitution. A constitution is that document whose provisions are sometimes referred to as "supreme," because no law can be enacted that conflicts with anything the constitution says. Many times a constitution will have a preamble that invokes its philosophical or moral basis. Both the Constitution of the United States and the Constitution of the State of California, for example, begin, "We, the People . . ." and thus make clear that their moral basis is found in the assent of the people. Simply put, a constitution is the touchstone by which a law will be deemed legitimate or illegitimate, and this is why our starting point for discussing law begins with recognizing the importance, indeed supremacy, of the Constitution.

The second category of laws are "statutes." Generally, statutes are written by the legislature whom we elect; the United States Congress is the legislature for the federal government. The representatives gather, spend much time collecting information, even more time arguing with one another, and then write a bill that, if signed by the Governor or the President, becomes a law. In California, the initiative process also allows citizens to create statutes without the aid of the legislature. A California law is sometimes referred to in an abbreviated form (called a "citation"), such as "Welf. & Inst. Code," which stands for "Welfare and Institutions Code." "Welf. & Inst. Code §5150," for example, the statutory reference to the section on involuntary psychiatric treatment in the Lanterman-Petris-Short Act, stands for section 5150 of the Welfare and Institutions Code. Other examples include "Evid. Code §1017" (section 1017 of the Evidence Code) and "Cal. Civ. Code §56.10" (section 56.10 of the California Civil Code).

The third group of laws is not written by the legislature at all and, in fact, these laws are not even called laws. These laws are called "regulations." Regulations are written by different groups of people, often those in charge of agencies, such as the California Department of Mental Health and the Federal Food and Drug Administration. Regulations get their legitimacy through the legislature, which generally has neither the time nor the expertise to get into the nitty-gritty of running an administrative agency. It is as if the legislature were to say, "Look, we can provide the general contours of your agency's work, but really know very little about what your agency does on a day-to-day basis. We therefore delegate to you the authority to run the agency and to carry out your mission in the way that makes most sense. You fill in the details about how things will get done." The details are the regulations written by the people who run the agency; generally, the legislature writes a statute authorizing the agency to write its regulations. Regulations must be consistent with the statutes they are designed to carry out. A California regulation is referred to by the abbreviation "Cal. Code Regs.," which stand for "California Code of Regulations." "15 Cal. Code Regs. §1207," for example, refers to the California Code of Regulations, title 15, section 1207. (The actual form of this citation may vary slightly; Cal. Code Regs. t. 15 §1207, for example, also refers to section 1207 of title 15. Sometimes the California Code of Regulations is abbreviated "CCR.")

The fourth and final group of laws are those found in court decisions. Laws that arise from court decisions are referred to as "case law." Case law is what many people most associate with the law, even though, as we've seen, much law comes from elsewhere. (In fact, technically speaking, no law should ever derive from the decision of a court, because the purpose of a court is to *interpret*, rather than to write, a law.)

In most instances relevant to our purposes, case law comes from a particular kind of court, an "appellate court." A court is an appellate court when it deals with cases "on appeal," that is, when someone doesn't like the decision of a lower court (usually a trial court) and so asks a higher court to review the lower court's decision. The holding of an appellate court is referred to as "law" because, like the Constitution, statutes, and regulations, the court's holding is legally binding; the court's holding is referred to as "case law" because it derives from a case. "Common law," a phrase you may have heard, is case law that has developed over a long, long time—many centuries, in fact.

In California there are two appellate courts: the California Court of Appeal and the California Supreme Court. The Supreme Court, the highest court in the state, is where one appeals a decision of the California Court of Appeal, although in certain circumstances a case can be appealed directly from a trial court to the State Supreme Court. In most instances, then, the Supreme Court is "the appeals court to the appeals court." The Supreme Court is thus the highest of the three tiers in the state's judicial system. Likewise, in the federal system there are federal appeals courts to which one may appeal the decision of a lower federal court. Above the federal appeals courts is the United States Supreme Court. The United States Supreme Court is the highest federal court.

California cases are cited in one of two ways: "Cal. App." is the abbreviation for cases from the California Court of Appeal; "Cal." is the abbreviation for cases of the California Supreme Court. The numbers before and after the initials refer to the volume, page number, and date of the opinion. 5 Cal. App. 3d 584 (1991), for example, means that the opinion was written by the California Court of Appeal in 1991, and can be found in volume 5, page 584 of the third edition of the *California Appellate Reports*, the series of volumes containing the opinions of the California Court of Appeal. 54 Cal. 3d 56 (1991) means that the opinion was written by the California Supreme Court in 1991, and can be found in volume 54, page 56, of the third edition of the *California Reports*, the series of volumes containing the opinions of the California Supreme Court. (Both the *California Reports* and the *California Appellate Reports* are currently in their fourth edition.) It is important to remember that when you see the abbreviation "Cal.," you will be reading an opinion of the California *Supreme* Court; "Cal. App." tells you the opinion was written by the California Court *of Appeal*, the court one step below the Supreme Court.

The laws we have discussed—the constitutions, statutes, regulations, and case law—can all be found in law libraries that are available to anyone who wishes to use them. Each county in the state has a trial court with its own library. In addition, most law schools have their own libraries that are open to the public. You should feel free to browse to your heart's content. If you'd like to find a law, simply go to the reference librarians, people who are more than happy—and sometimes literally ecstatic—to help you find what you're looking for. There are also numerous Web sites on the Internet that provide access to legal materials.

Our discussion of laws is not complete without mention of professional codes of ethical conduct. Codes of ethics are not considered law. They are written by private associations and may be amended without the consent or approval of an elected representative, judge, or government employee. Nevertheless, codes of ethics do establish acceptable standards of conduct and may be adopted by state licensing boards. Section 2936 of the Business and Professions Code, for example, provides that the California Board of Psychology "shall . . . establish standards of ethical conduct relating to the practice of psychology," and, in doing so, may consider the *Ethical Principles* of the American Psychological Association (1992). In addition, section 2960 of the Business and Professions Code states that a psychologist can be sanctioned by the Board if she is found to have deviated from her profession's code of ethics as adopted by the licensing board. For this reason, it behooves a mental health professional to be intimately familiar with his or her profession's code of ethical conduct, and to think of that code as if it were law because, in a way, it is—it is the law of the profession.

One final comment. As comprehensive as our discussions will be, there are probably one or two things that we will not cover but that you would learn if you spent $100,000 and three years in law school. Should you find yourself faced with a legal question, *consult a lawyer who has expertise in mental health law.* Cases involving law and mental health can be exceedingly complex and require legal expertise that no book, pamphlet, or review will provide. Educating yourself about the law by reading statutes and court decisions is an enormously worthwhile endeavor. Educating yourself about brain surgery is enormously worthwhile as well. But don't go after that tumor with your Swiss army knife.

# LAWS AFFECTING MENTAL HEALTH PRACTICE

I. Constitution
A. Supreme law of the land.
B. No law may conflict with the Constitution.

II. Statutes
A. Written by the legislature
1. United States Congress for federal laws
2. California legislature for California laws
B. California statutes referred to as, e.g., Welf. & Inst. Code §5150
(California Welfare and Institutions Code, section 5150)

III. Regulations
A. Written by agencies, with authority from the legislature
B. California regulations referred to as, e.g., 15 Cal. Code Regs. §1207
(California Code of Regulations, title 15, section 1207)

IV. Cases
A. Generally written by appellate courts
B. California cases referred to as, e.g.:
1. 54 Cal. 3d 56 (1991)
(1991 opinion of the California Supreme Court, found in volume 54 of the third edition of the *California Reports*, at page 56)
2. 5 Cal. App. 3d 584 (1991)
(1991 opinion of the California Court of Appeal, found in volume 5 of the third edition of the *California Appellate Reports*, at page 584)

V. Codes of ethics
A. Written by professional associations
B. Establish standards of conduct for profession
C. According to California law, may be used as a guide for regulatory boards (e.g., §§2936 and 2960 of the Business and Professions Code allow the California Board of Psychology to look to *Ethical Principles* of the American Psychological Association)

# 2

# *TARASOFF* AND ITS CALIFORNIA PROGENY

Most clinicians have heard the word "Tarasoff," usually uttered with some understandable, yet unfortunate, combination of anxiety and obligation. Of such magnitude is the aura surrounding *Tarasoff* that for many clinicians the very word has become synonymous with the concept of law and psychiatry. In reality, however, issues implicated by the *Tarasoff* case and its legal progeny account for a small percentage of forensic cases. Moreover, once the legal ruling is explained, much of the attendant anxiety usually disappears. Indeed, unbeknownst to many, *Tarasoff* entails a fascinating story.

Below is a discussion of the events that led to the *Tarasoff* case and an analysis of the law that California enacted as a response. Our discussion takes the California law apart, then puts it back together again, to show how the various elements of this law form a coherent whole around a particular set of values. The relevance of this discussion is that often a situation will arise that has no clear corollary in the law—no case, statute, or regulation will address directly what you should *do*. In fact, our experience is that most situations fall into this category. When faced with such a situation, *the process by which a clinician decides what to do* becomes as important as the decision itself. The documentation of this process should show that the clinician appreciates what values are at stake, and should demonstrate a thoughtful application of those values to the matter at hand. The appreciation and thoughtful application of the values embodied in a mental health law, together with the documentation of the decision-making process, will be a clinician's very best protection against liability.

## THE LEGAL LANDSCAPE

To understand why the *Tarasoff* case has so captured the imagination of clinicians, one must examine two aspects of our legal system: first, how the law views legal obligations ("affirmative duties") to third parties; and second, the concept of negligence. In terms of the former, the American legal system rarely imposes affirmative duties unless two or more individuals have freely entered into a legal agreement that creates corresponding responsibilities. In legal terms, one rarely owes a duty to third parties. Suppose that one morning I decide to go for a walk on the pier next to where I live and suddenly hear a cry for help. Should I see someone going under for the third time, there is no *legal* obligation that I do anything—I can simply keep on walking, without concern that I will be sued or charged with a crime.* Should there be a life preserver right beside me, a telephone for emergencies only feet away, I remain under no legal obligation whatsoever to act. I owe this third party no *duty*—he does not know me, I do not know him, and we have not entered into a relationship that creates affirmative duties to one another. From the law's point of view, our legal destinies are utterly independent.

An exception to this rule occurs should I begin a rescue, perhaps by picking up the life preserver and swinging it backward as if to throw it. In that case I have an obligation to make a reasonable attempt to complete the rescue. The reason behind the exception is that my commencing a rescue may serve to discourage others from acting—hence, if I begin to act in this instance, I have an obligation to follow through. This exception notwithstanding, the overriding principle is that the law will not impose a duty to act unless and until the individuals have entered into some relationship recognized by law.

A second important concept upon which the *Tarasoff* case is built is

---

* This manner of behaving will not, however, get one nominated for many humanitarian awards.

that of *negligence*. Negligence is a form of tort. Tort is the legal term for the sort of mistake that gives rise to lawsuits in civil, as opposed to criminal, courts. Malpractice is a form of negligence, and hence is a tort.

A malpractice lawsuit is often said to consist of the "four Ds," defined as the Dereliction of a Duty Directly causing Damages. Each of the four Ds is an essential element of a malpractice claim—if any one is missing, the lawsuit cannot succeed. You might think of the four Ds as the wheels on a car—if even one wheel is gone, the car stays put. In the example above, should the individual in the water drown and his estate attempt to sue me, my defense will be that I had no <u>d</u>uty toward him and so cannot be held liable for negligence. One of the wheels is missing, so the suit cannot go anywhere. Likewise, in cases where there is <u>d</u>ereliction of a <u>d</u>uty, yet no <u>d</u>amages, a suit for malpractice fails. This makes intuitive sense—no matter how bad my mistake, if you suffer no harm, you should not be able to collect moneys from me. Similarly, if I am <u>d</u>erelict in my <u>d</u>uty, yet my <u>d</u>ereliction does not <u>d</u>irectly cause your <u>d</u>amages, a suit in negligence cannot prevail. Again, this makes sense. If I make a mistake, and you happen to suffer a harm, yet it was not *my* mistake that caused your harm, I should not be held responsible for compensating you.

In a malpractice case, the plaintiff—the person who claims to have been harmed and is consequently bringing the lawsuit—must demonstrate by a preponderance of evidence, or 51% (see part II, question 4), that each of the four Ds is present. Each D has its own complexities; the manner in which one calculates damages, for example, can be enormously intricate, as can be showing direct causation. Dereliction of duty, also called "breach of duty," is somewhat unique, insofar as the standard by which to judge whether one is derelict remains constant—for those in the medical profession, one must provide care that is *reasonable*. One need not provide the best, most expensive, or most up-to-date care available; one only need provide care that is within the standard of practice of an average member of the profession practicing within her specialty. Should one provide care that falls below this standard, one can be considered derelict in one's duty.

Defining the fourth D, that of <u>d</u>uty, involves answering two questions. The first question is: *What* duty is owed? That is to say, I must determine precisely what my legal obligation entails. The second question is: *To whom* is the duty owed? Now that I know what I must do, to whose benefit must I do it? It was in answering these two questions that the *Tarasoff* case broke new ground.

## THE FOUR "Ds" OF NEGLIGENCE

I.  Dereliction
    A.  The mental health professional must provide care that is **reasonable**.
    B.  Care is considered reasonable if it is **within the standard of practice of an average member of the profession practicing within her specialty.**
    C.  If the care falls below what is reasonable, the mental health professional is derelict.

    *No dereliction = The lawsuit for malpractice fails.*

II.  Duty
    The mental health professional **has a legal relationship** with an individual that gives rise to a duty.
    A.  What is the duty? (An important point in *Tarasoff*)
    B.  To whom is the duty owed? (An important point in *Tarasoff*)

    *No duty = The lawsuit for malpractice fails.*

III.  Directly causing
    The dereliction of duty must directly cause the damages.

    *No direct causation = The lawsuit for malpractice fails.*

IV.  Damages
    The person bringing a negligence suit must have suffered harm.

    *No damages = The lawsuit for malpractice fails.*

# THE FACTS OF THE CASE

Early in July of 1969 a young man named Prosenjit Poddar arrived at an appointment to see a clinician at the University of California, Berkeley, student health center. Poddar, a 25-year-old graduate student, had come to the student health center at the urging of a friend who had become concerned over Poddar's obsession with a 19-year-old undergraduate, Tatianna Tarasoff. By the time Poddar arrived at the student health center that summer he had been transformed from a student with enormous potential and industriousness into a loner who spent hour upon hour in his room listening to secretly recorded audiotapes of his conversations with Tatianna. After meeting at a folk dance for international students nearly a year earlier, Poddar and Tatianna had shared a lingering flirtation but, to Poddar's great disappointment, no more.

Following his initial appointment at the student health center, Poddar began treatment with a clinical psychologist, Dr. Lawrence Moore. Poddar told Dr. Moore that he was going to kill a girl whom he did not name, but who was identifiable as Tatianna. Shortly thereafter, Poddar left therapy, almost certainly in response to Dr. Moore's statement that he would have to restrain Poddar should Poddar continue to talk of killing Tatianna. After consulting with colleagues, Dr. Moore wrote a letter to the Berkeley police that read, in part:

> He is at this point a danger to the welfare of other people and himself. That is, he has been threatening to kill an unnamed girl who he feels has betrayed him and has violated his honor. He has told a friend . . . that he intends to go to San Francisco to buy a gun and that he plans to kill the girl. . . . Mr. Poddar should be committed for observation in a mental hospital. (Winslade & Ross, 1983)

The campus police found and questioned Poddar. After extracting from Poddar a promise to stay away from Tatianna, however, the police released him. The director of the department of psychiatry then ordered that Poddar not be committed to a psychiatric hospital. Neither the campus police nor anyone at the student health center warned Tatianna or her parents of Poddar's threat. A short time later, on October 27, Poddar went to Tatianna's home and killed her.

Tatianna's parents brought a lawsuit against a number of individuals at UC Berkeley, including Dr. Moore and his colleagues. Their claim was based upon an action in negligence: The treaters had been derelict in their duty to warn Tatianna of Poddar's threat, a dereliction that directly caused Tatianna's death. The therapists—now defendants in the lawsuit—responded that they had no relationship with Tatianna, and so had no duty toward her. In the absence of a duty, they reasoned, a lawsuit could not succeed. They argued that, in addition to owing no duty to Tatianna, therapist-patient confidentiality prohibited them from disclosing this information. The defendants argued that the case was open and shut: What happened to Tatianna was a tragedy but, with one of the four Ds (duty) missing and with the constraints of confidentiality, a tragedy that had no place being decided in a court of law.

The lawsuit had an extremely high profile because of its possible implications. If Tatianna Tarasoff's parents were to prevail, therapists could have a duty toward people with whom they had no professional relationship, perhaps whom they had never met nor even seen. While courts had held psychiatrists responsible for damage done when their patients were prematurely released from an inpatient psychiatric facility, this case was different: Poddar was an outpatient and Dr. Moore was a psychologist, raising the specter that the ruling would encompass all mental health professionals, who could henceforth be held responsible for harms committed by *any* of their patients. The American Psychiatric Association (APA) judged the case to be of such import that it entered the fray as an *amicus curiae,* Latin for "friend of the court." An amicus curiae is an individual or an organization who, while neither a plaintiff nor a defendant, nevertheless has an interest in the outcome of a case. The APA, fearing that with the stroke of a pen the court might significantly increase the number of individuals who could sue a therapist and win, argued "that even when a therapist does in fact predict that a patient poses a serious danger of violence to others, the therapist should be absolved of any responsibility for failing to act to protect the potential victim" (*Tarasoff v. The Regents of the University of California,* 17 Cal. 3d 425 [1976] at 439). Put in other words, the APA wanted a blanket rule that a therapist is not liable to third parties whom a patient injures, even if the therapist could predict that the patient would be violent.

The court's first order of business was to examine whether there was any sort of relationship between Dr. Moore and Tatianna that the law would recognize. Such a relationship would give rise to a duty, and so supply the missing "D." To address this question the court reviewed case law that held that a duty may arise to a third party when there is a "special relationship" between two individuals. A "special relationship," the court explained, could give rise to affirmative duties toward third persons in cases where a third person is the foreseeable victim of some harm. The court examined the doctor-patient relationship between Dr. Moore and Poddar and concluded that it was indeed this sort of "special relationship."* Thus, the court reasoned, by virtue of Dr. Moore's "special relationship" to Poddar, Dr. Moore owed a duty to Tatianna Tarasoff, the foreseeable victim of Poddar's harm. Put another way, the court concluded *that Dr. Moore had a duty to Tatianna Tarasoff because she was the foreseeable victim of his patient's harm.* In less than two pages, the court had supplied the missing "D."

---

* Part of the court's thinking may well have been that the "special" nature of the therapist-patient relationship makes it likely that a patient would tell a therapist about feelings of wanting to hurt someone.

Having concluded that Dr. Moore and his colleagues did owe Tatianna a duty, the court's next order of business was to determine how that duty should be defined. Perhaps the greatest misunderstanding about the *Tarasoff* case is on precisely this point. The court stated,

> [O]nce a therapist does in fact determine, or under applicable professional standards reasonably should have determined, that a patient poses a serious danger of violence to others, he bears a duty to exercise reasonable care *to protect* [italics added] the foreseeable victim of that danger. (439)

The *Tarasoff* case held that the duty a therapist owes to third parties is the duty *to protect*—not, as is commonly misunderstood, the duty *to warn*.

The court was then presented with the question of how broad a circle of potential victims the duty to protect should encompass. Again the APA weighed in, arguing "that warnings must be given only in those cases in which the therapist knows the identity of the victim." The APA's approach could be characterized as, "Therapists should not be liable to third parties at all, but if the court decides they are, they should be liable only to those third parties who have been identified." The *Tarasoff* court was not so restrictive in its thinking. Addressing the question of whether a therapist must know exactly who the potential victim is before a duty to protect arises, the court explained,

> [I]n some cases it would be unreasonable to require the therapist to interrogate his patient to discover the victim's identity, or to conduct an independent investigation. But there may also be cases in which a moment's reflection will reveal the victim's identity. The matter thus is one which depends upon the circumstances of each case, and should not be governed by any hard and fast rule. (439)

The court left open the possibility that the duty to protect could extend to individuals whom the therapist had not yet identified, yet whose identity could be discovered after "a moment's reflection." This seemingly innocuous comment has given rise to an enormous debate over the extent to which a therapist must know, or be able to determine, who the potential victim is before a duty to that third person arises. Some states, for example, require that the potential victim be identified before any duty arises. Other states have been far more expansive, creating a duty to protect when it becomes clear that anyone—regardless who—will be harmed. Below we will see how California has dealt with this issue.

The *Tarasoff* case examined the second of the four Ds—duty—in a way that no court had done before. The court answered the two central questions about the duty owed by a therapist to a third party: The duty owed is the duty *to protect,* and the duty is owed to *foreseeable victims of harm who can be identified after "a moment's reflection."* The heart of the case, however, lies in how it directly pitted two values—confidentiality and public safety—against one another. There was no way to finagle. Given the way the court framed the issue, it had to choose one value at the expense of the other. The court came down decidedly in favor of public safety. In perhaps its most famous quotation, the *Tarasoff* court concluded,

> the public policy favoring protection of the confidential character of patient-psychotherapist communications must yield to the extent to which disclosure is essential to avert danger to others. *The protective privilege ends where the public peril begins* [italics added]. (442)

The balance struck by the court—that confidentiality must yield to public safety—is the foundation of the *Tarasoff* ruling. Before turning to see how the state of California has addressed the issues raised by the *Tarasoff* decision, we leave the reader with two historical notes on what happened to those most intimately involved with Tatianna's murder.

In the criminal matter, Poddar was charged with first degree murder. After a trial, at which much evidence concerning his mental status was heard, he was found guilty of second-degree murder and sent to a state prison. Poddar appealed and five years later the California Supreme Court overturned his conviction. The state was then in the position of putting Poddar on trial again for Tatianna's murder; instead, however, the prosecutor struck a bargain with Poddar's attorney. In exchange for not retrying the criminal case, Poddar's attorney would ensure that Poddar would return home and not come back to the United States. Today Poddar is married and living in India.

In the civil matter, the California Supreme Court announced its rule of law—that therapists have a duty to protect foreseeable victims of harm who can be identified after a moment's reflection—and instructed the trial court to apply this rule of law to determine whether Dr. Moore and his colleagues had been negligent in fulfilling their duty. Questions of fact before the trial court would therefore have been: Was Tatianna Tarasoff a foreseeable victim of Poddar's harm? If so, did Dr. Moore and his colleagues fulfill their duty to protect Tatianna by notifying the campus police? If notifying the police did *not* suffice to fulfill their duty to protect, did their failure to take additional steps directly cause Tatianna's death?

Before the case could make it back to the trial court, however, the parties reached a settlement for a sum of money, the amount of which was never disclosed. Tatianna's parents agreed to go home and leave the courts behind. As a consequence, no clinician involved in Prosenjit Poddar's care was ever held liable for negligence in a court of law.

## *TARASOFF* ARRIVES AT THE CALIFORNIA LEGISLATURE

*Tarasoff* was decided by the California Supreme Court. As a consequence, the *Tarasoff* ruling became the law of the state. As is often the case when courts announce a rule of law, however, many questions remained unanswered: How broad is the circle of potential victims encompassed by this duty? Must the victim be identified? Do spoken words threatening violence always give rise to a duty? What, in addition to warning the victim, does the duty to protect entail? Following the *Tarasoff* decision the California legislature, largely in response to pleas from professional organizations to answer these and other questions, attempted to clarify the duty created by the *Tarasoff* ruling.

---

### THE CALIFORNIA *TARASOFF* STATUTE

#### Cal. Civ. Code §43.92

(a) There shall be no monetary liability on the part of, and no cause of action shall arise against, any person who is a psychotherapist as defined in Section 1010 of the Evidence Code in failing to warn of and protect from a patient's threatened violent behavior or failing to predict and warn of and protect from a patient's violent behavior except where the patient has communicated to the psychotherapist a serious threat of physical violence against a reasonably identifiable victim or victims.

(b) If there is a duty to warn and protect in the limited circumstances specified above, the duty shall be discharged by the psychotherapist making reasonable efforts to communicate the threat to the victim or victims and to a law enforcement agency.

---

There are five elements of this law that you should note. The first element concerns the individuals to whom the statute extends: "any person who is a psychotherapist as defined in Section 1010 of the Evidence Code."

The definition of psychotherapist covers anyone who is entitled to the psychotherapist-patient privilege described in the Evidence Code. The definition is broad and extends to physicians who devote a substantial part of their practice to psychiatry; licensed psychologists; licensed clinical social workers when they are engaged in applied psychotherapy of a nonmedical nature; state-credentialed school psychologists; licensed marriage, family, and child counselors; supervised psychological assistants; supervised marriage, family, and child counselor interns; supervised associate clinical social workers; supervised individuals exempt from the psychology licensing law; supervised psychological interns; supervised marriage, family, and child trainees who are fulfilling their supervised practicum; individuals rendering mental health services under section 6924 of the Family Code (generally, any individual who provides mental health services to a minor, pursuant to the minor's consent); and registered nurses who possess a master's degree in psychiatric mental health nursing. If in doubt, and your clinical work requires a license from the state or you are supervised by a licensed mental health professional, it is best to consider yourself covered by section 43.92 until you can determine otherwise.

The second element is the manner in which the statute reads in clause (a), "There shall be *no* monetary liability on the part of, and no cause of action shall arise against, any person who is a psychotherapist . . . in failing to warn of and protect from . . . *except* [italics added] . . ." This language emphasizes the restrictive nature of the statute—liability is limited to the specific circumstances identified in the statute. The statute thus sends a clear message to courts: "We, the legislature, intend this statute to be restrictive, rather than expansive." Without this particular beginning, courts might be inclined to find liability over and above the situations spelled out in the text of the statute, something the legislature wished to discourage.

The third element is that the statute limits liability to specific circumstances in two realms: that of failing *to warn and to protect* a victim and that of failing *to predict* a patient's violence. The legislature is again clear in narrowing the duty—a psychotherapist will not be held responsible for failing to predict a patient's violent behavior unless the patient has "communicated" a "serious threat of physical violence." Psychotherapists, therefore, have a limited duty to predict violence, a duty that arises only in the context of a specific patient communication.

The fourth noteworthy element of the California statute indicates the conditions under which a therapist has an affirmative duty to act. Clause (a) is specific and, as such, in keeping with the restrictive nature of the law as a whole. For a duty to arise under clause (a): (1) the patient must have communicated to the psychotherapist a threat *of physical violence*; (2) the threat must be *serious* (e.g., the patient must have the intent and ability to carry out the threat); and (3) the victim or victims must be *reasonably identifiable*. Only when all three conditions are met does the therapist have a duty to protect and to warn a potential victim. Note how the California legislature has addressed issues raised by the *Tarasoff* decision. In doing so it tells the therapist what must occur before she must act: In the absence of a serious threat of physical violence against a reasonably identifiable victim, this clause will not impose a duty.

*An outline of the essential elements of California Civil Code section 43.92 can be found on page 21.*

In writing the statute, the California legislature has provided more guidance about when to act than did the *Tarasoff* decision itself. The California Supreme Court's decision directs clinicians to act when the harm is "foreseeable"—helpful, but not overly so. Many a debate could be held about when a particular act of violence is "foreseeable." The statute, by contrast, directs clinicians to act when there is a "serious" threat of physical violence against a "reasonably identifiable victim or victims." The specificity found in the language of the California statute narrows and defines the *Tarasoff* duty.

The specificity of the language notwithstanding, the statute leaves ample room for clinical judgment. A threat, for example, is *not* sufficient to create a duty. The threat must be serious, which would require the patient to have both the intent and the ability to carry out the threat. Often patients will bring into their therapies fantasies of wishing to harm or even kill another individual. Such rage may be the focus of your work with a patient. Obviously, every time a patient expresses the wish to kill, a duty is not created; many clinicians would spend most of their time on the phone were this the case. Rather, the clinician's task is to determine when patients are likely to *act* on their fantasies. Only then does the duty arise, and it is by relying on your clinical judgment that you will determine when a patient is likely to move from fantasy to action. What's important is that while the statute provides much helpful guidance, your clinical judgment will ultimately determine whether you must act. In moments of uncertainty, consult with an experienced colleague or an attorney who is knowledgeable in mental health law. Be sure to document your consultation, as well as your reasons for following the particular course of action you choose to follow. *Every bit as important as what you do will be a careful documentation of your consultation(s) and of the process by which you come to decide how to respond.*

The fifth noteworthy element of the California *Tarasoff* statute specifies how a clinician can satisfy her duty to warn and protect. The therapist must make reasonable efforts to communicate the threat to the potential victim or victims and to a law enforcement agency. Note the "and"; both the victim *and* the police must be notified. Note also that the duty entails making a "reasonable" effort to warn the victim; in circumstances where the victim is unreachable the therapist will satisfy her duty to protect by making "reasonable" efforts to communicate the threat. Whether an effort is "reasonable" will be judged against the standard of what a reasonable mental health professional of your discipline would do under similar circumstances. The limiting qualification of making "reasonable" efforts to warn is not similarly applicable to the police, since it will virtually always be possible to contact law enforcement officers.

## CONCLUSION

The California *Tarasoff* statute gives clinicians explicit guidance about when a duty to act arises and tells clinicians what actions fulfill their duty. As explicit as this statute is, however, mental health professionals face many situations that leave the clinician to wonder whether a duty has arisen and, if so, what she should do. Take, for example, the HIV positive patient who insists on having unsafe sex with an unsuspecting partner. It is unclear how—or whether—the *Tarasoff* statute applies (see part II, question 153, for our assessment of this case). In many instances, no statute, regulation, or case will completely address questions about a clinician's legal responsibility.

In circumstances that have no clear resolution, the process by which a clinician resolves the problem becomes crucial. The clinician's appreciation of what values are at stake and her thoughtful application of those values to the matter at hand are what will be important. While we have discussed the values behind the *Tarasoff* decision, the more significant point is that a clinician's greatest protection against liability is not found in a book of laws. Rather, what protects a clinician from liability is her capacity to see what values are relevant to a particular circumstance, and to apply those values in a thoughtful manner to a problem that may have no clear answer.

Having examined the *Tarasoff* statute in detail, we now turn to a series of statutes and regulations central to mental health law, those governing privacy, confidentiality, and testimonial privilege. Our discussion of these laws forms the body of the following chapter. As you read, notice both what the laws say and how they are put together. Your understanding of how these statutes and regulations embody a coherent set of values will be an invaluable resource when you are confronted with a dilemma in your own practice.

---

## *TARASOFF* COMES TO CALIFORNIA

### CAL. CIV. CODE §43.92

I. The duty arising under California Civil Code §43.92 applies to:
   A. "Psychotherapists" as defined by §1010 of the Evidence Code:
      1. Psychiatrists
      2. Licensed psychologists
      3. Licensed clinical social workers
      4. Licensed marriage, family, and child counselors
      5. State credentialed school psychologists
      6. Supervised assistants, interns, trainees, and students engaged in clinical work
      7. Registered nurses who possess a master's degree in psychiatric mental health nursing
      8. Individuals providing mental health services under Family Code §6924 (individuals providing mental health services to a minor, pursuant to the minor's consent)
   B. If in doubt, and your clinical work requires a license from the state, consider yourself covered by the statute until you can determine otherwise.

II. Psychotherapists are not subject to monetary liability for failing **to warn, to protect**, or **to predict**, except under the specific circumstance identified in the statute.

III. The duty is:
   A. To warn and to protect *and*
   B. To predict.

IV. A psychotherapist has a duty to warn, to protect, and to predict **only** when:
   A. A **patient** has **communicated to the psychotherapist**
   B. a **serious** threat of **physical violence**
   C. against a **reasonably identifiable** victim or victims.

V. A psychotherapist fulfills the duty under the statute by making **reasonable** efforts to communicate the threat:
   A. To the victim or victims *and*
   B. To the police.

# 3

# PRIVACY, CONFIDENTIALITY, AND TESTIMONIAL PRIVILEGE

Privacy, confidentiality, and testimonial privilege affect the day-to-day life of a clinician perhaps more than any other area of mental health law, yet they remain elusive concepts. We sense that each of these words captures something important, but we also feel a general fuzziness about what they share with one another and, perhaps more important, what is unique to each. And so we begin with definitions.

## DEFINITIONS

*Privacy* is a right that stems from an underlying value central to our society, that of *individual autonomy*. Autonomy is a highly valued right because, as a society, we believe in self-determination; that individuals have the right to lead their lives however they choose, provided their choices do not unreasonably interfere with the choices others wish to make. Autonomy is therefore an active concept.

The right to privacy that flows from the value of individual autonomy is more passive. In *Olmstead v. United States*, 277 U.S. 438 (1928), Justice Brandeis, a famous Justice of the United States Supreme Court, remarked that the right to privacy is "the right to be let alone—the most comprehensive of rights and the right most valued by civilized men" (478). Justice Brandeis's definition captures the notion that privacy is a right that prevents others, especially the government, from unduly interfering with our lives. Because the active right of autonomy (an individual's right to determine the course of her life) is so completely intertwined with its passive complement, the right to privacy (the right to be let alone), many aspects of autonomy, such as the right to decide how to educate one's children, the right to decide upon a profession, the right to travel where one pleases, the right to choose "what [one] eats, wears, or reads" (*Kent v. Dulles*, 357 U.S. 116 [1958] at 125–126), are commonly referred to as "privacy rights." Our focus, however, will be on the privacy right that allows us to be "let alone."

*Confidentiality* is an aspect, or subset, of privacy. Confidentiality in the clinical context is the right to have things that are communicated to a mental health professional kept in confidence, that is, not revealed to individuals who are outside the professional relationship. We refer to such individuals as "third parties." Confidentiality has legal, ethical, and interpersonal dimensions. From a *legal* perspective, a mental health professional has an obligation to ensure that what a patient communicates *to* her stays *with* her. From an *ethical* perspective, confidentiality is premised upon values our society holds dear, those of privacy and individual autonomy. Confidentiality ensures that patients are free to decide for themselves with whom they will share what is most intimate to them, and that what they choose to share will remain private. From an *interpersonal perspective*, confidentiality goes to the very heart of the professional relationship. To keep communications confidential is to treat the patient with dignity and respect, and so to build trust. Trust is the foundation that creates and defines the space where two people may work together toward a mutual goal.

*Testimonial privilege*, often referred to simply as "privilege," flows from the very same values as does confidentiality—privacy and individual autonomy—but is a concept narrower in both theory and practice. Testimonial privilege is the patient's right to keep confidential communications from being disclosed in a legal proceeding. Because of privilege, a patient has the prerogative to prevent a mental health professional from testifying or releasing records in a court of law, a deposition, or an administrative hearing. When a patient decides not to allow a mental health professional to disclose confidential information, the patient is said to "invoke privilege." When a patient invokes privilege, the mental health professional may not discuss the patient's confidential communications or release any of the patient's records unless ordered to do so by a court. A client who permits a mental health professional to testify or release records in a legal proceeding is said to "waive privilege."

Note the tension between the values that lie behind testimonial privilege and the truth-finding mission of a court. The tension arises because testimonial privilege keeps information out of the judicial system. When an individual invokes privilege, information that may be relevant to a legal proceeding is not admitted into evidence, which is why lawyers say that "privilege suppresses truth." Put another way, we could seek complete candor and truth in all legal proceedings were we willing to expose the most intimate details of relationships our society holds dear. However, because of the value we place on preserving the sanctity of certain relationships (such as that between a husband and a wife, a psychotherapist and a patient, a priest and a penitent, an attorney and a client), we declare these relationships "off limits" to the law. We call these relationships "privileged." Because testimonial privilege limits the amount of information available to the legal system, judges tend to stick very close to the letter of the law when they interpret testimonial privilege statutes. Generally, a judge will deem privileged only those relationships explicitly named by the statute; for the most part, a relationship not named in the law cannot hide behind the cloak of privilege to avoid exposure in a legal proceeding.

Like privacy, confidentiality and testimonial privilege respect the value of individual autonomy. Confidentiality and privilege ensure that the individual, and the individual alone, may determine the nature, content, and destination of his communications. Confidentiality and privilege serve another important purpose as well. Communication is the tool of a mental health professional's trade, the raw material of a clinician's work. Protecting the sanctity of a patient's communications provides a safe haven for the patient to share the most intimate aspects of her life experience. The promise of confidentiality and privilege is thus the foundation of a successful clinical relationship.

## FOUR GUIDELINES

The laws that govern privacy, confidentiality, and testimonial privilege can be enormously complex when applied in practice. It is therefore helpful to have certain general principles in mind when assessing your legal responsibilities to keep confidential—or to disclose—something your client has communicated to you. These four guidelines will help as you make your way through this important, yet complicated, area of mental health law.

First, numerous laws regulate privacy, confidentiality, and testimonial privilege. Some are general laws that apply to a variety of professionals, while others focus specifically on mental health practitioners, or even on specific areas within the mental health system. Because both general and specific laws cover the same basic legal issues, statutes often overlap. When a broad or general statute conflicts with a narrow or more specific statute, the specific statute governs, unless one of the statutes expressly states otherwise.

Second, the statutes that deal with privacy, confidentiality, and testimonial privilege are based on a presumption that with respect to privacy a mental health professional's foremost obligation is to her client. This presumption, however, is not absolute. In certain circumstances, the obligation a mental health professional owes to keep private what a patient reveals must be balanced against interests of our society as a whole. Examples of important societal interests are the public's safety, the efficient provision of mental health services, and the just administration of our legal system. The balance between privacy rights that belong to a client and interests that belong to society as a whole is somewhat like a teeter-totter: only in the most unusual circumstances is one end completely on the ground or completely up in the air. Most often, where the teeter-totter comes to rest represents a balance of the two ends.

The rights of the client and the interests of the state thus coexist along a continuum. At one end, the client's right to privacy is absolute. In these circumstances, a mental health professional will have a duty to keep in complete confidence what the client reveals. At the opposite end of the continuum, the interests of society override the client's right. In these circumstances, a therapist will have an obligation to disclose what the client reveals. In the middle, the rights of the individual and the interests of the state are roughly equal—neither the state's interest nor the client's right is controlling. When neither the interests of the state nor the privacy rights of the individual patient are given clear priority, a mental health professional is often allowed, but not required, to disclose what a client communicates. Our analysis of the California statutes that govern privacy, confidentiality, and testimonial privilege will span the length of this theoretical continuum.

Third, a mental health professional must not only pay attention to *whether* patient communications will be kept in confidence or disclosed, but also to *how* she will disclose information if the possibility—or necessity—of doing so arises. We have developed two rules to govern the disclosure of patient information: The Law of No Surprises and the Parsimony Principle. The Law of No Surprises and the Parsimony Principle apply to all mental health professionals and should be followed whenever a patient communication is disclosed.

The Law of No Surprises says simply that a clinician should take every reasonable step to inform a client about the circumstances that will warrant a disclosure of confidential information to a third party. The Law of No Surprises is founded upon a clinical truism: You never want your client to be surprised when you disclose confidential information. The Law is consistent with statutes and codes of ethics that require a mental health professional to tell a client at the beginning of the relationship what circumstances will necessitate a breach of confidentiality. A corollary to the Law of No Surprises says that, in order to minimize any possibility of surprise or confusion, a disclosure of information should be done together with the client whenever possible.

A clinician should be up front and honest with a client when the necessity of disclosing information arises. Such honesty will be greatly enhanced if the clinician informs her client at the outset that there may be situations in which they both decide—or safety requires—that information will be disclosed. Many clinicians use an informed consent letter to convey the circumstances that warrant a disclosure of information, and we recommend that all mental health professionals give serious consideration to using such a letter for this purpose (appendix B contains a sample informed consent letter; see question 133 for a discussion of the letter's advantages and disadvantages). Explaining the limits to confidentiality at the beginning of your work will lay the groundwork should the need to disclose confidential information arise. *The four words you never want a client to begin a sentence with are: "You didn't tell me . . ."*

Your aim should be to address the topic in a way that speaks to your particular client. For example, if your client has a history of serious suicide attempts or a history of violence, you will want to emphasize the necessity of disclosing information should you feel that safety is at issue. Your phrasing may be something like, "Safety is our bottom line, so should there come a time when I feel safety—yours or anyone else's—is in jeopardy, I may need to share some of the things we've talked about. If that happens, I'll make every effort to talk it over with you first and, if at all possible, we'll share the information together." This communication creates a frame for your work by conveying that safety is the foundation upon which the treatment rests. The communication also conveys that you and your client are working *together*. The latter communication is important because many clients will experience a disclosure as a rift, a break in the relationship, perhaps even a betrayal of faith. By emphasizing at the beginning of your work that any such disclosure will be done in the interests of your work and that it will be done *with* the client, you are "vaccinating" your treatment, as it were, against such an injury.

Our second rule that governs the disclosure of confidential information is the Parsimony Principle. The Parsimony Principle says that a mental health professional discloses only that information necessary to achieve the purpose of the disclosure, and no more. If, for example, you receive a call from an emergency room physician who needs to have certain information about a suicidal client, you provide information that will help the physician assess and formulate a plan to protect your client's safety. No more. If you are making a referral for an MRI, you may choose to share that your client suffers from an anxiety disorder, since her anxiety may make it difficult for her to tolerate lying in a long, dark tube. There is no reason to share that she also suffers from an eating disorder. To put the Parsimony Principle another way: Determine what information is necessary and sufficient to address the need for disclosure, and disclose only that information. An excellent example of the Parsimony Principle is found in the Welfare and Institutions Code. Section 5328.4 states that when a mental health professional suspects that a client has committed a crime covered by a mandatory reporting statute, the mental health professional must limit her disclosure to "information directly relating to the factual circumstances of the commission of the [offense] and not any information relating to the mental state of the patient."

*The Law of No Surprises and the Parsimony Principle govern all disclosures of confidential information.*

The fourth and final guideline is that every mental health professional must look to her profession's code of ethics before disclosing confidential information. Each major mental health discipline has its own code of ethics, and every ethics code speaks to the issue of confidentiality. If, in disclosing confidential information, a mental health professional violates that code, she runs several risks: that of being disciplined by her professional association, of being considered negligent for deviating from her profession's standard of care, and of being disciplined by a state regulatory board, when the law allows a regulatory board to look to specific codes, as California law allows the Board of Psychology to look to the American Psychological Association's *Ethical Principles*. Often codes of ethics require a more stringent standard of behavior than does the law (see question 104 for a discussion of a circumstance in which ethics may demand a higher standard of conduct). For this reason, *read and become familiar with your profession's code of ethics.*

An analogy perhaps best captures how these four guidelines are related. Imagine that someone builds a long hallway and places it on our teeter-totter. The hallway has a series of doors, all of which are closed. You are at the low end of the hallway; on the wall next to where you are standing is written, "Complete client confidentiality." You can neither see anyone nor speak to anyone as you stand still in a dark and quiet space. You look ahead and see a closed door immediately in front of you; suddenly you feel the hallway begin to change its balance. You are now looking up at a door marked "confidentiality," but only with a key marked "an exception" can you open it and walk through. You manage to find such a key in a box beside the door and you then move ahead. The balance continues to shift as you walk forward. The next door is marked "testimonial privilege." This door, too, is locked, although several keys marked "exceptions" can be found hanging nearby. You choose a key, open the door, and continue to move forward. The balance shifts again and you are now walking downward. At the very end of the hallway, a final door stands between you and the outside, a door marked "ethical considerations." Again, several keys can be found nearby; each key is labeled with a different discipline's name. You find the key tagged with your discipline, and see whether it opens the last door. If it does, you may open the door and walk out. But be careful—ahead of you is a moat, with an alligator named "The Law of No Surprises" and a crocodile named "The Parsimony Principle." You must have a fish to throw to each—no fish, and you can't get by the moat. This analogy captures (we hope) the idea that disclosing client communications is a *process*, to which there are several steps. You must consider each step along the way, and only when you have opened each door and fed our pets can you legally and ethically disclose what a client has revealed to you.

# CONFIDENTIALITY: DISCLOSURES OF INFORMATION

I. Presume that everything a patient communicates to you is confidential.

II. If the possibility of disclosing a patient communication arises, consider whether any exception to confidentiality will permit the disclosure.

III. If the disclosure is to take place in a court of law, a deposition, or an administrative hearing, consider whether any exception to testimonial privilege will permit the disclosure.

IV. The Law of No Surprises, Parsimony Principle, and professional codes of ethics govern all disclosures of patient communications.
  A. Law of No Surprises
    1. Inform client at outset that there are limits to confidentiality.
      a. Give general contours of limits to confidentiality at initial session.
      b. Tailor what you say to meet needs and circumstances of specific client.
      c. Emphasize that client will be notified of any disclosures.
      d. Document your discussion.
    2. Whenever possible, make client part of disclosure process, up to and including having client make the actual disclosure when appropriate.
    3. Consider giving client informed consent letter at first session.
  B. Parsimony Principle
    1. Determine what information is necessary and sufficient to meet purpose of disclosure.
    2. Disclose only that information.
  C. Professional codes of ethics
    1. Each major mental health discipline has a code of ethics.
    2. California law allows regulatory bodies to consider codes of ethics when evaluating whether professional misconduct has occurred.
    3. Often, codes of ethics require a more stringent standard of behavior than does the law.

# LAWS THAT GOVERN PRIVACY

The right to *privacy* is found in the United States Constitution. While the word "privacy" is not mentioned in the actual text of the Constitution, the Supreme Court has said that a number of the Constitution's amendments have penumbras—a word whose Latin roots mean "almost a shadow"— under which the right to privacy falls. Think of the Constitution as a great oak tree with sturdy limbs, long branches, and wide leaves. While no limb, branch, or leaf is emblazoned with the actual word "privacy," it is the oak's shade that creates, covers, and protects our right to privacy. Thus, the Supreme Court has reasoned that the term "liberty" in the Four-teenth Amendment implies certain privacy rights, even though the word "privacy" is not found in that, or in any other specific clause.

The California Constitution explicitly names a right to privacy. Article I, section 1 of the California Constitution states: "All people are by nature free and independent and have inalienable rights. Among these are en-joying and defending life and liberty, acquiring, possessing, and protect-ing property, and pursuing and obtaining safety, happiness, *and privacy* [italics added]." To emphasize and reinforce this constitutional right to privacy, the California legislature wrote the Information Practices Act of 1977, which begins at section 1798 of the Civil Code. The Information Practices Act states that "the right to privacy is a personal and fundamen-tal right protected by Section 1 of Article I of the Constitution of Califor-nia and by the United States Constitution" (Civ. Code §1798.1). Thus, citizens of California hold an implied right to privacy under the United States Constitution, an explicit right to privacy granted by the California Constitution, and a statutory right to privacy found in the California Civil Code. It is upon this firmly anchored right to privacy that confidentiality and testimonial privilege laws are founded.

# LAWS THAT GOVERN CONFIDENTIALITY

*Important California confidentiality laws can be found in appendix A.*

Laws that govern confidentiality are found in court decisions, statutes, and regulations. In *Davis v. Superior Court,* 7 Cal. App. 4th 1008 (1992), and *Lantz v. Superior Court,* 28 Cal. App. 4th 1839 (1994), California courts held that the constitutional right to privacy applies to a relation-ship between a patient and a health care professional, and supersedes nearly all other statutory provisions. In the Confidentiality of Medical Information Act (CMIA), which begins at section 56 of the Civil Code, the California legislature provided a comprehensive right to privacy that covers all medical relationships and patient communications. The Welfare and Institutions Code contains similar statutory provisions that govern the confidentiality of mental health information for patients who receive services in the public mental health system, or who are hospitalized in a psychiatric facility on a voluntary or involuntary basis. These more narrowly focused statutory sections are found in the Lanterman-Petris-Short Act (LPS), beginning at section 5328. In addition, section 4514 of the Welfare and Institutions Code affords individuals with developmental disabilities the same confidentiality protections found in LPS. Together, these statutes create an overriding presumption that all information concerning a mental health client is confidential, and may not be released absent very specific circumstances.

Although both the Confidentiality of Medical Information Act (CMIA) and the Lanterman-Petris-Short Act (LPS) protect the confidentiality of mental health information, they contain notable distinctions. In *Loder v. City of Glendale*, 14 Cal. 4th 846 (1997), the California Supreme Court explained that the purpose of CMIA is to "protect confidentiality of individually identifiable medical information obtained from a patient by a health care provider, while at the same time setting forth limited circumstances in which the release of such information to specified entities or individuals is permissible." (859) Thus, the Court held that CMIA was designed to keep confidential any information that could lead to a patient's identity, and to be clear about when it is permissible to disclose otherwise confidential information. The *Loder* Court's characterization of CMIA reveals some key similarities and distinctions between the confidentiality requirements of CMIA and LPS.

First, like CMIA, LPS prohibits mental health professionals from disclosing patient information except under very specific circumstances. While the language of LPS specifies that "*all* [italics added] information and records . . . shall be confidential" (Welf. & Inst. Code §5328), CMIA says that all "*medical* [italics added] information" (Civ. Code §56.10) is confidential. This subtle distinction means that CMIA, unlike LPS, allows some general information about a patient to be released, provided the information is *nonmedical*. (According to section 56.05(c) of the Civil Code, medical information is "any individually identifiable information in possession of or derived from a provider of health care regarding a patient's medical history.") In addition, CMIA allows a health care provider to release a patient's name, age, gender, address, general description of the reason for treatment, general nature of the injury or condition, and the patient's general condition. LPS prohibits disclosure of this information, as do laws that govern the treatment of individuals with developmental disabilities. In accordance with the underlying value of patient autonomy, however, CMIA recognizes a patient's right to prevent a treater from releasing this information, by allowing the patient to request in writing that such information not be disclosed (Civ. Code §56.16).

Second, the scope of CMIA is broad, while that of LPS is comparatively narrow. CMIA applies to *all* medical licensing and certification boundaries (that is, CMIA applies to all mental health professionals). LPS, on the other hand, was drafted specifically for the public mental health system and for inpatient psychiatric facilities. CMIA states explicitly that its provisions do *not* cover records and information obtained in the course of providing services under LPS, or to individuals with developmental disabilities (Civ. Code §56.30). LPS therefore governs when the two statutes conflict over records and information of patients in the public mental health system or in inpatient psychiatric facilities.

Finally, neither CMIA nor LPS provide for absolute confidentiality; both list exceptions. As we hope our continuum illustrates, the exceptions to confidentiality are the result of a balance between the patient's right to privacy (the autonomy interest) and a competing societal interest (such as public safety). Some exceptions to confidentiality are permissive, others are mandatory. Whether an exception is permissive or mandatory generally depends on the importance of the societal interest at stake; as an example, because society places great value upon protecting children, the duty to break confidentiality is mandatory when a child's safety is at issue. Note when reading the statutes that the permissive exceptions use the language "*may* disclose" and the mandatory exceptions use the language "*shall* disclose."

## EXCEPTIONS TO CONFIDENTIALITY

In the past few years, many people have argued that confidentiality is more the exception than the rule. Despite appearances, confidentiality is maintained in the majority of treatments conducted by mental health professionals. Essential to your work, however, is a clear understanding of when you are *not* bound by confidentiality, as well as when you are bound to *break* confidentiality.

Keep in mind that every exception to confidentiality represents a balance of some value against the value of keeping clinical material confidential. Put another way, every time there is an occasion to disclose confidential information to third parties, *there is another interest at stake that is equal to or trumps confidentiality.* If you can hold on to this point as you read through the exceptions to confidentiality, you are well on your way to understanding this area of law. The occasions outlined by CMIA and LPS that permit or require treaters to disclose otherwise confidential patient information fall into the following nine categories:

1. client consent
2. treatment emergencies
3. public safety
4. treatment
5. provision of mental health services
6. the legal system
7. crimes committed by hospitalized patients
8. research
9. mandatory reporting statutes

## CLIENT CONSENT

The value behind confidentiality is individual autonomy. Autonomy dictates that an individual is free to decide for herself with whom she will communicate and what the content of her communications will be. The first exception to the rule of confidentiality is entirely consistent with individual autonomy: An adult client who is competent may *consent* to allow the mental health professional to share communications with specified third parties. In the case of client consent, the disclosure of information furthers the client's wishes, and so reinforces the value of individual autonomy.

Both CMIA and LPS name client consent as an exception to confidentiality, and this underscores an important, yet often overlooked, point: Confidentiality belongs to *the client.* Consistent with the value of autonomy, it is for your client—not you—to decide with whom to share otherwise confidential information.

A patient's consent to release confidential information should be in writing. Written consent makes clear the nature and extent of the disclosure, and will serve as a record if any unclarity or disagreement about the consent arises. A client's written consent must be legible and must give the name of the individual who is authorized to disclose the information, the individual or agency to whom the disclosure may be made, the date on which the consent to release ceases to be valid, and any limitations on how the released information may be used (Welf. & Inst. Code §§5328.6, 5328.7; Civ. Code §56.11). In practice, many clinicians, especially when they have a good working relationship with a client, rely on an oral consent, and perhaps would even consider it patronizing or demeaning to ask a client to sign a release. While the vast majority of these clinicians will never encounter any clinical or legal difficulties from releasing information without a written consent, it is important to remember that should any misunderstanding arise, the dispute will degenerate into the clinician's word against that of the client, a position in which no clinician would want to find herself. At the very least, the clinician will want to document the patient's oral consent.

Mental Health professionals should be aware that LPS limits a patient's right to consent to the release of information by requiring "the approval of the [mental health professional] in charge of the patient" (Welf. & Inst. Code §5328(b)) before information can be disclosed to a third party. The Patient's Access to Records chapter of the Health and Safety Code, however, specifies that a patient may obtain her own records, unless doing so would entail a "substantial risk of significant adverse or detrimental consequences to the patient" (H. & S. Code, §123115). The different values behind these provisions of LPS and the Health and Safety Code are apparent: LPS makes the disclosure of information subject to a mental health professional's approval, thus subordinating the client's autonomy to the clinician's judgment. The Health and Safety Code, on the other hand, provides for greater client autonomy by narrowing professional discretion. Because the legislature stated that the provisions of the Health and Safety Code were intended to trump the parallel LPS provisions, the Health and Safety Code governs when a client asks to review her chart (H. & S. Code, §123110). (For a further discussion of a client's request to review records, see chapter 11, Records and Record-Keeping.)

## TREATMENT EMERGENCIES

The second exception to confidentiality, that of a treatment emergency, is likewise consistent with the value of autonomy. Whereas client consent is the direct expression of a client's wishes, the disclosure of confidential information in an emergency is *presumed* to be the expression of a client's wishes. The presumption is that most people would give the emergency precedence over confidentiality. This presumption is honored for the duration of the emergency—even if the client expressly states a wish that confidentiality *not* be broken. The idea behind this exception is that an emergency is no time to sort these things out, to decide whether a client's judgment is intact or whether his words are a true expression of his desires—all that can wait until after the emergency is resolved. During the course of the emergency, confidentiality will yield to treatment, because that is the way most people would want it.

A treatment emergency is a circumstance in which information must be shared with health care providers to protect an individual's health and physical well-being from immediate harm. In practice, you can go by the rule that an emergency is a circumstance in which a reasonable person would judge that an individual's health and physical well-being are at significant risk. You may disclose confidential information for the purpose of attenuating that risk; let the Parsimony Principle be your guide as you do so. As an example of an emergency communication, personnel in an ambulance may talk to people in an emergency room, regardless of whether the patient has authorized the communication (Civ. Code §56.10(c)(1)).

Two points about the emergency exception to confidentiality merit discussion. First, beware of strangers claiming "emergency." Many a clinician has been duped into disclosing confidential information by a caller stating that an "emergency" necessitates releasing client information. Before discussing any client on an "emergency" basis, ask *who* needs to know, and *what emergency* necessitates disclosure. If a true emergency exists, this information can be passed on in a matter of seconds. If you have doubts, attempt to confirm the emergency before discussing your client.*

Second, when faced with a possible emergency, *pay attention to the process by which you decide what to do.* Your protection from a breach-of-confidentiality claim will be your documentation of the process by which you come to a decision about whether to break or to maintain your client's confidentiality. As your decision-making process unfolds, you should consider the facts as they are known to you, the reliability of your sources, the imminence of harm, alternatives to breaking confi-

* We owe a debt to Jay Patel, M.D., for emphasizing this important point to us.

dentiality, and consultations which, in an ambiguous situation, agree with the degree of the emergency and the necessity of breaking confidentiality. Your documentation should indicate that you have made a reasoned decision about what to do—what will *not* help is a note in the record that reads, "Emergency, disclosed confidential patient information." Although there may be very good reasons for doing so, your protection from liability—the documentation of how you came to your decision—is nowhere to be found in such a note. Rather, your note should indicate clearly why you shared information with a third party: "Received call from emergency personnel at approximately 3 p.m. Patient L.S. was found unconscious at her residence; attempts to revive L.S. were under way at that time. EMT asked what medication L.S. was prescribed, and whether I was aware of any other substances L.S. may have ingested. I provided EMT names and doses of medication, and stated that L.S. had a recent history of abusing benzodiazepines." The necessity of disclosing confidential information is immediately apparent upon reading such a note.

*PUBLIC SAFETY*

A third category of exceptions to confidentiality balances the state interest in public safety against the patient's privacy interest. It is helpful to distinguish "safety emergencies" from "treatment emergencies." Exceptions for *treatment* emergencies are designed to allow a mental health professional to assess a patient's condition and to provide necessary treatment. Exceptions for *safety* emergencies allow a mental health professional to prevent a client from harming himself or some other individual. As always, a mental health professional should document the process by which she decides whether to break or maintain confidentiality.

Perhaps the most well-known safety exception to patient confidentiality is the *Tarasoff* statute, California Civil Code, section 43.92 (see chapter 2 for a discussion of the *Tarasoff* statute). The *Tarasoff* statute states that a psychotherapist has a duty to break confidentiality when a patient makes a serious threat of physical violence against a reasonably identifiable victim. When such a threat is made, the psychotherapist has a duty to communicate the threat to both the victim and the police. In addition, LPS provides that "when the patient, in [the mental health professional's] opinion, presents a serious danger of violence to a reasonably foreseeable victim or victims, then any [patient information] *may* be released to that person or persons and to law enforcement agencies as [the mental health professional] determine[s] is *needed* [italics added] for the protection of that person or persons" (Welf. & Inst. Code §5328(r)). Notice that LPS uses the permissive "may," rather than the mandatory language of the *Tarasoff* statute, "shall." In addition, LPS allows the mental health professional to make a subjective judgment as to what information is *needed* to attenuate the risk. Thus, LPS affords greater discretion in deciding when to act and what to do than does the *Tarasoff* statute. However, because section 43.92 creates a *duty* to act, a psychotherapist should always consider herself to have a duty to disclose when a patient makes a serious threat of physical violence against a reasonably identifiable victim, and should act accordingly. The effect of LPS is to give a mental health professional permission to release information when she determines that doing so is necessary to protect a victim.

The law creates another public safety exception to confidentiality when an individual is in danger of spreading the HIV virus. Section 121015 of the Health and Safety Code states that a physician may disclose a patient's HIV positive status for "the purpose of interrupting the chain of [HIV] transmission." Section 121015 is permissive rather than mandatory, and allows a physician to disclose HIV status to a patient's spouse, sexual partner, or someone with whom the patient has shared a needle. The physician may *not* reveal any information that identifies the patient; rather, the physician may share that the individual to whom the disclosure is made has been exposed to the HIV virus. Before disclosing any information, however, the physician must first discuss the HIV test results with the patient, offer the patient educational and psychological counseling relating to HIV and AIDS, try to obtain the patient's voluntary consent to the disclosure, and tell the patient that the physician intends to notify the patient's contacts. (See also part II, question 153.)

Other public safety exceptions to confidentiality involve persons found not competent to stand trial or criminally insane, as well as mentally disordered sex offenders (MDSOs). According to LPS, a mental health professional must disclose information to a law enforcement agency when a court has determined that the importance of obtaining records outweighs the potential injury to such a patient of releasing confidential information. In addition, LPS allows mental health professionals to provide information to law enforcement agencies for the protection of elected officials and their families (Welf. & Inst. Code §5328(g)). Finally, Welfare and Institutions Code section 5328.01 requires that a mental health professional disclose certain information to law enforcement agencies when a crime is being investigated.

## TREATMENT

The fourth category of exceptions to confidentiality is designed to facilitate the treatment process. Section 5328(a) of the Welfare and Institutions Code allows the disclosure of patient information "between qualified professional persons in the provision of services." The statute further states that to share information without client consent, the professionals involved must be employed by the same facility, or be responsible for the same patient's care. Thus, section 5328(a) promotes the value of providing treatment, by allowing mental health professionals involved in a particular client's care to discuss treatment information. Note that because treatment information can be shared without the client's consent, this exception to confidentiality places the value of providing treatment ahead of the patient's autonomy. Similarly, section 56.10(c)(1) of the Civil Code states that information may be disclosed to "providers of health care or other health care professionals or facilities for purposes of diagnosis or treatment of the patient." Through these exceptions to confidentiality, the law recognizes that good treatment sometimes requires that treaters communicate with one another; the treatment exceptions allow a clinician to do so regardless of whether the client consents.

Note that the exception to confidentiality found in section 121015 of the Health and Safety Code (see the "public safety" section of this chapter) is also a treatment exception, insofar as the purpose of disclosure is both to break the chain of HIV transmission, as well as "for the purpose of diagnosis, care, and treatment of persons notified."

## PROVISION OF MENTAL HEALTH SERVICES

The fifth category of exceptions to confidentiality ensures that clients will receive mental health services of an acceptable quality. Exceptions necessary to achieve this end involve payment and insurance and peer and administrative review.

Both CMIA and LPS allow disclosure of patient information for payment or insurance purposes. Because payment requires patient information, an exception to confidentiality is warranted. Note, however, that a mental health professional should never release information to a third party payor over a patient's explicit objection; a patient retains the prerogative to pay out of pocket or to stop treatment. Although a mental health professional may have legal permission to release information, the ethical obligation to maintain confidentiality remains. A treater should release information to a third party payor only after having discussed the matter with the patient and after having made clear to the patient how such requests would be handled (see appendix B for an example of an informed consent letter).

The language found in the insurance and payment exceptions under CMIA and LPS are similar. Under CMIA, "information may be disclosed . . . to the extent necessary to allow responsibility for payment to be determined and payment to be made" (Civ. Code §56.10(c)(2)). For recipients of public mental health services or hospitalized mental patients, LPS allows disclosure "to the extent necessary for a recipient to make a claim, or for a claim to be made on behalf of a recipient for aid, insurance, or medical assistance to which he or she may be entitled" (Welf. & Inst. Code §5328(c)). Note that the statutes do not wholly abandon the sanctity of the patient's privacy right. Both CMIA and LPS use identical language, "*to the extent necessary*," to limit the information that may be disclosed for payment or insurance purposes. This example of limited disclosure illustrates the Parsimony Principle: Disclose only that information necessary to accomplish your purpose.

Another exception to confidentiality necessary to ensure that mental health services of an acceptable quality are delivered is administrative or peer review. Administrative review serves a number of essential purposes. First, by monitoring the ethical and legal standards to which health professionals are subject, administrative review helps make sure that patients receive adequate care and treatment. In addition, review agencies serve as watchdogs to help prevent professional misconduct. Agencies, such as Protection and Advocacy, Incorporated,* and licensing boards investigate treatment practices. When appropriate, such agencies are able to take remedial action. By investigating reports of misconduct, review boards also help protect against mental health practice that falls below the standard of care.

Both CMIA and LPS specify agencies to which information can be disclosed for the purpose of reviewing the quality of care provided. According to CMIA, information may be released to:

> organized committees and . . . professional standards review organizations . . . or to utilization and quality control peer review organizations . . . if the committees, agents, plans, organizations, or persons are engaged in reviewing the competence or qualifications of health care

---

* Protection and Advocacy, Incorporated is set up pursuant to federal law (The Protection and Advocacy for the Mentally Ill Individuals Act of 1986). Its purpose and functions in California are outlined by the Welfare and Institutions Code, beginning at section 4900.

professionals or in reviewing health care services with respect to medical necessity, level of care, quality of care, or justification of charges.
(Civ. Code §56.10(c)(4))

LPS authorizes disclosure to certain licensing personnel who are employed by, or who represent, the State Department of Health Services.
LPS also allows information to be disclosed to Protection and Advocacy, Incorporated and "to any board which licenses and certifies professionals in the fields of mental health pursuant to state law, when the
director of mental health [believes] that there has occurred a violation
of any provision of law subject to the jurisdiction of that board and the
records are relevant to the violation" (Welf. & Inst. Code §5328.15(b)).
That both CMIA and LPS allow information to be disclosed to these
organizations speaks to the importance lawmakers attribute to ensuring
that consumers of mental health services receive care and treatment
that is acceptable.

## THE LEGAL SYSTEM
The legal system needs information to work effectively. This need sometimes conflicts with the value of keeping client communications confidential. The exceptions to confidentiality which involve the legal system
thus represent a balance: In certain, specific situations, the needs of the
legal system will outweigh a client's right to privacy.

Both the CMIA and LPS explicitly state that a mental health professional
must provide information when ordered to do so by a court. Under CMIA,
a health care provider "shall disclose medical information if the disclosure
is compelled by . . . a court pursuant to an order of that court" (Civ. Code
§56.10(b)(1)). LPS states that patient "Information and records shall be disclosed . . . to the courts, as necessary to the administration of justice"
(Welf. & Inst. Code §5328(f)). Other exceptions under CMIA include when
a lawyer writes a subpoena to obtain clinical records or to compel a mental health professional to testify under oath, and when a court issues a
search warrant (Civ. Code §56.10(b)(3)–(7)). Likewise, LPS contains numerous provisions for disclosure under the legal system exception. Mental health
providers may be required to disclose confidential information to Senate
and Assembly Rules Committees or to lawyers with signed releases. These
exceptions to confidentiality recognize that, at times, the needs of the legal
system will outweigh a client's right to privacy—the balance swings away
from privacy and toward this important societal interest. (See chapter 7 for

specific questions regarding how a mental health professional should respond to a subpoena or a court order.)

## CRIMES COMMITTED BY HOSPITALIZED PATIENTS
The seventh exception to confidentiality involves crimes committed when a patient is hospitalized. Welfare and Institutions Code section 5328.4 provides that a mental health professional has a duty to disclose client information when there is probable cause to believe that certain serious crimes (e.g., murder, manslaughter, rape) have been perpetrated either by or upon a patient. When a mental health professional has probable cause to believe that any of these crimes has occurred, the institution's head mental health professional "*shall* [italics added] release information about the patient to governmental law enforcement agencies." In keeping with the Parsimony Principle, this section of LPS limits disclosure to information directly relating to the factual circumstances regarding the commission of the offense. No information regarding the patient's mental status should be released.

## RESEARCH
Exceptions to confidentiality found in the Civil Code and in the Welfare and Institutions Code allow disclosure of patient information for the purpose of research. Effective medical research relies on detailed patient information. Without this sharing of information, advances due to research would slow considerably. Under CMIA, medical information may be disclosed to legitimate researchers without client consent. Researchers are prohibited from further discussing the information in any way that would permit identification of the patient (Civ. Code §56.10(7)). LPS is more specific in its restrictions; under LPS, research must be approved by an institutional review board, and researchers must both sign an oath of confidentiality and obtain informed consent from their subjects (Welf. & Inst. Code §5328(e)).

## MANDATORY REPORTING STATUTES
The final exceptions to confidentiality are found in California's mandatory reporting statutes. To the extent the law serves as a balance for competing interests, mandatory reporting statutes provide an excellent illustration of our jurisprudence at work. Mandatory reporting statutes require that information pertaining to the safety of certain groups of individuals *not* be kept confidential. These are groups society has deemed

particularly vulnerable—children, the elderly and dependent adults, and individuals in need of hospital care. Because these groups are less able to protect themselves than other groups in society, we place a higher value on ensuring their health and well-being than we do on keeping information revealed in a clinical setting confidential. As a consequence, information about harm or abuse to individuals in these groups is made available to agencies charged with their protection. Mandatory reporting statutes make clear the societal balance of values: For individuals belonging to especially vulnerable groups, well-being and safety trump confidentiality. Thus, mandatory reporting statutes reside on the furthest end of the continuum—the interests of society outweigh the individual's right to privacy.

## MANDATORY REPORTING STATUTES

California's mandatory reporting statutes are remarkably similar to one another in both structure and content. We will comment upon seven elements of these statutes.

*The central elements of California's mandatory reporting laws can be found in appendix A.*

*An outline of the essential elements of the mandatory reporting statutes is found on pages 46–47.*

The first of the seven elements is perhaps the most obvious, and for that reason all the more likely to be overlooked: Individuals are *required* to report when certain criteria are met. That is why these statutes are called "mandatory," rather than "discretionary," reporting statutes. The statutes are quite specific about both the mandatory nature of the reporting, and the nature, circumstances, and timing of the reports that must be made.

The second of the seven elements is the list of mental health professionals upon whom the statutes impose a duty to report. This list, found at the beginning of each of the statutes, covers most professionals who would come into contact with the individuals at issue. In addition to mandating that certain individuals report, the statutes also *permit* any individual to report. The permissive element is expansive, insofar as there are no restrictions on who may file. Thus, the statutes have both mandatory and permissive elements. Certain individuals *must* report, any other individual *may* report.

The third element involves the definition of the individuals on behalf of whom a mandatory report would be made. A *child* is defined as anyone under the age of 18 years of age (Penal Code §11165), while an *elder* is defined as any person 65 years of age or older (Welf. & Inst. Code §15610.27). The definition of *dependent adult* has three factors: The person is between the ages of 18 and 64, the person has a mental or physical disability and, as a result of the mental or physical disability, the person is restricted in "her ability to carry out normal activities or to protect . . . her rights" (Penal Code §15610.23). Note how the first two groups are defined solely by age, while the third is defined by a dependency that stems from a disability. The reporting statutes that deal with assaults and injuries from neglect or abuse also require that a report must be made for individuals who are patients in hospitals and have been transferred to a hospital from a health or community care facility (e.g., a nursing home) (Penal Code §§11160(a), 11161.8).

The fourth element involves the definition of the conditions that must be reported. For children, a mental health professional must report "any act or omission that would constitute willful cruelty or unjustifiable punishment or emotional injury . . . which causes harm or substantial risk of harm to the child's health or welfare including sexual abuse, or . . . neglect, including malnutrition, or . . . dependen[ce] upon an addictive drug at birth" (Penal Code §11165.6). For children (individuals under 18 years of age), injuries that cause harm or substantial *risk* of harm, sexual abuse, neglect, or addiction at birth are the conditions to be reported. For elders or dependent adults, the definition of abuse is "physical abuse, neglect, fiduciary abuse, abandonment, isolation, abduction, or other treatment with resulting physical harm or pain or mental suffering, or the deprivation by a care custodian of goods or services that are necessary to avoid physical harm or mental suffering" (Welf. & Inst. Code §15610.07).

The legislature recognizes that certain kinds of abuse are endemic to certain groups of people. For example, the elderly are more likely to suffer fiduciary abuse—financial exploitation—than are children. As a consequence, the legislature included fiduciary abuse in the list of conditions that warrant a report when the victim is an elderly person. As another example, dependent adults are particularly susceptible to being cut off from the outside world by caretakers, who may refuse to allow visitors and telephone calls. The statute thus includes isolation as a form of abuse that requires a report. The statute dealing with patient injury from neglect or abuse defines those terms as a "physical injury or condition [that] appears to be the result of neglect or abuse" (Penal Code §11161.8). This statute ensures that hospitals will be alert to patients who have been abused or neglected in a health care facility, such as a nursing home, and require hospital level or emergent care as a result. Often such patients are dependent upon their caretakers, and so would be hesitant to report an injury if they must return to the same facility after discharge from the hospital. Each of these instances illustrates how the legislature addresses the needs of the specific population.

The fifth element identifies the standard by which reports must be made. The language of the statutes is virtually identical: A health care provider who "knows or reasonably suspects," that harm has occurred must report. The statute regarding mandatory reports for patients has a slight variation: A treater shall report if "*in* [*her*] *opinion . . .* [the injury] *reasonably appears* [italics added] to be the result of neglect or abuse" (Penal Code §11161.8). The statutes do not require that a reporter know definitively, or confirm, that the reportable condition—be it abuse, neglect, or sexual abuse—is present. Rather, the statutes only require that the reporter *reasonably suspects* that the necessary conditions are present. This represents a conscious decision of the legislature. Once a mandated reporter reasonably suspects that a reportable condition exists, she will turn the matter over to a state agency that will initiate an investigation. This wording encourages reporters to act without waiting for definitive evidence, thus *increasing* the likelihood that a report will be made. If a mental health professional is unsure of whether to make a report, she can call a child protective agency to ask whether a report is necessary. The mental health professional should give the facts of the case without providing any identifying information and without identifying herself. Thus, if a report is not necessary, no confidential information has been disclosed.

The sixth element involves the timing of the report. Each statute requires two types of reports: an oral report (which may be made by telephone) and a written report. The oral report must be made "immediately, or as soon as practically possible," while the written report must be made within 36 hours (for child abuse and patient neglect or abuse), or within 2 working days (for elder and dependent adult abuse). Reports about child abuse are made to a child protective agency. The term "child protective agency" includes a police or sheriff's department, a county probation department, or a county welfare department (Penal Code §11165.9). Reports concerning abuse of elderly or dependent adults are made to the local ombudsman (if the abuse occurred in a long-term care facility), to designated investigators of the State Department of Mental Health or the State Department of Developmental Services (if the abuse occurred in a state mental health hospital or a state developmental center), or to the adult protective services agency. In addition, reports concerning the abuse of elder or dependent adults can be made to a local law enforcement agency. Reports regarding patient injuries resulting from assaults, abuse, or neglect are made to the local police authority and to the county health department. *If you suspect that abuse has occurred, but are unsure of where to report, call your local police and ask whom you should contact.*

The seventh and final element is the penalties for not reporting when one is mandated to do so, and release from liability when a report is actually made. Each statute states that if a mandated reporter who reasonably suspects abuse fails to report, the reporter can be found guilty of a misdemeanor (a crime). The crime of failing to report is punishable by up to six months in the county jail, a fine of up to one thousand dollars, or both. On the other hand, each statute releases from both criminal and civil liability any individual who makes a report in good faith. The clear message is that penalties will attach if a reporter has reasonable cause to suspect abuse and does nothing, whereas such an individual who goes forward in accordance with the law and contacts the appropriate agency will not incur a penalty. Be careful: The statutes further indicate that an *in*appropriate disclosure—to an individual or agency not named in the statute—is a misdemeanor that can be punished by up to six months in jail, a fine of five hundred dollars, or both. Thus, although mandated reporters are required to disclose specified information to specific individuals or agencies, the information otherwise remains confidential. *If you work with individuals to whom a mandatory reporting statute applies—children, the elderly, dependent adults, or patients in a hospital—it is always best to know beforehand to whom a mandatory report would be made. Few experiences are worse than rushing around trying to figure out whom you should call or where you should send the mandatory report you have just written.*

One final mandatory reporting statute applies to a condition, rather than to a group of individuals. Health and Safety Code section 103900 states that physicians must report disorders "characterized by lapses of consciousness" (e.g., alcoholic blackouts, lapses of consciousness due to a head injury), including Alzheimer's disease. The purpose of section 103900 is to provide information to the Department of Motor Vehicles in order for the Department to determine who should be allowed to drive. Section 103900 has many of the elements of the other mandatory reporting statutes: The statute applies when any individual 14 years or older has been diagnosed with such a disorder; the report must be made to the local health officer; the report must be made "immediately"; and a man-

# MANDATORY REPORTING STATUTES

I.  **Mandated** reporting for certain groups:
    A.  Children (individuals under the age of 18) (Penal Code §11164)
    B.  Elderly (individuals 65 or over) (Welf. & Inst. Code §15610.27)
    C.  Dependent adults (individuals between the ages of 18 and 64 with a mental or physical limitation as a result of which they are dependent on others) (Welf. & Inst. Code §15610.23)
    D.  Hospital patients who have been transferred from a health or community care facility (Penal Code §11161.8)

II.  Conditions for reporting:
     A.  Children
         1.  Physical injury inflicted by other than accidental means
         2.  Sexual abuse (including sexual assault or sexual exploitation)
         3.  Act or omission that constitutes willful cruelty or unjustifiable punishment
         4.  Neglect
         5.  Physical dependence upon addictive drug at birth
     B.  Elderly and dependent adults
         1.  Physical abuse (assault, battery, unreasonable restraint, sexual abuse)
         2.  Misuse of physical or chemical restraint
         3.  Neglect, abandonment, or isolation
         4.  Fiduciary abuse (misappropriation of money or property)
     C.  Patients
         1.  Abuse
         2.  Neglect
         3.  Assaultive injuries (e.g., from a firearm)

III.  Standard for reporting: **Know or reasonably suspect** that condition for reporting is present

IV.  When reports must be made:
     A.  Oral reports (immediately, or as soon as possible)
     B.  Written reports
         1.  Children and patients (within 36 hours)
         2.  Elderly and dependent adults (within 2 working days)

V.  To whom reports must be made when report involves:
    A.  Children (a child protective agency or local law enforcement)

*continued*

---

      B.  Elderly/dependent adults (long-term care ombudsman, local law enforcement, or county adult protective services)

      C.  Patients (local police authority and county health department)

  VI.  Failure to report: Possible criminal sanctions, civil sanctions, and professional discipline

  VII.  Release from liability: No civil or criminal sanctions attach when report is made in good faith

  VIII.  One mandatory reporting statute applies to a condition: **disorders characterized by a lapse of consciousness** (H. & S. Code, §103900)

      A.  Physicians are mandated reporters.

      B.  Reports must be made on any individual 14 years of age or older.

      C.  Reports must be made "immediately."

      D.  Reports must be made to the local health officer.

      E.  Release from liability for making a report pursuant to the statute.

---

dated reporter who discloses information pursuant to the statute is released from liability.

After reading about the exceptions to confidentiality, it might seem as though the exceptions have swallowed the rule. The length of this section, however, attests to the enormously complex interplay between a patient's right to privacy and interests belonging to society as a whole. Keep in mind that every disclosure of confidential information arises from a balance of these competing interests.

## LAWS THAT GOVERN TESTIMONIAL PRIVILEGE

The purpose of testimonial privilege is to allow a sacred space—a hallowed ground—that is protected from the scrutiny of the legal system. The California Supreme Court first created a psychotherapist-patient privilege in the case of *In re Lifshutz*, 2 Cal. 3d 415 (1970). Subsequently, the California legislature wrote laws that specified how privilege works for mental health professionals of various disciplines; these laws are found in the California Evidence Code, beginning at section 1012.

Testimonial privilege is created by statute, and only when a statute specifically names a discipline should a mental health professional assume that testimonial privilege applies. In other words, only when a statute explicitly names your discipline should you assume that your client may rely on privilege to prevent you from disclosing information in a legal proceeding. As an example of how testimonial privilege statutes are exclusive, the psychotherapist-patient privilege includes *licensed* clinical social workers within the definition of "psychotherapist." Confidential communications shared with an *un*licensed social worker might not be covered by privilege; that is, a client may not have the prerogative to prevent an *un*licensed social worker from discussing what was said in a treatment, if the social worker were given a subpoena to do so. So—know whether the privilege statute applies to your discipline.

Three additional points about testimonial privilege. First, consistent with the value of individual autonomy, *privilege belongs to the client.* It is the client's prerogative to decide whether to invoke or to waive privilege, as section 1013 of the Evidence Code makes clear. Second, testimonial privilege, like confidentiality, is not absolute; exceptions to privilege allow patient communications to be disclosed in a legal proceeding. If you think of testimonial privilege as a cloak that hides confidential communications from the scrutiny of the legal system, you can think of the exceptions to testimonial privilege as holes in the cloak that let the law "peek through" and see what happened in a relationship normally hidden from its eyes. Finally, keep the concept of testimonial privilege separate from the concept of mandatory reporting. A mandatory reporting statute tells a mental health professional to *do* something; privilege indicates whether a patient's communication can be revealed in a legal proceeding. Privilege has to do with lawyers, courts, and judges; mandatory reporting tells a mental health professional to pick up the phone.

## EXCEPTIONS TO TESTIMONIAL PRIVILEGE

The exceptions found in the testimonial privilege statutes are perhaps more appropriately referred to as "potential exceptions." The reason for this qualification is that no exception to testimonial privilege is automatic; when the possibility of an exception is raised, a judge will review the materials in his chambers (called an in camera review). In the review the judge will determine whether some exception to privilege will allow the materials to be disclosed in the legal proceeding. Only when the materials fall under an exception to privilege will the judge order that they be disclosed.

The first exception to privilege arises when a client presents her mental or emotional condition as an issue in court (Evid. Code §1016). The reasoning behind this exception is straightforward: If an individual wishes to make his mental or emotional state an issue in a legal matter, that claim must be given a full and fair hearing. A full and fair hearing requires that information gathered by a mental health professional be heard. Thus, if, following an accident of some sort, a patient makes a claim based on emotional suffering, his therapy records may no longer be protected by privilege. Why? Because he has made his emotional state an issue in a legal matter and it would be unfair to allow the patient to hide behind the cloak of privilege to protect information that might disprove his claim.

The second exception to privilege is communications made during a psychiatric evaluation for the purpose of determining a criminal defendant's state of mind. This exception is premised *upon the mental health professional having informed the client that his communications are not confidential.* If, for example, a mental health professional is asked by a court to examine a criminal defendant for the purpose of determining whether the defendant was sane at the time of a crime, the mental health professional must tell the client that their conversation will *not* be kept in confidence. If the mental health professional fails to do so, the defendant's testimony cannot be admitted into evidence. Note how this exception is really a variation on client consent; if the mental health professional does not explain to the defendant the purpose of the examination, namely, that it is to help the court or the jury determine his mental state at the time of the crime, the client will *not* have consented to the disclosure and the examination cannot be submitted in court. This exception to privilege does not apply when the court orders the examination "in order to provide the lawyer with information needed so that [she] may advise the defendant whether to enter or withdraw a plea based on insanity or to present a defense based on [her] emotional condition" (Evid. Code §1017). In such a case, the purpose of the examination is to help the defendant and his lawyer plot legal strategy, and society will allow this information to remain between the lawyer and her client.

The third set of exceptions to psychotherapist-patient privilege is designed to ensure that invoking testimonial privilege does not hide criminal or civil wrongdoing from the legal system. Section 1018 of the Evidence Code states, "There is no privilege . . . if the services of the psychotherapist were sought or obtained to enable or aid anyone to commit or plan to commit a crime or a tort or to escape detection or apprehension after the commission of a crime or a tort." Other circumstances also fall outside privilege due to potential criminal activity. If, for example, you have a patient under the age of 16 and you have reasonable cause to believe that she "has been a victim of a crime and that disclosure of the communication is in the best interest of the child," the psychotherapist-patient privilege does not apply (Evid. Code §1018). As a consequence, your patient cannot invoke privilege to keep this information out of a legal proceeding. Thus, if your patient is the child victim of a crime, testimonial privilege will not keep information relevant to the crime out of the court.

The fourth category of exceptions to privilege involves deeds, wills, transfers of property, and other claims having to do with patients who have died. Communications relevant to the validity of a deed or the will of a deceased patient are not privileged (Evid. Code §§1019, 1021, 1022). Nor is there privilege when two people are having a legal disagreement that involves some interest—for example money or property—of a patient who has died. The reasoning behind these exceptions is that the patient is no longer alive and the information is needed to settle a legal dispute.

The fifth exception to privilege allows for disclosure of communications relevant to a claim that a psychotherapist has been negligent in her duties (Evid. Code §1020). If, for example, a patient brings a legal action against his treater, and confidential information is necessary, or even relevant, to the treater's defense, the patient will not be allowed to invoke privilege in order to prevent the information from being admitted into the legal proceeding. The law will thus not permit a client to use testimonial privilege as a way of rendering the mental health professional defenseless against the client's accusation.

Finally, section 1024 of the Evidence Code states that there is no privilege when the psychotherapist has "reasonable cause to believe that the patient is in such mental or emotional condition as to be dangerous to himself or to the person or property of another." Section 1024 states further that disclosure is allowed only when "*necessary* [italics added] to prevent the threatened danger." Section 1024 is similar to the exception to confidentiality created by the *Tarasoff* statute; note, however, that privilege falls away either if the person is merely "dangerous" (the threat does not have to be one of "serious physical violence"), or if the person is dangerous to *himself* (the *Tarasoff* statute concerns a threat of serious physical violence to *others*). Section 1024 takes away privilege when the threat is to another's person *or* property; again, however, the information remains protected by privilege unless disclosure is *necessary* to prevent the danger.

Part I, our introduction to the law, closes here. Part II, 175 Questions on California Mental Health Law, is really nothing more than the application of the concepts put forth in the first part of the book. As you read part II, keep in mind that behind every statute or regulation lies an important value; behind every exception to a statute or regulation lies another important value.

When faced with a problem that has no clear solution, think through what values are at stake. Remember as you do so that any statute or regulation can be analyzed in the same way as we've done in chapters 2 and 3. If you can break a law down into its smaller parts, the law's mystique will soon evaporate. So will lingering anxieties about your legal rights and responsibilities.

# OVERVIEW OF PRIVACY, CONFIDENTIALITY, AND TESTIMONIAL PRIVILEGE

I. Privacy: The right to decide how to live one's own life
   A. Constitution of the United States (penumbras of amendments to the Constitution)
   B. Article I, section 1, of the California Constitution
   C. Information Practices Act of 1977 (beginning at Civ. Code §1798)

II. Confidentiality: The client's right to have communications kept within the bounds of the professional relationship
   A. All health services providers must maintain the confidentiality of all medical information (Confidentiality of Medical Information Act; Civ. Code §56).
   B. Confidentiality is maintained for all clients in the public mental health system and in public and private psychiatric hospitals (Lanterman-Petris-Short Act; Welf. & Inst. Code §5328).
   C. Confidentiality is maintained for developmentally disabled individuals (Welf. & Inst. Code §4514).

III. Testimonial privilege (or simply privilege): The client's right to prevent the mental health professional from revealing confidential communications in a legal proceeding
   A. Psychotherapists (Evid. Code §§1010, 1014)
      1. Psychiatrists
      2. Licensed psychologists
      3. Licensed clinical social workers
      4. Licensed marriage, family, and child counselors
      5. State credentialed school psychologists
      6. Supervised assistants, interns, trainees, and students engaged in clinical work
      7. Registered nurses who possess a master's degree in psychiatric mental health nursing
      8. Individuals providing mental health services under Fam. Code §6924 (individuals providing mental health services to a minor, pursuant to the minor's consent)
   B. Consistent with the value of individual autonomy, privilege belongs to the patient.
   C. A client is said to "waive privilege" when she allows a mental health professional to reveal communications in a court of law, a deposition, or an administrative hearing.
   D. A client is said to "invoke privilege" when she does not allow a mental health professional to reveal communications in a court of law, a deposition, or an administrative hearing.
   E. If the client is unavailable, the mental health professional should invoke privilege on the client's behalf.

# Part II

# *175 QUESTIONS ON CALIFORNIA MENTAL HEALTH LAW*

Part II consists of 175 questions mental health professionals often ask about the law. For the most part, the questions are self-explanatory, so only a brief word of introduction is in order.

First, our questions represent a fraction of what could be asked—the list is virtually endless. What we have done is to divide the questions into ten topic headings that cover the essential areas of California mental health law, and then to present those questions that, in our experience, most concern clinicians. Familiarity with these answers will provide an excellent overview of what clinicians need to know in California. If, after reading part II, you don't have a particular answer you are looking for, you will at the very least have a way to think about the question, which is often nearly as good as having the answer itself.

Second, the questions refer to a number of statutes, regulations, and court cases. We therefore thought it would be helpful to review how California laws are cited:

- *Statutes*: Welf. & Inst. Code §5150 refers to the California Welfare and Institutions Code, section 5150.

- *Cases of the California Supreme Court:* 54 Cal. 3d 56 (1991) refers to the 1991 opinion of the California Supreme Court, found in volume 54 of the third edition of the *California Reports*, at page 56.
- *Cases of the California Court of Appeal:* 5 Cal. App. 3d 584 (1991) refers to the 1991 opinion of the California Court of Appeal, found in volume 5 of the third edition of the *California Appellate Reports*, at page 584.
- *Code of California Regulations:* 15 Cal. Code Regs. §1207 refers to the California Code of Regulations, title 15, section 1207.

Finally, don't read all the questions at once. It's too much. Part II covers a lot of territory, much more than can be absorbed in one sitting. At most, read a single topic at a time. Responses are designed for easy access and are well-suited as references—but they can be dense. Take your time, enjoy what you read, and let us know what you think. Part II of this book will serve its purpose well if our readers find our responses to these questions helpful in their clinical practice.

# 4

# THE LEGAL SYSTEM AND LEGAL PROCESS

*Mental health professionals find no topic more shrouded in mystery than the legal system and legal process: the law's way of doing things. Remember, though, that lawyers find what mental health professionals do equally mystifying—and intriguing. The questions below, which discuss particular aspects of how the legal system works, are written to illuminate the method behind the law's seeming madness. As you read, try to keep in mind both the legal rule and whatever value the rule, or its exception, is designed to promote.*

## QUESTIONS DISCUSSED IN THIS CHAPTER

1. What is the difference between civil law and criminal law?
2. What is a tort?
3. What does it mean to say that our system of law is "adversarial"?
4. What is a standard of proof?
5. What is a burden of proof?
6. What does it mean to say that a court has "jurisdiction"?

7. Why do lawyers seem so different from mental health professionals?
8. What is a deposition?
9. Why is a deposition important?
10. What is an interrogatory?
11. What is the difference between an expert witness and a fact witness?
12. Who decides who qualifies as an expert witness?
13. If I receive a subpoena and must testify at a deposition about a therapy case, am I an expert witness or a fact witness?
14. What should I know if I am called to testify as a fact witness?
15. Does whether I am an expert witness or a fact witness make any difference in what I am paid?
16. I've heard that a "writ of habeas corpus" can play an important role in protecting the rights of a psychiatric patient. What is a writ of habeas corpus?
17. What is a patients' rights advocate, and how is a patients' rights advocate different from a lawyer?
18. I hear lawyers refer to what seems a dizzying array of laws—for example, the Welfare and Institutions Code, the Penal Code, the Health and Safety Code, the Evidence Code, and the Probate Code. How do all these different codes fit together?
19. What is a statute of limitations?
20. What is the statute of limitations for malpractice lawsuits in California?
21. What is the discovery rule?
22. How do the statute of limitations and the discovery rule apply to cases involving minors?
23. What is the Americans with Disabilities Act?

# DISCUSSION

**1. What is the difference between civil law and criminal law?**
Criminal law is based on the notion of *moral blameworthiness*. In a criminal court a person may be found "guilty," given a fine, and sentenced to jail or prison because he has violated the criminal law and so must be morally sanctioned. Murder and manslaughter are two examples of crimes for which society punishes wrongdoers.

The civil law is much further removed from the notion of moral blameworthiness. The purpose of a civil lawsuit is to assign responsibility for harm and to make an injured party whole. Thus, the purpose of a malpractice suit is to determine whether a treater is responsible—in civil court parlance, "liable"—for the harm suffered by a patient. If the treater is found liable, the civil court will then determine the remedy for that harm, that is, what is required to make the patient whole. The remedy is referred to as the "award."

### 2. What is a tort?

In the words of Black's Law Dictionary, a tort is "A private or civil wrong or injury . . . for which a court will provide a remedy in the form of an action for damages." To explain, a tort is a *civil* wrong—a private individual has been harmed and goes to court to seek compensation. A tort action differs from a criminal action, which is brought by a prosecutor or district attorney to redress a wrong against society. At times the parties in a tort action will agree to *settle*. To settle a case means that the parties agree to some amount of damages without waiting for a court to decide for them. Malpractice is a type of tort (the elements of a malpractice claim are discussed in chapter 2).

### 3. What does it mean to say that our system of law is "adversarial"?

Legal actions, whether civil or criminal, pit one party against another. The parties to a lawsuit are thus *adversaries*. Our adversarial system of law is built on the assumption that having two parties on opposite sides of an issue is the way most likely to yield what is true, right, and fair. In criminal cases, one party is the government. The idea is that an individual has harmed society as a whole by his crime, and the government has the responsibility of ensuring that the individual is held accountable for what he has done. Note how, by taking on this responsibility, the government also precludes private individuals from exacting retribution—vengeance belongeth to the state. Thus, the title of a criminal case in California is always along the lines of *People v. Saks,* showing that the people of the State of California are the aggrieved party bringing suit. Saks is the criminal *defendant,* who may go to jail if she is found guilty. (The "People" are referred to as the *prosecution* or simply as the *State.*) In civil law, private individuals who have been harmed may bring the action, and are referred to as *plaintiffs.* The second name in the title of both civil and criminal lawsuits, the name on the other side of the "v." (for "versus") is the defendant. What's important to remember is that lawsuits consist of adversaries, two parties with competing interests, only one of whom will prevail.

### 4. What is a standard of proof?

Think of a "standard of proof" as a hurdle. If someone told you that on your way to work tomorrow you would have to jump over a hurdle, you might well ask, "How high is the hurdle?" Exactly the same question is asked in the law. The height of the "proof hurdle" in a legal proceeding is called the standard of proof. The standard of proof depends on the importance of the issues at stake. For example, criminal trials, in which a defendant's personal liberty is at stake, require our system's highest standard of proof, *beyond a reasonable doubt.* The reason for this strict standard of proof is that our society will deprive an individual of his liberty only when his guilt is certain. Thus, society's values are reflected in the choice of the standard of proof. Proof *beyond a reasonable doubt* is considered proof in the 99% range. Proof *by clear and convincing evidence* is considered to be proof in the 75% range. The lowest standard of proof, *a preponderance of the evidence,* is 51%, or *more likely than not.* Malpractice cases involve the lowest standard of proof, *a preponderance of the evidence.*

### 5. What is a burden of proof?

While the *standard* of proof refers to the height of the proof hurdle, the *burden* of proof refers to which party must jump the hurdle to win the case. In a criminal case, the prosecutor—the attorney for the government—bears the burden of proof. It is therefore the prosecutor who must prove beyond a reasonable doubt that the defendant is guilty. In a malpractice case, the plaintiff bears the burden of proof. It is therefore the plaintiff who must show by a preponderance of the evidence that all the elements of a malpractice claim (see chapter 2) are present.

Any legal proceeding will involve both a standard and a burden of proof. A mental health professional who becomes involved in a legal proceeding will therefore want to know what standard of proof the case requires, and which party bears the burden of proof. In other words, the mental health professional will ask "How high is the hurdle?" and "Who must jump the hurdle to win the case?"

### 6. What does it mean to say that a court has "jurisdiction"?

Jurisdiction is the legal way of saying "who gets to decide." The person who has the T.V. clicker has *jurisdiction* over which programs are watched; the person in the driver's seat has *jurisdiction* over what radio station is played in the car; the birthday boy or girl has *jurisdiction* over what kind of cake gets served. Jurisdiction indicates in whose domain a particular matter rests. Generally, a statute will indicate which court has jurisdiction over a given matter. California statutes, for example, provide that the probate court has jurisdiction over guardianships, the superior court has jurisdiction over malpractice cases, and the juvenile court has jurisdiction over cases involving abused and neglected children. Jurisdiction is always relevant because a party must determine *which* court has jurisdiction before it can proceed with a legal action.

**7. Why do lawyers seem so different from mental health professionals?**
Lawyers, by training, are professional skeptics who take nothing at face value and will insist that a mental health professional support a position by concrete evidence. To complicate matters, lawyers see themselves as representing the patient's wishes. To a lawyer, representing the patient's wishes translates into what the patient says he wants at a given time.

The skepticism displayed by lawyers is part of their professional training and serves them well in legal proceedings, where evidence must be supported by standards of proof. Recall that the lowest standard of proof is a preponderance of the evidence. That standard requires lawyers to marshal enough evidence to demonstrate that their argument is *more likely than not* correct. Mental health professionals are rarely held to even the lowest legal standard of proof—appropriately, since their work is different. Perhaps, however, mental health professionals sacrifice a thoroughness by not being more rigorously challenged.

A number of years ago one of us attended a clinical case conference in the Midwest. A consultant was interviewing a patient who had been admitted to a psychiatric hospital for having jumped off a rather high bridge. Despite the height of the bridge, the patient had suffered no injuries whatsoever. The discussion following the interview centered on the level of this patient's suicidality. As the case conference went on, one of the clinicians rather timidly asked whether there was any independent confirmation that this young woman had indeed jumped off the bridge. Not surprisingly, there was not. The patient had shown up at an emergency room in soaking wet clothes and every clinician from that point on had simply taken her story at face value. The remarkable issue was not that this young woman did—or did not—jump off the bridge. Rather, it was that her treating clinicians did not know and had not attempted to find out or confirm whether she had or hadn't, yet were proceeding as if this part of her history were certain. Clearly the clinical assessment would be quite different depending on whether this woman actually jumped off the bridge, or whether she *claimed* that she jumped off the bridge, but had not. A bit of lawyerly skepticism at the outset might have been useful for the treatment.

Lawyers apply their skepticism all the time. They will ask how a clinician *knows* that a patient will hurt himself if released from the hospital, how a clinician *knows* that a particular treatment will work, or how a clinician *knows* that a patient cannot perform a certain job or task. While the questions may seem abrasive, insensitive, and not fully appreciative of the mental health professional's expertise, it is based on the legal model: At least a preponderance of the evidence, or 51% of the available data, must supply the foundation for any position, statement, or opinion.

Another matter to consider is that a lawyer is a patient's (and, for that matter, a mental health professional's) legal representative. For a lawyer, proper representation means vigorously advocating for what the client says he wants. Therein lies a friction with mental health professionals. Clinicians are trained in the complexity of human behavior. They regard a patient's oral expression of a desire as only one aspect of what the person truly wants. Often mental health professionals will counsel an individual to delay acting until ample time has been devoted to exploring all the advantages and disadvantages of a particular course of action. Other times, mental health professionals will probe a patient's unexpressed feelings. Thus, the posture of the mental health professional—to delay and to explore—is often directly at odds with that of the lawyer—to act. This difference can be intensified by the lawyer's skepticism, by virtue of which the lawyer may discount a mental health professional's reasons for caution and delay. The consequences of this friction are mental health professionals who feel devalued professionally, and frustrated that lawyers are helping patients accomplish what mental health professionals consider not necessarily in the patients' best interests.

Despite these differences, there are many successful lawyer-clinician teams who do excellent work. If you are called upon to work with an attorney, try to keep three things in mind: First, both you and the lawyer are working on behalf of the patient. While you may disagree about goals, each of you has been trained to assist your client within the scope of your expertise. Second, find the time to ask yourself the sort of questions the lawyer might ask. Clinicians rarely engage in this sort of activity, partly because they are rarely called upon to explain the rationale behind their treatment. Ask yourself questions like: What is my treatment plan? What facts in the history support my use of this plan? What facts in the history would be inconsistent with this plan? Might there be other plans that I have not considered and that may be helpful? If I have made an intervention, such as an involuntary hospitalization, on what basis have I made that intervention? How certain am I that the intervention will be successful? On what facts or observations do I base my certainty? In other words, try to place yourself in the shoes of the lawyer and ask the skeptical questions she would ask. Third, find a time to sit with the lawyer to understand better what she thinks about the case. Ask what the lawyer intends to do and why she intends to do it. Explore the reasons behind her plan of action. As you discuss the case with the lawyer, remember that she will hold your reasoning to a standard of evidence, so be prepared to explain the reasons behind *your* thinking as well. Above all, keep in mind that the more you and the lawyer work *together*, the better each of you will serve your mutual client.

## 8. What is a deposition?

Depositions are part of a legal process called "discovery." "Discovery" is just that—a process whereby one party in a lawsuit discovers facts and information from another party in the lawsuit. The discovery process has several purposes: The facts and information garnered during discovery allow the parties to focus the issues that will be addressed at trial; facts and information that may be lost or forgotten before the trial actually takes place are recorded and thereby preserved; the parties may be more disposed to settle the lawsuit after certain facts and information come to light. The process of discovery allows a party literally *to discover* the nature, strengths, and weaknesses of the lawsuit. Depositions are an important part of the discovery process. The purpose of taking a deposition is consistent with the purpose of discovery—for a party to learn *what it does not know.*

Depositions are particularly well suited to uncovering unknown facts and information. Depositions consist of oral questions and oral responses. Lawyers can ask questions from a wide range of topics. Furthermore, the rules of admissibility—rules that can exclude certain evidence from a trial—are much less strict for depositions. Wide latitude is given to lawyers regarding the types and scope of the questions. If an objection is raised to a particular question, the objection is noted and reviewed at trial. The question itself is answered during the deposition.

Most depositions take place at an attorney's office—the attorney who wants the deposition—at a time that all the parties agree on. Testimony at a deposition takes place under oath and a court reporter is present to record the proceedings. A deposition may last from half an hour to several days, depending on the importance of the testimony being taken.

It is wise to consult your malpractice carrier any time you testify, to determine whether the presence of a lawyer is indicated. If you receive a subpoena, be sure to check with your malpractice carrier and follow their advice on whether you should have legal representation. One instance will always require an attorney's presence: when you are the defendant (that is, the person being sued). When an issue of confidentiality or testimonial privilege is likely to arise, you should seriously consider having a lawyer present, insofar as answering a question may expose you to a claim that you have breached your client's confidentiality (see chapter 7, Subpoenas and Court Orders).

**9. Why is a deposition important?**
We cannot overemphasize the significance of a deposition. Deposition testimony is taken under oath. Consequently, false or misleading statements can lead to a charge of perjury. In addition, if what you say at trial differs from what you said at a deposition, the opposing counsel can use your deposition to contradict—in legal parlance, "impeach"—you at trial. It is extremely useful to obtain a copy of the transcript following the deposition, for two reasons: First, you will want to check the transcript for accuracy and correct any mistakes for the final version; second, having a copy of the transcript will allow you to review what you said at the deposition before you testify at trial.

**10. What is an interrogatory?**
An interrogatory is the *written* equivalent of a deposition. An interrogatory is sent only to the parties in the lawsuit, not to expert witnesses. When a party receives the interrogatory, she must respond in writing and sign a sworn statement that the responses are true.

**11. What is the difference between an expert witness and a fact witness?**
A fact witness is an individual who has *personal knowledge* of some

situation or event relevant to a legal proceeding. An expert witness need not have personal knowledge of the matter. Rather, an expert witness is called to testify because he has *special knowledge that can help the jury in making its decision.* While a fact witness testifies to *facts,* of which he has direct knowledge, an expert witness gives expert *opinions* that derive from his unique expertise.

As an example, consider that one day you are walking down the aisle of the grocery store. You slip on a banana peel and aggravate that old knee injury so that you are unable to participate in the big croquet tournament this weekend. You sue the store for your injury. You will call as a *fact witness* anyone who was in the store who witnessed the events surrounding your accident, such as the baker who saw the banana on the floor immediately before you fell, the person at the cash register who saw you go down, the butcher who heard your bloodcurdling scream. All of these people have personal knowledge of what happened—they will testify about the events that lead to your injury based on what they personally saw and heard. Courts allow fact witnesses to testify solely about what they personally experienced. If they attempt to testify to matters of which they have no direct experience, the lawyer on the other side will become apoplectic and ask the judge to please tell the witness to stop speaking immediately.

You will call as an *expert witness* Dr. Peal, the world-famous authority on injuries suffered during banana falls. Dr. Peal did not see or hear you fall, but he has special knowledge regarding how the knee turns in an unusual manner during a banana fall and the injuries unique to those dreadful contortions. Dr. Peal will testify about the severity of your injury, your likely prognosis, and your inability to participate in the upcoming croquet tournament. Note that Dr. Peal was not in the store when you fell, and he has no personal knowledge of what occurred. Rather, Dr. Peal's knowledge about your injury derives almost entirely from second-hand information: your description of the fall, the X-rays, the report of the emergency room physician, and the reports submitted by your treating physician.

Two comments about expert witnesses. First, the expert is allowed to speak only on those matters his expertise covers. Dr. Peal will not be allowed to speak about the sorts of injuries that result from garbanzo-bean falls, because he is only a banana-fall expert. Garbanzo beans lie outside his area of expertise. Note how this restriction is somewhat like the restriction on fact witnesses, who are allowed to testify only as to matters of which they have personal knowledge. All witnesses—fact and expert—may speak solely to those matters that lie within their direct experience (fact) or within their expertise (expert).

Second, the expert must testify as to the facts that underlie his expert opinion. Describing the facts upon which the expert opinion is based is called "laying the foundation." Dr. Peal, for example, will base his expert opinion—that you must wait one year before you play croquet again—on his examination of your knee, his review of your knee's medical record, and his exploration of the sprawling and sometimes treacherous croquet fields on which you compete. He will begin his testimony by describing in great detail his examination, his review, and his exploration. He will then say (in an appropriately ponderous tone), "Based on these facts, I am of the opinion that . . . " Dr. Peal has laid his foundation.

### 12. Who decides who qualifies as an expert witness?
The judge decides who will qualify as an expert witness. Judges have a great deal of discretion in this regard; there isn't any list of names or qualifications that determine who is an expert. Rather, the trial judge asks two questions: Does the expert know things that the jury most likely does not? Will what the expert knows help the jury in making its decision? If the answer to both these questions is "yes," the judge is free to qualify the person as an expert and allow her to give expert opinions at trial.

### 13. If I receive a subpoena and must testify at a deposition about a therapy case, am I an expert witness or a fact witness?
You can be "subpoenaed" as either, so *be clear about whether you are being called to testify as an expert or as a fact witness.* A lawyer will not send a subpoena to his own witness. Therefore, if you receive a subpoena, it is from the *other* side. A lawyer would subpoena you as an expert only if you had already been identified as an expert by *your* side. So if you receive a subpoena and are confused about whether you are an expert or a fact witness, you are almost certainly a fact witness.

### 14. What should I know if I am called to testify as a fact witness?
The following five points may be helpful if you receive a subpoena to testify as a fact witness.

First, you are not required to prepare for a deposition, either by reading your notes or reviewing the therapy. Preparing may lessen your anxiety, but time so spent will not be compensated. So if you do decide to prepare, it's on your own time.

Second, should you decide to prepare, know that any documents you make regarding your patient's treatment—including personal notes made in contemplation of your testimony—are subject to a subpoena! In addition, an attorney can question you about *conversations* you had in preparation for the deposition, with whomever, including your patient and your patient's attorney. The sole exception is that you do not have to answer questions about conversations you had with your own attorney.

Third, respond only to the questions. Volunteer nothing and speculate even less. "I don't recall" or "I don't know" are fine answers, if true. A deposition is neither an intelligence test nor a memory competition. Attempts to impress the opposing attorney with your memory may get you into trouble at trial, when written documents show exactly the opposite of what you testified under oath at the deposition.

Fourth, although you are being called as a fact witness, the opposing attorney will very likely ask you to give an expert opinion. If you are asked a question that demands *more than your personal knowledge of this treatment and this patient,* give your attorney time to object before beginning your answer. If, for example, you are asked to explain the usual prognosis for patients with this diagnosis, to discuss the controversy surrounding what medication should be given to such patients, or to give your opinion on the debate over the treatment of choice, you are being asked to provide expert testimony. Because this testimony is not based on your knowledge of this singular treatment and this particular patient, your attorney will object. Subsequently, the court will limit your testimony to the facts of which you are personally aware.

Finally, you must have permission (preferably in writing) from your patient or an order from the court (see chapter 7, Subpoenas and Court Orders) before you disclose any information or release any records. Only your patient's permission or an order from the court will allow you to disclose confidential information or communications that are protected by testimonial privilege. A subpoena alone will not suffice.

### 15. Does whether I am an expert witness or a fact witness make any difference in what I am paid?

Whether you are a fact witness or an expert witness makes an *enormous* difference in how much you are paid. *Expert witnesses* generally charge an hourly fee for their services, which may consist of interviewing the patient, reviewing the record, speaking with current or former treaters, discussing the case with lawyers, and traveling to and from where the testimony is taken. An expert witness who is subpoenaed by the lawyer for the opposite side is entitled to payment by the opposition. Matters of payment will be settled before the expert testifies.

*Fact witnesses* are paid a fee established by Government Code section 68093. The fee in California is $35.00 per day (*not* per hour) and $.20 per mile of traveling. That said, many clinicians who are called as fact witnesses attempt to negotiate a reasonable hourly fee—usually through an attorney—for time spent at the deposition and any time spent in preparation for the deposition. Both sides have an incentive to negotiate in these circumstances. The clinician who is testifying would obviously like to get paid more than $35.00 per day, especially since she will almost certainly have to cancel appointments. The attorney who has issued the subpoena does not want a clinician who is angry at having to cancel appointments, frustrated about pay, and eager to say as little as possible to expedite the process and get back to her office. The negotiated payment may be the clinician's hourly treatment fee.

### 16. I've heard that a "writ of habeas corpus" can play an important role in protecting the rights of a psychiatric patient. What is a writ of habeas corpus?

A writ of habeas corpus is a procedure that comes from centuries-old English law. The writ of habeas corpus, often referred to as the "Great Writ" because of its enormous legal and social significance, was used to request that a judge review the legality of an individual's incarceration. The drafters of the United States Constitution included the Great Writ as a means of having a judge review the decision of a state to incarcerate an individual.

When current mental health laws were enacted in California, the writ of habeas corpus was incorporated into California law to allow for a judge to review an individual's involuntary hospitalization. The power of a writ of habeas corpus is that it affords an individual the opportunity to go before a judge and say, "I am being confined illegally." The judge will then review the detention.

### 17. What is a patients' rights advocate, and how is a patients' rights advocate different from a lawyer?

A patients' rights advocate is an individual who is responsible for assisting recipients of mental health services. A patients' rights advocate may be an attorney, or anyone who acts on behalf of a mental health client. Certain patients' rights advocates are specifically recognized by section 5520 of the Welfare and Institutions Code, which requires each county to appoint or contract for the services of one or more patients' rights advocates. Generally, patients' rights advocates protect the rights and secure treatment or other services to which patients are entitled. Patients' rights advocates thus investigate complaints, monitor mental health facilities for compliance with patients' rights provisions, and provide training and education about mental health law. Patients' rights advocates also provide representation at hearings that involve involuntary treatment and detention.

**18. I hear lawyers refer to what seems a dizzying array of laws—for example, the Welfare and Institutions Code, the Penal Code, the Health and Safety Code, the Evidence Code, and the Probate Code. How do all these different codes fit together?**
To deal with the complexity of laws regulating modern society, the legislature has categorized laws according to general areas. Because mental health intersects with a wide array of these general areas, laws affecting mental health are found in a variety of codes.

Ideally, all of the separate categories of laws enacted by the legislature are consistent with one another. In practice, however, statutes (see chapter 1) sometimes don't work together so well. Under section 1801 of the *Probate* Code, for example, an individual who cannot properly provide for his or her own personal needs may have a conservator appointed. Under the Lanterman-Petris-Short (LPS) Act, which is part of the *Welfare and Institutions* Code, a person who is gravely disabled as a result of a mental disorder may also have a conservator appointed. Thus, it may happen that a person has both a probate and an LPS conservator at the same time. Prior to 1986, it would have been unclear which conservator governed treatment decisions. In this instance, the Legislature has (thankfully) clarified the ambiguity by granting superiority to the LPS conservator. Because ambiguities in the law remain, however, it is always recommended that you consult an attorney when it is unclear which law governs your situation.

**19. What is a statute of limitations?**
The law seeks to promote justice. If one individual injures another, justice requires that the injured party be allowed to seek compensation for that injury. But how long should the injured party be allowed to wait before she brings a lawsuit? Some might argue that she should be able to

wait as long as she likes. She was harmed and therefore deserves compensation, regardless of when she seeks it.

The law takes a different position. The law limits the amount of time that may pass before you bring a suit, for two reasons. First, even though someone harmed you, that person has a right eventually to proceed with her life, without fear of being brought into court. A limitation on when a plaintiff can bring suit allows people to continue with their lives without worrying that events from the distant past could return to burden them. Thus, laws that limit the time within which a plaintiff can bring suit promote efficiency. Second, evidence becomes stale with time. A lawsuit affords a plaintiff an opportunity to prove that another person harmed her. The accused, in turn, has the opportunity to defend herself. If too much time elapses before a plaintiff files the suit, the accused person's ability to defend herself proportionately diminishes—memories fade, physical evidence deteriorates, and people helpful to a defense become old and die. For these reasons, the law imposes a time limit following an injury within which a plaintiff must bring suit. If the time expires, the lawsuit will not be heard. The *statute of limitations* specifies the length of this time period.

### 20. What is the statute of limitations for malpractice lawsuits in California?

The California statute of limitations for medical malpractice lawsuits, Code of Civil Procedure section 340.5, requires that any action be filed within one year of the patient's discovery of the harm. If, however, the patient is unaware of the injury for a period of time, the statute of limitations allows three years to file suit (see the following question). In a single instance the time for bringing suit can exceed three years—when the plaintiff can prove fraud, intentional concealment, or the presence of a foreign body that has no therapeutic or diagnostic purpose. So be sure to count those sponges.

One note: Under section 364 of the California Code of Civil Procedure, a patient must give notice to a mental health professional 90 days prior to filing a malpractice suit. This 90-day period allows the mental health professional time to review the case to decide whether it can be settled without litigation. (See question 2.)

### 21. What is the discovery rule?

The California statute of limitations for malpractice gives an individual one year from the time of an injury to file a lawsuit. The *discovery rule* applies when an individual does not realize that she has been harmed or, although realizing that she has been harmed, does not realize that a particular treater was the cause of her harm. California courts have reasoned that in such cases it would be unfair for the statute of limitations to start at the moment the injury occurs. The discovery rule says that the one-year limitation period commences only after a patient discovers, or reasonably should have discovered, that she has been harmed by her treater. Section 340.5 of the Code of Civil Procedure makes clear, however, that even in cases where the discovery rule applies, a plaintiff must still file suit within three years. (See question 20 for the single exception to this rule.) Thus, if a patient discovers that she has been harmed by her physician two and a half years after a medical procedure, she has only six months left within which to file a malpractice suit.

## 22. How do the statute of limitations and the discovery rule apply to cases involving minors?

Section 340.5 permits a minor to bring a negligence action against a health care provider either within three years of the injury, or prior to the minor's eighth birthday—whichever period is longer. In *Kelemen v. Superior Court of Sacramento County*, 136 Cal. App. 3d 861 (1982), a seven-year-old (with her parents' help) sued for malpractice during her birth. Although the statute of limitations had run out, the court held that the minor had until her eighth birthday to file suit; the seven-year-old was thus still within the statute of limitations.

## 23. What is the Americans with Disabilities Act?

The Americans with Disabilities Act was signed by President Bush in 1990. This Act provides sweeping federal protection for individuals with disabilities, including mental disabilities, in areas of employment, public services, and private services that accommodate the public. To be eligible for protection under the Act, an individual must have an impairment, a record of an impairment, or be regarded as having an impairment that substantially limits one or more major life activities. Thus, it protects both individuals who have an actual impairment and individuals who, because of stereotypes, may be kept out of the mainstream of their community's social and economic life.

Under the Americans with Disabilities Act, an employer may not refuse to hire and may not fire an individual because of a disability if that individual can perform the "essential functions" of the job, either with or without "reasonable accommodation." The essential functions of the job are those duties that are necessary to the task; it would be necessary for an individual working as a hotel receptionist, for example, to interact with hotel guests. A reasonable accommodation is a modification that allows the individual to perform the essential functions of the job. A person with a mental disability, for example, may need time during working hours to see a therapist; such time would be a reasonable accommodation. A more severe mental disability may require several days off for a brief inpatient stay; additional unpaid leave for the purpose of a hospitalization could also be considered a reasonable accommodation.

# 5

# Involuntary Hospitalization and Treatment

*The involuntary hospitalization and treatment of psychiatric patients is sometimes referred to as "civil commitment." In California, however, civil commitment is not the appropriate term for describing how a patient is placed in a psychiatric hospital against his will. The reason this term is inappropriate in California is that while true civil commitment involves a judicial proceeding, in which a judge determines whether a person can be hospitalized and treated despite his wishes to the contrary, in California <u>mental health professionals</u> make this important decision.*

*When placing individuals in a psychiatric hospital, mental health professionals act under the authority of a state statute. The California statute allows mental health professionals to deprive an individual of his civil liberties when a risk of harm arises from mental illness. Just as in the criminal context, this deprivation of civil liberties is limited by a safeguard called "due process." Due process requires that when we deprive an individual of his liberty, whether because that individual is a*

suspected criminal or because that individual is mentally ill, we make
sure that certain procedures, such as the right to be represented by a
lawyer and the right to a hearing before a judge or hearing officer, are
in place. The amount of process—that is, how many safeguards—the
Constitution requires depends on a balance of the individual's interest
to be free and the state's interest to promote public health and to
protect the safety of its citizenry. The state protects its interests by
invoking two separate types of power: the parens patriae power, the
authority to act like a parent and care for a citizen who is not able to
care for herself, and the police power, the authority to detain an
individual who is a danger to herself or to someone else.

For many years in this country, mental illness alone was enough to
justify depriving an individual of his liberty. Thus, were an individual
simply "in need of treatment," he could be placed against his will in a
psychiatric hospital. Times have changed, however, and today an
individual's mental illness must present an issue of safety before he
may be placed involuntarily in a hospital. Put another way, the state
(often directed by court decisions) has grown less comfortable in using
its parens patriae power to govern the treatment of psychiatric patients;
the police power now provides the basis for most state interventions
into the lives of individuals with mental illness.

## QUESTIONS DISCUSSED IN THIS CHAPTER

24. **Where does one find the laws and regulations that govern
    psychiatric hospitalizations?**
25. **What is the standard for involuntary hospitalization in Califor-
    nia?**
26. **The requirements for involuntary hospitalization and treatment
    under section 5150 are based on a person's "mental disorder."
    Does the law define "mental disorder"?**
27. **How long can a person be hospitalized against his will?**
28. **Who can authorize a 72-hour hold for evaluation and treatment?**
29. **Does anyone review the decision to place an individual in the
    hospital against his will?**
30. **What review is available to a person who has been involuntarily
    detained over and above the initial 72-hour hold?**
31. **Which court has jurisdiction over cases involving involuntary
    hospitalization and treatment?**

32. How does a certification review hearing work?
33. What is the standard of proof in long-term involuntary hospitalization cases?
34. How does a person receive *voluntary* psychiatric hospitalization and treatment?
35. When may a voluntary patient be held against his will?
36. What rights does a psychiatric inpatient have?
37. Can any rights of a psychiatric inpatient ever be denied?
38. Do psychiatric patients have the right to refuse antipsychotic medication?
39. LPS gives a great deal of authority to psychiatrists, psychologists, and peace officers. Could a patient who has been involuntarily hospitalized ever have cause to sue one of these individuals?
40. Can alcohol or substance abuse (rather than mental illness) provide the basis for involuntary hospitalization?
41. May seclusion and restraint be used for therapeutic purposes?
42. If a client who clearly meets the criteria for involuntary hospitalization gets up to walk out of my office, should I attempt physically to restrain him?
43. Does California have a law providing for outpatient commitment?

# DISCUSSION

## 24. Where does one find the laws and regulations that govern psychiatric hospitalizations?

The laws relevant to psychiatric hospitalizations are found in three places. First, the Lanterman-Petris-Short Act (LPS), in the California Welfare and Institutions Code (beginning with section 5000), covers a wide range of topics, including voluntary and involuntary treatment, patients' rights, confidentiality, and conservatorship. The heart of LPS consists of the rules that govern the involuntary treatment of individuals with serious mental illness.

Second, also in the Welfare and Institutions Code (beginning at section 5750), is the Bronzan-McCorquodale Act (formerly the Short-Doyle Act). The Bronzan-McCorquodale Act sets forth the administration of the mental health system and explains how the system is to be funded.

Third, the mental health statutes provide that the Department of Mental Health may write regulations for carrying out its responsibilities. These regulations are found in the California Code of Regulations (Cal. Code Regs.), title 9. If you have questions about the Department of Mental Health or about psychiatric hospitalizations, look first at Welfare and Institutions Code, section 5000 and following, and then try the California Code of Regulations, title 9.

Happy hunting.

### 25. What is the standard for involuntary hospitalization in California?

Section 5150 of LPS defines the circumstances under which an adult may be involuntarily placed in a psychiatric hospital designated by the county. There are two requirements for involuntary hospitalization: First, that the individual has a mental disorder; and second, that as a result of that mental disorder, the individual is a danger to herself, a danger to others, or is gravely disabled. LPS defines grave disability as the inability to take care of one's basic needs, such as those for food, clothing, or shelter. "Grave disability" cannot be based on mental retardation alone. (See question 156 for the definition of "grave disability" that governs the involuntary hospitalization of children.)

### 26. The requirements for involuntary hospitalization and treatment under section 5150 are based on a person's "mental disorder." Does the law define "mental disorder"?

The law does not specifically define mental disorder for purposes of involuntary hospitalization or treatment. Perhaps the law recognizes that our understanding of mental illness is constantly evolving and that a precise legal definition of mental disorder may need continual adjustment. Courts generally turn to experts on this subject, most often to the American Psychiatric Association. Thus, in California, courts have typically interpreted mental disorder to include any significant mental disorder identified in the current edition of the *Diagnostic and Statistical Manual of Mental Disorders (DSM-IV)*.

### 27. How long can a person be hospitalized against his will?

Initially, a person who fulfills the requirements for involuntary hospitalization under section 5150 may be placed into custody and hospitalized for a 72-hour treatment and evaluation period. (Section 5585.25 governs 72-hour holds for minors.) If at the end of the 72-hour period the person is still dangerous to self or others or is gravely disabled, section 5250

---

## INVOLUNTARY HOSPITALIZATION

### Welf. & Inst. Code §5150

I.  Individual has a "**mental disorder**."
    A.  Law does not give explicit definition of "mental disorder."
    B.  Courts look to the current edition of *DSM* to determine what constitutes a mental disorder.

II. Individual, **as result of mental disorder**, is:
    A.  A danger to herself *or*
    B.  A danger to others *or*
    C.  Gravely disabled, defined as:
        1.  Unable to provide for **food, clothing, or shelter**.
        2.  Grave disability cannot be based **solely on mental retardation**.

---

allows him to be placed on an additional 14-day hold for intensive treatment. It is important to note that the patient must be given the opportunity to accept treatment on a *voluntary* basis before the period of *in*voluntary hospitalization and treatment can be extended. This opportunity for the patient to become a voluntary patient reflects the intent of the legislature to reduce the number of involuntary hospitalizations. The legislature's intent notwithstanding, if the patient is unwilling to accept treatment and he continues to meet the criteria for involuntary hospitalization, he may be "certified" for an additional 14 days. If at any time an individual no longer meets the criteria for involuntary detention, he should be released, even if the initial 72-hour or 14-day hold has yet to expire. Beyond the additional 14 days of treatment, a patient's involuntary hospitalization and treatment may be extended if he continues to be dangerous or gravely disabled as a result of a mental disorder. Extended hospitalization requires a stronger showing of dangerousness than the original 14-day certification. Holds beyond the 14-day certification are sometimes referred to as postcertification holds.

After the original 17 days (the initial 72-hour hold and the additional 14-day hold), the length of extended hospitalization depends upon which criteria the involuntary hold is based. Under section 5260 of the Welfare and Institutions Code, individuals who threaten or attempt to take their own life during the initial 72-hour treatment and evaluation period or during the 14-day intensive treatment may be held for a *second* 14-day intensive treatment. If the person was originally detained for suicidal behavior, the second 14-day treatment period may be imposed if the person continues to present an imminent threat of taking his own life. Note that the criteria for the second 14-day hold requires suicidal *behavior* (threats are considered behavior) rather than just general dangerousness to self.

Individuals who pose a demonstrated danger of inflicting substantial physical harm on others may be confined for further treatment (up to 180 days), after the initial 14-day period of intensive treatment. The danger must be based on actual infliction, attempt, or serious threat of harm during or just prior to the initial hold. Because a 180-day hold is renewable if a person remains a demonstrated danger during the expiring 180-day hold, and thus involves a significant deprivation of liberty, a court hearing and other procedural safeguards are required.

Finally, a person who is gravely disabled may be certified for an additional 30 days of intensive treatment or placed on a temporary conservatorship following the initial 14-day hold. Because the additional 30-day hold is used in only a few counties, most often a temporary conservator is appointed. The temporary conservator only has the authority to authorize an additional 30 days of hospitalization. Following a temporary conservatorship, a renewable one-year conservatorship can be established by the court (see chapter 8).

### 28. Who can authorize a 72-hour hold for evaluation and treatment?

Under section 5150 of LPS, only certain individuals may place a person in custody and initiate a 72-hour hold. These individuals include police officers, members of the attending staff of an evaluation facility designated by the county, members of a mobile crisis team, or other professional persons designated by the county.

### 29. Does anyone review the decision to place an individual in the hospital against his will?

There is no judicial or administrative review for the first 72-hour period of treatment and evaluation. Additional holds beyond the first 72 hours, however, are subject to either administrative review (review by a hearing officer), judicial review (review by a judge), or both, depending on the nature of the hold.

### 30. What review is available to a person who has been involuntarily detained over and above the initial 72-hour hold?

If, at the end of the 72-hour hold, the patient is certified for a 14-day

# TERMS OF INVOLUNTARY HOSPITALIZATION UNDER THE LANTERMAN-PETRIS-SHORT ACT

## Welf. & Inst. Code §§5000–5550

I. **72-hour hold (§5150)** for evaluation and treatment requires:
   A. As a result of mental disorder a person is
      1. Dangerous to self *or*
      2. Dangerous to others *or*
      3. Gravely disabled.
   B. At conclusion of 72-hour hold
      1. Patient is released *or*
      2. Given the opportunity to accept treatment voluntarily *or*
      3. If patient still refuses needed treatment, see II.

II. **14-day certification (§5250)** for intensive treatment requires that after the original 72-hour hold the patient remains:
   A. Dangerous to self *or*
   B. Dangerous to others *or*
   C. Gravely disabled.

III. **Holds following the initial 14-day hold** (postcertification holds)
   A. **Second 14-day hold (§5260)** for intensive treatment requires that the patient:
      1. Threatened or attempted to take his own life during the previous (72-hour and 14-day) holds *or*
      2. Was originally detained for suicidal behavior and still presents imminent threat of taking his own life.
   B. **180-day hold (§5300)** requires that the patient:
      1. Continues to pose a demonstrated danger of inflicting substantial physical harm on others.
      2. The danger must be based on actual infliction, attempt, or serious threat of harm.
      3. 180-day hold periods are renewable if patient has attempted, inflicted, or made a serious threat of harm on others during expiring 180-day hold.
      4. 180-day hold requires a court hearing.
   C. **30-day hold (§5270.15)** for intensive treatment (available only in limited number of counties):
      1. Patient is gravely disabled *and*
      2. Unwilling or unable to accept treatment.
   D. **Temporary conservatorship (§5352)** (instead of 30-day hold):
      1. Patient remains gravely disabled.
      2. Temporary conservator authorizes up to 30-day hold if patient is unwilling to follow the conservator's decisions.
   E. **Conservatorship (§5350) following a temporary conservatorship due to grave disability**:
      1. Patient remains gravely disabled.
      2. Appointment of a conservator requires a court hearing.
      3. Remains valid for renewable one-year periods.

hold, then he is entitled to a review of the certification of the 14-day hold. The review is conducted at a hearing called a "certification review hearing" because its purpose is to review the necessity for a 14-day detention over and above the 72-hour hold. It is also known as a "Gallinot" hearing because it was in the case of *Doe v. Gallinot,* 657 F.2d. 1017 (9th Cir., 1981), that a federal court required such a hearing to be held. Finally, it is sometimes referred to as a "probable cause" hearing because its purpose is to determine whether probable cause exists to justify continued involuntary detention.

The certification review hearing, over which a "hearing officer" generally presides, provides protection for the patient's greater liberty interest that is now at issue. The hearing must be held within four days of the date on which the person is certified for the 14-day hold. At the patient's request, however, the hearing officer may allow a 48-hour continuance. As a consequence, the hearing may not actually take place for up to six days.

The avenue for judicial review is a writ of habeas corpus (see question 16). Section 5275 of the Welfare and Institutions Code gives patients the right to challenge the legality of additional holds in a habeas corpus proceeding. A hearing on a writ of habeas corpus—always conducted by a judge—must be held within two days of the request by the involuntary patient. In the habeas proceeding, the government bears the burden of proof, but the standard is merely a preponderance of the evidence (see question 4). Thus, the state will need to show only *more likely than not* that the patient presents a danger to self, to others, or is gravely disabled, in order for the 14-day hold to be upheld.

*Hospital staff have an obligation to convey to the court as soon as possible a patient's wish—however that wish may be expressed—to leave the hospital.*

Unlike other holds, a 180-day hold for imminently dangerous individuals *requires* a court hearing. Furthermore, if the person asks for a jury trial, the trial must be granted within 10 days of when the request is filed. During the trial, the patient is entitled to an attorney. In addition, the burden of proof borne by the state is subject to a higher standard—rather than proof by a preponderance of the evidence, the standard of proof at a trial for a 180-day hold is proof beyond a reasonable doubt. The reason for these extra safeguards is the greater deprivation of liberty that a renewable 180-day hold entails.

### 31. Which court has jurisdiction over cases involving involuntary hospitalization and treatment?

The superior court for the county in which the facility providing intensive treatment is located has jurisdiction over cases of involuntary hospitalization and treatment. If, however, the patient or a person acting on the patient's behalf informs the staff of the evaluation facility (in writing) that the patient will seek judicial review, jurisdiction will be in superior court of the county in which the 72-hour evaluation was conducted. In addition, if the staff of the evaluation facility has been informed in writing that a judicial review will be sought, the patient cannot be transferred from the county providing evaluation services to a different county for intensive treatment until the judicial review is complete.

### 32. How does a certification review hearing work?
Certification review hearings are informal proceedings that usually take place at the treatment facility. Either a court-appointed commissioner or referee, or a certification review hearing officer, conducts the hearing. All relevant evidence regarding the basis for the continued hold must be admitted.

During the hearing, a patient retains certain rights. The patient is entitled to assistance by an attorney or a patients' rights advocate. The patient also has the right to present evidence on his own behalf and to cross-examine opposing witnesses. In addition, the patient may make reasonable attendance requests, such as the attendance of any facility staff who participated in or who has knowledge of the 14-day certification. Finally, if the patient was given any medication within 24 hours prior to the hearing, the hearing officer must be notified of the possible effects of the medication. These statutory rights reflect how the legislature attempts to balance patient liberty with the need to provide involuntary treatment when a risk arises because an individual is mentally ill.

### 33. What is the standard of proof in long-term involuntary hospitalization cases?
California statutes do not explicitly state what standard of proof involuntary hospitalization and treatment cases require. In *Addington v. Texas,* 441 U.S. 418 (1978), however, the United States Supreme Court ruled that clear and convincing evidence (see question 4) is the federal Constitutional standard required for involuntary hospitalization and treatment. California cases have established an even higher standard of proof, beyond a reasonable doubt, in cases involving long-term holds. As an example, California courts have gone beyond the United States Supreme

Court by holding that, because a conservator may place a person in a psychiatric hospital against his will for up to one year, the state must show *beyond a reasonable doubt* that the criteria for conservatorship are met before a court will appoint a conservator. (See question 78.)

### 34. How does a person receive *voluntary* psychiatric hospitalization and treatment?

The Welfare and Institutions Code, beginning at section 6000, sets only minimal requirements for voluntary treatment; these requirements are designed to protect the patient rather than limit admission. The medical director or person in charge of a state hospital, neuropsychiatric institute, county psychiatric hospital or private institution, hospital, or clinic providing mental health treatment who receives a written application for admission may admit any person suitable for treatment. An adult seeking admission must be competent at the time of the application to make the decision. In addition, the application must be voluntary. If the adult has a conservator (see chapter 8) who holds the right to place him in a hospital, then the conservator may apply for admission on his behalf. In the case of a minor, a parent, guardian, or conservator may apply for his admission. Any person admitted in one of these ways is considered a voluntary patient.

Voluntary patients who give notice and complete normal hospital departure procedures may leave the hospital or institution at any time. Likewise, a conservatee (the person over whom the conservator is appointed) may leave if notice is given by his conservator. Also, a minor who is a voluntary patient may leave the hospital or institution after the parent, guardian, or conservator gives appropriate notice to the superintendent or person in charge.

These requirements are simple and unrestrictive on purpose. The legislature wants to facilitate admission and treatment for those who need it, especially for those who seek treatment voluntarily. The preference for voluntary, rather than involuntary, hospitalizations is reflected in section 5250 of the Welfare and Institutions Code, which authorizes a 14-day certification for involuntary intensive treatment only after a "person has been advised of the need for, but has *not been willing or able to accept treatment on a voluntary basis* [italics added]." By affording involuntary patients the opportunity to become voluntary patients, section 5250 helps reduce the number of involuntary hospitalizations.

### 35. When may a voluntary patient be held against his will?

Generally, a voluntary patient must be released upon request. A patient may be held involuntarily only when he both meets the requirements of LPS for involuntary treatment *and* insists on leaving the treatment facility. Although the distinction between involuntary and voluntary status may seem academic, it is significant.

Welfare and Institutions Code section 5258 states that if after an involuntary commitment begins, a patient switches from involuntary to voluntary status and then requires continued involuntary hospitalization, his total term of hospitalization cannot exceed the maximum allowable period of detention had the hold been entirely involuntary. For example, if after a 72-hour involuntary hold, a patient who remained suicidal wished to continue treatment voluntarily, he would become a voluntary patient. However, if after 10 additional days, the patient decided to leave but was still suicidal, he could then be involuntarily held for only 18 more days (14-day hold + 14-day additional hold due to threat of suicide = 28 days total; 28 days – 10 days already spent in the hospital = 18 days). It is important to note that a patient who originally admits himself voluntarily cannot begin counting down until he becomes an involuntary patient for the first time. If, in our example, the patient had initially gone into the hospital on a *voluntary* basis and then wished to leave at the very same time as above, he could be held for *28*, rather than 18 days, since the clock would not begin ticking until his initial *in*voluntary status.

### 36. What rights does a psychiatric inpatient have?

Patients retain the same rights that federal and state laws guarantee to all other citizens except those rights that are compromised by involuntary hospitalization. To illustrate this point, sometimes the law balances the rights of the patient against competing state interests. When state interests are sufficiently compelling, the law may limit the patient's rights accordingly. For example, if a patient is dangerous to others as a result of a mental illness, he may be placed in temporary custody for treatment and evaluation. Under Welfare and Institutions Code section 5325.1, however, a psychiatric inpatient may not be denied any of the following rights: (1) the right to treatment services that promote the patient's independent functioning and are least restrictive of the patient's liberty; (2) the right to dignity, privacy, and humane care; (3) the right to be free from harm, including unnecessary or excessive physical restraint, isolation, medication, abuse, or neglect; (4) the right to religious freedom and practice; (5) the right to participate in appropriate public education programs; (6) the right to social interaction and participation in community activities; (7) the right to physical exercise and recreational opportunities; (8) the right to be free from hazardous procedures; and (9) the right to an attorney and a patients' rights advocate.

### 37. Can any rights of a psychiatric inpatient ever be denied?

Certain specific rights may be denied under appropriate circumstances. Welfare and Institutions Code sections 5325 and 5326 state that the following inpatient rights may be denied when "good cause" exists: (1) the right to wear one's own clothes; (2) the right to keep and use one's own personal possessions, including toilet articles; (3) the right to keep and spend a reasonable sum of one's own money for canteen expenses and small purchases; (4) the right to have access to individual storage space for private use; (5) the right see visitors each day; (6) the right to have reasonable access to telephones, both to make and to receive confidential calls; and (7) the right to have ready access to letter-writing materials, including stamps, and to mail and receive unopened correspondence.

Good cause for denial of these specific rights exists when the patient's exercise of the right would injure him, seriously infringe upon the rights of others, or seriously damage the facility. Because the law recognizes the importance of inpatients' rights, it details various safeguards in addition to the good cause standard that help prevent the inappropriate denial of rights. First, there must be no less restrictive means of protecting the interests specified under the good cause standard. Second, the patient's parent, guardian, or conservator may not waive any of these rights or authorize seclusion and/or restraint. Third, seclusion and/or restraint cannot be used as punishment or as a substitute for a less restrictive form of treatment. Finally, whenever a right is denied or seclusion and/or restraint is used, the staff must make a detailed record in the patient's file of what occurred.

### 38. Do psychiatric patients have the right to refuse antipsychotic medication?

Yes. In *Riese v. St. Mary's Hospital*, 209 Cal. App. 3d 1303 (1987), the California Court of Appeal held that psychiatric patients have a statutory right under LPS to refuse antipsychotic medication. This right is not, however, without limits. The right extends neither to emergency situations nor to instances where the court has determined that the patient is incompetent to make treatment decisions. An emergency is defined in Welfare and Institutions Code section 5008(m) as a situation in which action to impose treatment over the person's objection is immediately necessary for the preservation of life or the prevention of serious bodily harm to the patient or others, and it is impracticable first to gain consent.

If an involuntary patient is refusing antipsychotic medication and it is not an emergency, the hospital staff may request an administrative hearing to determine competency by filing a petition with the superior court. The patient is entitled to representation by the county patients' rights advocate or an attorney. The competency hearing must be held at the facility within 24 hours of filing the petition. If the judge or court-appointed hearing officer determines the patient is incompetent, the patient can, even when objecting, be forced to take antipsychotic medication prescribed by his physician. (If the patient has a durable power of attorney for health care [see question 91], the agent must consent before the medication can be administered.) Either the patient or the hospital may appeal the hearing decision to the superior court.

### 39. LPS gives a great deal of authority to psychiatrists, psychologists, and peace officers. Could a patient who has been involuntarily hospitalized ever have cause to sue one of these individuals?

The Welfare and Institutions Code contains statutory provisions that protect from lawsuits individuals who are authorized to detain, hospitalize, and treat an individual against that individual's will. Section 5278 provides that authorized individuals who act in accordance with the law regarding involuntary hospitalization and treatment will not be held civilly or criminally liable for their actions. In addition, section 5154 states that directors of treatment facilities, psychiatrists who are directly responsible for the patient's treatment, and peace officers responsible for the patient's detention are exempt from any criminal or civil liability for any action of a person released before or at the end of a 72-hour hold. Note, however, that the exemption from liability in section 5154 hinges on *proper adherence to statutory requirements* for involuntary hospitalization and treatment outlined in LPS. Since exemption from liability depends on observance of the statutory requirements for involuntary hospitalization and treatment, clinicians authorized to admit and treat patients must carefully adhere to those requirements. *It is therefore well worth your time and effort to become familiar with LPS if you intend to work with individuals who are likely to need involuntary psychiatric hospitalization.*

### 40. Can alcohol or substance abuse (rather than mental illness) provide the basis for involuntary hospitalization?

Welfare and Institutions Code section 5230 states that if a person is a danger to himself, to others, or is gravely disabled because of chronic alcoholism or substance abuse, he may be detained in a facility for 72-hour treatment and evaluation. Notice that this section mirrors section 5150, which governs the involuntary hospitalization and treatment of patients with mental disorders. The only significant difference between the statutes is that mental illness in section 5150 is replaced by chronic alcohol or substance abuse in section 5230 as the cause of dangerousness to self, to others, or grave disability. Section 5230 demonstrates that while the legislature does not regard chronic alcohol or substance abuse as a mental illness, it does recognize that its effects can be equally debilitating. Thus, LPS attempts to provide for prompt evaluation and treatment of persons who are impaired by chronic alcoholism or substance abuse.

Note that section 5230 does not provide for additional involuntary holds after the original 72-hour hold. Thus, an individual can be held only for 72 hours if the basis for the hold is chronic alcoholism or substance abuse.

**41. May seclusion and restraint be used for therapeutic purposes?**
No. Whatever value seclusion and restraint have (their purpose and effect are often disputed; some argue a therapeutic value because they can help calm a patient or remove excess stimuli that might intensify agitation), the law sets clear guidelines regarding their use. Seclusion and/or restraint may only be used in treatment facilities that are authorized to use them. In addition, seclusion and/or restraint may only be used when a patient's behavior poses a serious threat of injury to self or others. As soon as the threat no longer exists, the patient must be released. Seclusion and/or restraint can never be used as a punishment or in place of a less restrictive alternative treatment, and they may only be used after receipt of a written order from a physician or in a legally defined emergency. Any use of seclusion and/or restraint must be accompanied by proper documentation.

Mental health professionals should note, however, that restraint refers to the unreasonable confinement of an individual's freedom to move. Restraint does not refer to orthopedically prescribed appliances necessary for treatment, supportive body bands, protective helmets, or physical holding when necessary for surgical purposes, medical treatment, or to achieve functional bodily position or proper balance to protect a patient from falling out of bed.

**42. If a client who clearly meets the criteria for involuntary hospitalization gets up to walk out of my office, should I attempt physically to restrain him?**

The vast majority of mental health professionals are neither trained in the technique, nor legally authorized, to restrain a client. From a practical point of view, this lack of training *increases* the likelihood that someone will get injured if you attempt to restrain a client. From a legal point of view, you risk being sued for assault and battery should you attempt physically to restrain a client. *Do not attempt to do what you are neither trained nor legally authorized to do.*

If a client who appears to meet commitment criteria insists on leaving your office, call the people who are trained and authorized to use restraints: mental health workers at a community mental health center, security at a hospital, or the local police. Apprise the appropriate agency of the situation. Although it is difficult to watch such a client walk out of your office, it is best to use *your* expertise (in formulating a clinical assessment) to inform others so that they may use *their* expertise (in using restraints) to place your client in a safe setting.

**43. Does California have a law providing for outpatient commitment?**

There is only limited outpatient commitment in California.

Outpatient commitment requires an individual to comply with a treatment plan when *outside the walls of* a psychiatric unit. As an example, say that a patient, Elyn, was discharged from the hospital back to her group home under an outpatient commitment. Under her treatment plan, Elyn is required to attend therapy sessions and to take medication. If Elyn stopped taking her medication, her doctor could contact the police, who would pick Elyn up and bring her to the hospital. Once there, Elyn would be given her medication, by force if necessary. With outpatient commitment, *noncompliance with a treatment plan is sufficient to initiate state intervention.*

According to section 5305 of the Welfare and Institutions Code, outpatient commitment in California is limited to individuals who have been placed on a 180-day hold because they present a demonstrated danger of inflicting substantial physical harm upon others. Such a patient may be placed on outpatient status if the professional in charge of the facility and the county mental health director advise the court that the person will no longer be dangerous, will benefit from outpatient status, and will participate in an appropriate program of supervision and treatment.

For individuals who are gravely disabled, LPS conservatorships (see chapter 8) may be used in a way similar to outpatient commitment. A conservator may require a conservatee to take antipsychotic medication while living in the community. If the conservatee refuses, and hospitalization is necessary because the conservatee poses an immediate and substantial danger to herself or others, the conservator can place the conservatee in a psychiatric hospital against the conservatee's wishes.

# 6

# CRIMINAL LAW

*Mental health professionals may be called upon to assess whether a criminal defendant is competent to stand trial or responsible for a crime he has committed. Competency to stand trial and criminal responsibility are often confused with one another. They are alike insofar as both require assessing a criminal defendant's state of mind. They differ insofar as competency to stand trial speaks to the defendant's state of mind <u>at the time of trial</u>, while criminal responsibility speaks to the defendant's state of mind <u>at the time of the crime</u>. An individual who is found not criminally responsible is referred to as "criminally insane," or "not guilty by reason of insanity" (NGI). Insanity is thus a <u>legal</u> concept with <u>legal</u> consequences.*

## QUESTIONS DISCUSSED IN THIS CHAPTER

44. What is the California test for criminal insanity?
45. What happens to a person in California who is found criminally insane (NGI)?
46. When is a person in California not competent to stand trial?
47. What happens to a person in California who is found not competent to stand trial?
48. What is "diminished capacity"?

49. **How is a diminished capacity defense different from an insanity defense?**
50. **Does California have a defense based on diminished capacity?**
51. **What happens if someone in a jail or prison becomes depressed, has a psychotic break, or otherwise needs mental health services?**
52. **Who is a "sexually violent predator"?**
53. **Once a sexually violent predator has served his criminal sentence, how can a court impose further detention?**

# DISCUSSION

### 44. What is the California test for criminal insanity?
When should society not blame an individual for his actions? If a person becomes psychotic and assaults a stranger, is he criminally insane? If a person steals a car while in a manic state, should he be sent to jail? If a person commits a murder while dissociating and later remembers nothing, is incarceration an appropriate response?

The original test for criminal insanity in California was the M'Naghten rule, derived from England's M'Naghten case of 1843. To establish an insanity defense under the M'Naghten rule, a defendant must prove that, at the time of the act, he was laboring under such a defect of reason from mental illness as not to know the nature and quality of the act or not to know that the act was wrong. In *People v. Drew*, 22 Cal. 3d 333 (1978), the California Supreme Court rejected the M'Naghten test in favor of the American Law Institute (ALI) test:

> A person is not responsible for criminal conduct if at the time of such conduct as a result of mental disease or defect he lacks substantial capacity either to appreciate the criminality (wrongfulness) of his conduct or to conform his conduct to the requirements of the law. (ALI Model Penal Code §401)

Three principal changes distinguish the ALI test from the M'Naghten test. First, the ALI test adds a volitional element, the "capacity . . . to conform . . . to the requirements of the law." Second, the ALI test avoids M'Naghten's "all or nothing" language by allowing an insanity defense based on a defendant's "substantial" rather than complete mental impairment. Third, mental impairment may be *either* cognitive (the capacity to appreciate) *or* volitional (the capacity to conform); it need not be both to excuse criminal responsibility. The ALI test proved short-lived in California.

In 1982, California adopted Proposition 8, which added section 25(b) to the Penal Code. Section 25(b) replaced all previous definitions of criminal insanity. While section 25(b) purported to reinstate the M'Naghten test, its language actually misstates the previously accepted version of M'Naghten. Historically, M'Naghten required that a defendant prove by a preponderance of the evidence (see question 4) that he was *either* unable to understand the nature of the act *or* incapable of distinguishing right from wrong. The language of section 25(b) requires a defendant to prove that, at the time of the crime, he was *both* incapable of understanding the nature of his act *and* of distinguishing right from wrong. California currently uses this slightly more restrictive version of the M'Naghten test to determine criminal insanity.

### 45. What happens to a person in California who is found criminally insane (NGI)?

The answer to this question has generated vigorous debate in recent years. The debate is fueled by the belief that too many people are found not criminally responsible; simply put, too many defendants are judged criminally insane and therefore go free. This belief is not supported by fact. Only about 1% of criminal defendants plead insanity, and the plea is successful in only 25% of those cases. Thus, the insanity plea is relevant to only one quarter of one percent of criminal defendants. Moreover, defendants are not released after a court finds them criminally insane. On the contrary, criminal defendants found insane often receive lengthy commitments to maximum security treatment facilities.

Penal Code section 1026.5 states that when a criminal defendant is judged not guilty by reason of insanity (NGI) he shall be handed over to the Department of Mental Health. The length of time he is committed to the Department of Mental Health may not exceed the maximum prison sentence he could have received for his offense. The catch, however, is that at the end of the original commitment period, the district attorney may petition the court for a two-year commitment extension, *an extension that can be renewed* <u>*indefinitely*</u>. To extend the commitment, the court must find that the individual constitutes a substantial risk of harm to others due to mental disease or defect.

The recommitment hearing need not afford the patient the same protections as a criminal trial. The reason that fewer safeguards are required at a recommitment hearing was explained by the Court of Appeal in *Juarez v. Superior Court,* 196 Cal. App. 3d 928 (1987). According to *Juarez,* a recommitment hearing is civil, rather than criminal, in nature, because it focuses on *treatment,* rather than on *punishment.* The upshot is that the *commitment* term may be extended well beyond the maximum allowable *prison* term for the original criminal offense. Because there is no limit on the number of extensions, the commitment is virtually interminable, and will last as long as the courts consider the patient a substantial threat of harm to others.

### 46. When is a person in California not competent to stand trial?

To be competent to stand trial, a person must be able to assume the role of a criminal defendant. This role, according to Penal Code section 1367, requires the capacity to understand the nature of the criminal proceedings and to assist one's attorney in conducting the defense in a rational manner. In other words, if a person is not able to understand what's going on around her or to help her attorney put on a defense, the trial isn't a fair trial and therefore should not go forward. Such a person is incompetent to stand trial (IST).

The above test is derived from the United States Supreme Court case *Dusky v. United States,* 362 U.S. 402 (1960). In *Dusky,* the U.S. Supreme Court held that, in determining whether a criminal defendant is competent to stand trial, a court should ask:

> whether [the defendant] has sufficient present ability to consult with his lawyer with a reasonable degree of rational understanding and whether he has a rational as well as factual understanding of the proceedings against him. (402)

Examples of questions which would help to assess competence to stand trial would therefore be: Is the defendant able to understand that the prosecutor thinks she has done something wrong? Is the defendant able to understand that her attorney is there to help her? Is the defendant able to understand that she may be put in jail or told to pay a fine if she is found guilty? Is the defendant able to sit in court and comprehend what other people say about her, or about what people claim she did? Is the defendant able to answer questions her attorney may need to ask in order to put on a defense?

Notice how the first three questions begin with "Is the defendant able to understand . . ." rather than "Does the defendant know that . . ." The reason for beginning the questions in this manner is that competency to stand trial is based on what the individual is *able* to understand about the judicial process, not on what she *actually* understands. If a person does not actually understand something about the trial, but is able to understand this information, one can educate her and the trial can proceed.

## 47. What happens to a person in California who is found not competent to stand trial?

Penal Code section 1370 states that if an individual is found incompetent to stand trial, the criminal process shall be suspended and the individual entrusted to a mental health facility until she regains her competence. Before the court commits the defendant to a treatment facility, the court orders a community program director to recommend whether the defendant should be treated on an outpatient basis or admitted to a locked facility. If the recommendation is for a locked facility, the facility director must report to the court within 90 days of commitment regarding the patient's progress. If the initial 90-day evaluation finds no substantial likelihood that the patient will regain mental competence, the court will hold a hearing to determine whether to appoint a conservator (see chapter 8).

If the patient has not regained her competence, but appears likely to regain competence in the foreseeable future, she will continue treatment. Subsequently, the treatment facility will apprise the court of the patient's progress every six months until she regains competence. If the patient is still incompetent after three years from the date of commitment, or a period equal to the maximum sentence for the alleged crime, and she does not seem likely to regain competence in the foreseeable future, the court will hold a hearing to decide whether to appoint a conservator.

This process is essentially the same for a defendant who is found not competent to stand trial due to a developmental disability. If a director of a regional center gives the recommendation to treat, the patient is committed to a facility that treats people with developmental disabilities (rather than mental disorders). A developmental disability, according to section 4512(a) of the Welfare and Institutions Code, is any substantial handicap that originates before age 18 and is expected to continue indefinitely; the definition of developmental disability includes mental retardation and autism. For people with developmental disabilities, the regional director reports to the court after 60 days. If the director finds that the patient is likely to regain competence within an additional 90 days, the court can order that the patient continue treatment. If, however, the patient is unlikely to regain competence within the 150 (60 + 90) days she must either be released by the court or placed in a hospital.

If, at any time during this process, the defendant becomes competent to stand trial, she returns to the court and criminal proceedings resume. Thus, like defendants found criminally insane, those judged incompetent to stand trial are not simply released. Various provisions allow for their continued confinement either in jail or in a hospital.

---

## COMPETENCE TO STAND TRIAL AND CRIMINAL RESPONSIBILITY IN CALIFORNIA

I.   Involve **criminal** proceedings (person has been charged with a crime).

II.  Involve assessment of person's mental state at a given point in time:
   A.  At **time of conduct alleged to be a crime** (criminal responsibility):
   B.  At **time of trial** (competence to stand trial)

III. Involve assessment of **mental capacity**.
   A.  Person not criminally responsible (insane) if, **at the time of the criminal conduct**
      1.  Incapable of knowing or understanding the nature and quality of her act *and*
      2.  Incapable of distinguishing right from wrong.
   B.  Person not competent to stand trial if, **at the time of trial**:
      1.  Unable to understand the nature of the criminal proceedings *or*
      2.  Unable to assist counsel in conducting a defense in a rational manner.

---

### 48. What is "diminished capacity"?

When a criminal case comes to trial, an individual—the defendant—has been charged with a crime. To win a criminal case, the prosecutor, who bears the burden of proof, must show beyond a reasonable doubt that the defendant is guilty of the crime with which he has been charged. Every crime consists of two elements: an actus reus (a guilty act) and a mens rea (a guilty mind). If either an actus reus or a mens rea is missing, no crime has been committed and the defendant must be found not guilty. To win, the prosecutor must therefore show that the defendant both did something wrong (actus reus) and had the necessary criminal state of mind (mens rea) while he was acting.

Certain crimes require a specific state of mind. Assault with intent to kill, for example, requires that the defendant placed a victim in fear of bodily harm (assault) and intended to kill the victim (assault with intent to kill). To convict a defendant of this crime, the prosecutor must therefore show beyond a reasonable doubt that the defendant both performed certain acts and, while doing so, had the necessary mens rea—the intent to kill.

The defense of diminished capacity comes into play when evidence is introduced at trial that shows the defendant lacked the capacity to form the necessary mens rea—mental state—at the time of the crime. Say, for example, the defense introduced psychiatric testimony showing that this defendant lacked the capacity to form an intent to kill; perhaps the defendant was of exceedingly limited intelligence or suffered from a delusion affecting his capacity to understand and appreciate the significance of someone dying. This testimony would then be used to argue that the defendant was not guilty of the crime of assault with intent to kill. Why? Because a necessary element of this crime, the requisite mens rea—intent to kill—could not have been present, since the defendant was incapable of forming this intent. Note that the defendant may still be found guilty of a lesser offense, that of assault, because he may very well have intended to place the victim in fear of bodily harm. Because of the defense of diminished capacity, however, he will not be found guilty of the greater offense, assault with intent to kill.

### 49. How is a diminished capacity defense different from an insanity defense?

Diminished capacity addresses whether a specific criminal intent is present. It says, "Look, to find this defendant guilty, you have to show that he had this specific criminal intent at the time of the crime. But *he didn't have the capacity to form that intent*—so he can't be found guilty of that crime." Note how this argument does not preclude the defendant being found guilty of another crime—perhaps the intent necessary for another crime, one that required a more general intent, was indeed present. If so, the defendant can be found guilty for something, just not the crime with which he had been charged. Thus, diminished capacity generally acts as a *partial* defense to criminal guilt. The insanity defense acts as a *complete* defense to criminal guilt. When using an insanity defense, an individual claims that he lacked *any* criminal responsibility at the time of the crime. The implication of a successful insanity plea is that the defendant does not belong in the criminal justice system at all.

The final disposition may be very different for defendants who use an insanity defense and for those who rely on the defense of diminished capacity. An individual found not guilty by reason of insanity (NGI) is committed to the Department of Mental Health (for what could be an indefinite period of time). Individuals who successfully argue diminished capacity, on the other hand, may be able to reduce the offense, but may still be guilty of something, and so may remain in the criminal justice system. It sometimes happens that an individual relies on diminished capacity, and there is no lesser offense of which he could be held guilty. In such a case, a successful diminished capacity defense acts as a complete defense and will result in acquittal and release.

### 50. Does California have a defense based on diminished capacity?

Until 1981, the California Supreme Court allowed the defense of diminished capacity. In 1981, however, the California Legislature enacted section 28 of the Penal Code, which eliminated the diminished capacity defense. Section 28 specifically prohibits the admission of evidence of mental impairment to negate the *capacity* to form any mental state—a defendant can no longer argue diminished capacity on the basis of an inability to form a specific intent. Evidence of mental impairment is still admissible, however, on the issue of whether the accused *actually* formed a required specific intent. Today, therefore, a defendant will argue that he did not have the specific intent required by the crime. Put another way, the argument is no longer that, because of a mental impairment, a criminal defendant was not *able* to form the necessary intent. The argument now is that the criminal defendant *did* not form the intent.

### 51. What happens if someone in a jail or prison becomes depressed, has a psychotic break, or otherwise needs mental health services?

Many inmates have mental or emotional disabilities that are insufficient to support findings of not guilty by reason of insanity. Nevertheless, these inmates require some form of mental health care. Section 1200 of title 15 of the California Code of Regulations requires that some mental health services be provided in jails. Penal institutions differ, however, in their requirements and ability to treat mentally disturbed inmates.

Although the terms "jail" and "prison" are often used interchangeably, the two institutions serve some distinct purposes. County jails typically house pretrial detainees (individuals waiting for their trial) and inmates who are incarcerated for up to one year. State prisons hold prisoners for much longer sentences, and therefore need more substantial medical and mental health treatment facilities. California Penal Code section 4007 states that when a county inmate requires medical treatment that is unavailable at the jail and the prisoner's past or present behavior poses a serious custodial problem, the inmate may be transferred to the nearest prison or other correctional facility capable of providing the necessary treatment.

According to Penal Code section 4011.6, an inmate in a county jail or a juvenile detention facility who appears mentally disordered may be transferred to a mental health facility for 72-hour evaluation and treatment. The transferring authority must send the treatment facility a confidential report detailing the prisoner's condition. If the treatment facility wishes to retain the prisoner, it must forward the report to the judge. Once the inmate has been transferred, the Welfare and Institutions Code on involuntary treatment and detention governs (see chapter 5). For inmates who are significant security risks, some jails provide involuntary treatment in psychiatric facilities within the jail.

### 52. Who is a "sexually violent predator"?
The California legislature recently created a new form of civil commitment for sexually violent predators (SVPs). A sexually violent predator is a person with a diagnosed mental disorder who has been convicted of a sexually violent offense against two or more victims (Welf. & Inst. Code §6600). In addition, a court must find beyond a reasonable doubt that the person's likelihood to commit sexually violent crimes presents a continued danger to the health and safety of others. When a court finds beyond a reasonable doubt that an individual is likely to commit future acts of sexually violent criminal behavior, that individual may be confined and treated until it can be determined he no longer presents a threat to society.

### 53. Once a sexually violent predator has served his criminal sentence, how can a court impose further detention?
Although individuals whom the law labels as sexually violent predators may have completed their sentences handed down by the court, the law still views them as a continued threat to society. The law's determination that SVPs pose a continued threat is based on an SVP's currently diag-

nosed mental disorder. On the basis of their mental disorder and perceived dangerousness, SVPs can be involuntarily hospitalized and treated for as long as the disorder persists. Because, according to the United States Supreme Court, a commitment hearing is for the purpose of *treatment* and not for the purpose of *punishment*, a commitment hearing is not considered a criminal proceeding. A commitment hearing, therefore, does not violate the law's prohibition against double jeopardy (trying an individual for the same crime twice). Note, however, that the *California* Supreme Court has not ruled on this issue, and could decide that the *California* Constitution would not permit indefinite detention of SVPs.

The burden of proof in the commitment hearing is on the state to show beyond a reasonable doubt that the person is an SVP. If the court determines that the person is an SVP, the person shall be committed for a renewable period of two years to the custody of the State Department of Mental Health for appropriate treatment and confinement. Some have argued that renewable hold periods could result in indefinite detention, thus constituting cruel and unusual punishment. Again, however, the law views the involuntary hospitalization of SVPs as treatment, not punishment. By definition, then, indefinite detention of an SVP does not constitute cruel and unusual punishment.

Because renewable periods of extended commitment present serious risks to a person's liberty, the law does provide numerous due process safeguards to protect individuals who have been labeled sexually violent predators. A person committed under the sexually violent predator statute shall have a mental evaluation at least once a year. In addition, an SVP may appoint an expert to review all his records. Unless the person affirmatively waives his right to a hearing, the superior court must set a hearing each year to determine if the person's condition has changed. If the court finds that the person no longer presents a danger to the health and safety of others, the person is entitled to a full trial. At trial the SVP will have the same rights that were afforded at the initial commitment hearing. Furthermore, any time that the Department of Mental Health reasonably believes that the person is no longer an SVP, it must ask the court to review the commitment. Finally, if the court finds that the person is not likely to engage in sexually violent criminal acts while under supervision and treatment in the community, he can be placed on conditional release. These safeguards reflect the legislature's intent to balance the important liberty interests of the individual against the compelling state interest of public safety.

# 7

# SUBPOENAS AND COURT ORDERS

*As you read these questions, recall (from chapter 3) the close relationship between confidentiality and testimonial privilege. To say that a communication is "confidential" means that the mental health professional cannot disclose the communication without the client's consent. To say that a communication is "protected by testimonial privilege" means that the mental health professional cannot disclose the communication in a legal proceeding without the client's consent. When a client allows a mental health professional to disclose communications that are protected by testimonial privilege, the client is said to "waive privilege." If a client "invokes privilege," the mental health professional may not reveal the communication unless ordered to do so by a court.*

## QUESTIONS DISCUSSED IN THIS CHAPTER

59. What if I cannot locate my client?
60. What if the subpoena asks for the records of a client who has died?
61. Once my client has invoked privilege, or I have invoked privilege on my client's behalf, do I need to do anything else?
62. Please clarify—do I appear in court and *then* claim privilege, or do I refuse to appear in court at all?
63. Is a client's consent necessary for me to appear at a legal proceeding, or is a client's consent necessary only in order for me to testify or to release records?
64. If the client is a criminal defendant and his lawyer needs the treatment records to prepare a defense, is the client's consent to release this information necessary or may the defense attorney waive privilege on the client's behalf?
65. If my client waives privilege, how do I actually go ahead and comply with the subpoena?
66. What if a patient decides to waive privilege for only *part* of the record?
67. Having received a subpoena duces tecum, may I refuse to provide parts of the record that have nothing whatsoever to do with the matter under investigation, and that contain sensitive and possibly embarrassing information?
68. What if the client waives privilege, thereby allowing me to comply with the subpoena, yet at the legal proceeding I am asked questions that have nothing to do with the matter at hand?
69. Is a court order different from a subpoena?
70. Is a court order like a subpoena insofar as either the entire record or none of the record at all will be released?
71. I work as the custodian of records at a busy mental health center. What are my legal responsibilities when I receive a subpoena in my official capacity?
72. I work as the medical director of a community mental health center. How should we respond when a subpoena arrives for a mental health professional who no longer works here?
73. I do not believe judges fully understand the importance of confidentiality to the therapeutic relationship, and believe strongly that mental health professionals should always refuse to release confidential information, even if ordered by a court to do so. What power does a judge have if a mental health professional refuses to testify or release records?

# DISCUSSION

### 54. What is a subpoena?

The word "subpoena" comes from the Latin words "sub" and "poena" which, taken together, mean "under a penalty." A subpoena is a legal process granted to lawyers in order to conduct discovery (see question 8) or to have a witness appear at a legal proceeding. An individual who does not comply with a subpoena may be placed under a penalty, which may be a fine, arrest, and even jail. A special kind of subpoena, a subpoena *duces tecum*, requires that an individual bring certain materials with him to the proceeding. It is important to note that a subpoena is a requirement: that you appear at a given place at a given time (subpoena), or that you appear at such place and time with specified materials (subpoena duces tecum).

A sample subpoena duces tecum is included in appendix B.

### 55. If an individual comes to my office to deliver a subpoena, or a subpoena arrives through the mail, should I simply accept it?

To be valid and effective, a subpoena must be served *in person* on the individual whose appearance is desired. Thus, service by mail is not valid service and the subpoena may be ignored. Note that, according to section 1985.3 of the Code of Civil Procedure, a copy of the subpoena must also be served on the *patient*, prior to the date when the records must be provided.

If an individual arrives at your office to serve a subpoena, you could attempt to avoid service (e.g., by hiding under your desk, behind the water cooler, or on the window ledge). The problem with avoiding service is that the people who deliver subpoenas are professionals. They get paid to find you, and they are very good at their job. Bottom line: You can run, but you can't hide. Another incentive not to evade service is that the attorney who issued the subpoena has the authority to adjust the time when you are legally required to appear. An attorney may even be willing to keep you on "standby," requiring an appearance in court or at a deposition only if you are notified (either by phone or by page). So keep in mind that by attempting to avoid service you may be aggravating someone who has the power to make the whole process less burdensome for you. A final reason not to evade service is found in section 1988 of the California Code of Civil Procedure. Under section 1988, the court may permit the sheriff to break into a building where a witness is concealed, when an attorney is able to demonstrate that the witness is attempting to avoid service. Now, it would be a bit difficult to explain to a client exactly why that sheriff has just come crashing through your front door . . .

### 56. Once the subpoena is in my possession, should I do whatever it says?

No—you need to worry about your client's confidentiality! A subpoena is a demand for your *appearance*; once you have *appeared* you have complied with the subpoena. Although a subpoena is a very scary looking piece of paper, it *neither requires nor allows you to reply to questions or to produce materials that are protected by testimonial privilege.* You may only answer questions or produce materials if your client grants you permission (waives privilege) or if a court orders you to do so. If your client decides to waive privilege, you will ask him to do so in writing (see question 65).

Lawyers who do not understand or who choose to ignore the concept of testimonial privilege may insist (rant and rave, jump up and down, threaten you with contempt) that you provide the information they want. Simply explain that you are not able to do so without your client's consent or a court order, and ask the lawyer to contact your—or your patient's—attorney with any further questions.

### 57. What's the first thing I *should* do if I receive a subpoena?

Inform your client that you have received the subpoena and indicate what the subpoena demands. Next, determine if your records and testimony are protected by testimonial privilege (see chapter 3). If your client is willing to waive privilege, that is, to allow you to disclose information protected by testimonial privilege, you may then go ahead and do what the subpoena asks. Make sure your client waives privilege in writing (see question 65). If your client invokes privilege—does *not* allow you to testify or release records—have your client's lawyer contact you and proceed as directed. If your client does not have a lawyer, contact your own lawyer.

Under no circumstances should you contact the lawyer who issued the subpoena, except in writing and only then for the purpose of stating that, unless you receive the patient's permission or an order from the court, you will not release or disclose any information protected by testimonial privilege. You may also request to be released from the subpoena (see question 61).

## 58. What if I don't think my client is competent to waive privilege?

Evidence Code section 1013 makes clear that the patient is the holder of the privilege—that is, that the patient has the right to decide whether you may testify or release records in a legal proceeding. This rule holds unless the patient has a conservator or a guardian, or is deceased—in which case the conservator, guardian, or personal representative of the estate holds the privilege.

If the person who holds the privilege is unavailable, you may not release records or testify in court (see the following question), unless a judge orders you to do so. In the absence of evidence to the contrary, the law generally assumes that individuals are competent—that they appreciate the consequences of what they do and can act accordingly. A strong argument can be made, however, that a mental health professional is in a good position to determine whether a client is indeed competent, and that when evidence to the contrary arises the mental health professional should consider the client "unavailable" to waive privilege.

Our advice is the following: If, in your professional judgment, you determine that your client is unable to understand the implications of waiving privilege, do not release any information. Bring the matter to the attention of the court. The court will then determine whether the individual is competent and, based on this determination, will decide whether to appoint a guardian ad litem (see question 89) to act as holder of the privilege.

## 59. What if I cannot locate my client?

Remember that privilege belongs to the client. You therefore cannot waive privilege for your client—only your client may give you permission to testify or to release records. If you cannot find your client (perhaps because the treatment has terminated and your client has moved), you should invoke privilege on your client's behalf. In this case you do not testify or release records until a court orders you to do so.

## 60. What if the subpoena asks for the records of a client who has died?

Confidentiality and testimonial privilege survive death. A client's death does not in any manner lessen a mental health professional's obligation to keep that client's communications confidential. A mental health professional needs to be every bit as careful about releasing information after a client's death as she does about releasing information while the client is living.

The circumstances in which the records of a deceased client may be released are similar to those in which the records of an incompetent client may be released. These circumstances arise when an individual with the appropriate authority allows the mental health professional to release records, or when a court orders the mental health professional to release records. In the case of a deceased client, the individual with the appropriate authority is the executor or administrator of the estate; this individual may waive privilege and may consent to the release of records. A mental health professional should always confirm the appointment of the individual as the executor or administrator of the estate before disclosing any information about the client, and should get the consent or waiver in writing. If the mental health professional does not have the consent or waiver of the executor or administrator of the estate or, even with this individual's consent or waiver, does not believe the records should be released, perhaps because of ethical concerns (see question 104), the mental health professional should claim privilege and let the matter go before a court. A judge will make a ruling and issue an order that says what, if any, material to disclose.

### 61. Once my client has invoked privilege or I have invoked privilege on my client's behalf, do I need to do anything else?

Even though your client has invoked privilege or you have invoked privilege on your client's behalf, the subpoena remains valid insofar as a subpoena's demand is for your *appearance*. Once privilege is invoked, you may contact the attorney who issued the subpoena and request that you be "released" from the subpoena. If you are able, get the release in writing; if you are not able to get the release in writing, make a note of the day and the time of the release in your records. Most lawyers will not force you to appear at a deposition or trial until it has been determined what materials will be disclosed.

### 62. Please clarify—do I appear in court and *then* claim privilege, or do I refuse to appear in court at all?

The law requires that you respond to a subpoena. The response required is that you *appear* at a given place, at a given time (with records, if the subpoena is a subpoena duces tecum). Separate from your legal obligation to respond to the subpoena are matters that pertain to testimonial privilege. Put another way, once you have fulfilled your obligation under the subpoena through your appearance at the legal proceeding, it remains to be determined whether you will then testify and what records you will release. Thus, from the law's point of view, your legal obligation to respond to a subpoena and your client's testimonial privilege are separate and distinct matters, and you must treat them as separate and distinct. Bottom line: You respond to the subpoena by appearing as directed. Once you have fulfilled your obligation to respond to the subpoena, you then claim privilege.

### 63. Is a client's consent necessary for me to appear at a legal proceeding, or is a client's consent necessary only in order for me to testify or to release records?

Because your legal obligation to respond to a subpoena and your client's testimonial privilege are separate and distinct legal issues (see the question above), you do *not* need your client's consent to appear at a legal proceeding. You *do* need your client's consent to disclose information protected by testimonial privilege. Put more simply, you don't need your client's permission to show up at court, because the subpoena says you have to. You do need your client's permission to talk or to release records once you get there.

### 64. If the client is a criminal defendant and his lawyer needs the treatment records to prepare a defense, is the client's consent to release this information necessary or may the defense attorney waive privilege on the client's behalf?

Only the client may waive privilege. An attorney is a client's representative in a legal matter; this representation does not, however, give the attorney the authority to waive privilege on the client's behalf. The situation is complicated, of course, because the attorney is working for the client and may need treatment records to assist in the client's defense. And you may pick up the phone, only to hear a very hurried and harassed attorney explaining that yes, of course, privilege is important, but unless you fork over the records *this* morning the client may actually wind up in jail. The attorney's rush notwithstanding, only a client has the authority to waive privilege. Disclosure of material protected by privilege must rest on your client's consent.

### 65. If my client waives privilege, how do I actually go ahead and comply with the subpoena?

When your client says that he intends to waive privilege, tell him that you would like a letter to that effect, and that you will provide a copy of the subpoena to review and attach to the letter. The letter need not be long—essential ingredients are: the date, a statement that your client waives privilege and thereby allows you to comply with the attached subpoena, and your client's signature. It is important to remember that unless your client is under conservatorship or guardianship, only he can waive privilege, so that only *his* signature on the letter will suffice.

### 66. What if a patient decides to waive privilege for only *part* of the record?

Privilege cannot be waived in part. This point is important and separates privilege from confidentiality. A patient may ask that a treater only discuss certain confidential information with, for example, an employer or a family member. Testimonial privilege is different. A patient either waives privilege or she does not. If a patient voluntarily testifies to a privileged matter, then the matter may be opened to a full inquiry, testimonial privilege notwithstanding, as section 912 of the Evidence Code (see appendix A) makes clear. For this reason, patients must be extremely careful when they speak in any sort of legal proceeding. Once the floodgates have opened, it may be impossible to close them. (See also the following question.)

### 67. Having received a subpoena duces tecum, may I refuse to provide parts of the record that have nothing whatsoever to do with the matter under investigation, and that contain sensitive and possibly embarrassing information?

This question provides an excellent illustration of why matters involving testimonial privilege need to be handled with care. Remember that a subpoena, in and of itself, does not grant the authority to disclose information. Rather, a client's consent is necessary. Once a client waives privilege, thereby allowing the mental health professional to disclose confidential information, the client may be prevented from "picking and choosing" which information gets released. For this reason, clients must be *very* thoughtful when choosing to waive privilege.

Our advice is the following: If client does not want certain information in the record disclosed, he should not waive privilege. Rather, the client's lawyer should go to a judge and ask that the court issue an order that specifies which parts of the record will be released. The judge, who has the authority to give access to specific parts of the record, will then make a decision about what information will be disclosed (see question 69). It is *not* within the mental health professional's discretion to decide which aspects of the record to release and which to withhold.

**68. What if the client waives privilege, thereby allowing me to comply with the subpoena, yet at the legal proceeding I am asked questions that have nothing to do with the matter at hand?**

Unfortunately, it is neither your role nor your prerogative as a witness to determine what information is relevant and what questions you should answer. The judge and the attorneys decide what will be discussed in the courtroom or at a deposition. That said, it is good practice when testifying to pause before you respond to a question. A pause allows your client's attorney time to object before you answer. If the attorney's attention seems elsewhere and the questioning turns to matters patently irrelevant to the matter before the court, say, "I'm not sure what that has to do with what we're here for," and then stare intently in the attorney's direction. At that point the attorney should object, and the judge will tell you whether you have to answer the question.

**69. Is a court order different from a subpoena?**

Yes—while an *attorney* issues a subpoena, a *judge* issues a court order after a proceeding called a "fair hearing." At a fair hearing a judge decides if the communication under review is protected by testimonial privilege. To make this determination, the judge may ask: Is the mental health professional licensed? Did the communication take place in the context of a professional relationship? Does the mental health professional belong to a discipline named by one of the privilege statutes? If the answer to any of these questions is "no," the judge may decide that the communication is *not* protected by privilege, which means that it may be introduced into the legal proceeding. If the judge determines that the communication *is* protected by privilege, she will then determine whether any exception to privilege applies. An exception to privilege would permit the communication to be introduced (see chapter 3).

If the judge determines that the communication is not privileged, or that the communication falls under an exception to privilege, she will order all or part of the record to be produced. If the judge determines that the communication *is* protected by testimonial privilege, and that no exception applies, she will "quash" (think "squash") the subpoena, and you need not do anything else.

Bottom line: The judge will either order you to produce all or part of the record or she will "quash" the subpoena. Her word is final, and you do what she says.

### 70. Is a court order like a subpoena insofar as either the entire record or none of the record at all will be released?

No, and this difference is extremely important. A court order will specify what material from the record is to be released. *You only release material specified in the court order.* Whenever you receive an order from a court, you must read the order carefully and follow its instructions exactly.

### 71. I work as the custodian of records at a busy mental health center. What are my legal responsibilities when I receive a subpoena in my official capacity?

When a custodian of business records (including mental health records) receives a subpoena, Evidence Code section 1560 requires her to prepare the records in sealed double envelopes or wrappers and to submit the records, along with a sworn statement, to the judicial officer specified in the subpoena. No privileged or confidential records, however, should be included. The custodian should note in her sworn statement that records that would have been responsive to the subpoena were withheld because they were privileged, confidential, or both. The attorney who sent the subpoena can request a court hearing to attempt to gain access to the records that were withheld. Note that, unless the subpoena duces tecum explicitly says so, the custodian of records does not need to deliver the records in person, so that she need not "appear" anywhere.

### 72. I work as the medical director of a community mental health center. How should we respond when a subpoena arrives for a mental health professional who no longer works here?

If a subpoena is delivered to a mental health center, intended for a mental health professional who no longer works at the center, the person delivering the subpoena should be so informed. The reason is that the subpoena cannot be enforced unless it is served *in person* on the individual named. If, however, the name on the subpoena is the center itself—for records of a mental health professional who no longer works there—the center should assert privilege on behalf of the patient. Because the patient holds the privilege (see chapter 3), it does not matter where the professional is.

# RECEIVING A SUBPOENA

I. What **not** to do:
 A. Do not attempt to avoid service (that is, avoid receiving the subpoena itself).
 B. Do not disclose **any** information (or release **any** records) protected by testimonial privilege.
 C. Do not contact the attorney who issued the subpoena (except to ask that you be released from the subpoena).

II. What to do:
 A. Contact your client and indicate that you have received a subpoena.
 B. Find out whether your client wishes to **waive** or **invoke** privilege.
  1. If client **waives** privilege
   a. Get waiver in writing.
   b. You may now disclose client information in the legal proceeding.
  2. If client **invokes** privilege
   a. Ask to be released from the subpoena.
   b. If not released from the subpoena, you must comply with the subpoena by appearing at the specified time and place.
   c. If the subpoena is a subpoena duces tecum, you will take the physical documents requested with you to the legal proceeding.
   d. At the proceeding you will state that your client has invoked privilege. You will not say anything else, and you will keep your arms tightly wrapped around the physical documents.
   e. The judge will determine whether you must disclose client information. The judge will issue an order telling you what to do.

III. If you are unsure of what to do (e.g., because you cannot find your client), invoke privilege.
 A. The question of whether you must testify or release records will go before a judge.
 B. The judge will determine whether the material is "protected by privilege."
 C. If the judge decides that the material is protected by privilege, she will "quash" (squash) the subpoena.
 D. If the judge decides that the material is not protected by privilege, or that the material falls under an exception to privilege, she will issue an order.
 E. Follow the judge's order exactly.

**73. I do not believe judges fully understand the importance of confidentiality to the therapeutic relationship, and believe strongly that mental health professionals should always refuse to release confidential information, even if ordered by a court to do so. What power does a judge have if a mental health professional refuses to testify or release records?**

Some mental health professionals believe that a client's confidentiality should be protected and preserved at all costs. The strength of their convictions is rarely tested, but may well be when they are faced with a court order to testify or to release records. A court order has the force of law. A mental health professional who refuses to follow the order may be found in contempt of court and may be given a fine or even placed in jail. When you refuse to follow the order of a court because you believe a greater value is at stake, you are—by definition—engaging in civil disobedience; like all who engage in civil disobedience, you may be required to pay a price for your convictions.

# 8

# CONSERVATORS, GUARDIANS, AND SUBSTITUTE DECISION-MAKING

*A fundamental value upon which our society is built is <u>individual autonomy</u>. Individuals are allowed great leeway in the choices they may make: how to worship, what to read, where to live, whom to marry. In our society these and many, many other choices belong to the individual. Because of the value we place on individual autonomy, we presume that individuals are competent to make choices about how to live their lives in whatever fashion they reasonably choose.*

*The presumption of competence holds until we have evidence to the contrary. When such evidence comes to light and we have reason to believe that an individual is not competent to make important decisions, the state looks to its <u>parens patriae</u> power, its authority to take care of individuals who are not capable of caring for themselves. Under the <u>parens patriae</u> power the state may appoint a substitute decision-maker, such as a guardian or a conservator. Also, through such instruments as a durable power of attorney, the law allows an individual to anticipate and plan for his own incapacity to make decisions.*

# QUESTIONS DISCUSSED IN THIS CHAPTER

74.  What is the difference between a conservator and a guardian?
75.  What is the purpose of a conservator?
76.  Where does one find the laws that govern conservatorships?
77.  What is the difference between a conservator of the person and a conservator of the estate?
78.  What are the differences between a probate conservator and an LPS conservator?
79.  Who may ask that a conservator be appointed?
80.  What happens when an individual wants a conservator for herself?
81.  Who may serve as a conservator?
82.  What practical steps should I take when I believe that a client needs a conservator?
83.  What is a temporary conservator?
84.  What is a limited conservator?
85.  When can a conservator place a conservatee in a psychiatric hospital?
86.  What medical treatment may a conservator authorize?
87.  How can medical treatment be provided to a person who lacks the capacity to provide informed consent, but who does not have a conservator?
88.  What is a guardian?
89.  What is a guardian ad litem?
90.  What is a durable power of attorney?
91.  What is a durable power of attorney for health care?
92.  Why might someone who had written a DPAHC need a conservator?
93.  What is a representative payee?

# DISCUSSION

**74. What is the difference between a conservator and a guardian?**
Conservatorships and guardianships are protective relationships that a court establishes for people who need specialized supervision. Prior to 1957, the only protective relationship the court would provide an adult was a guardianship. In order to appoint a guardian, the court had to find that the adult was "incompetent." Because the consequences of being

found incompetent were thought to be too sweeping, California law currently appoints guardians only for minors, and previously existing adult guardianships are now considered conservatorships. The court may appoint a conservator for an adult who is unable either to manage her affairs or to provide for her basic personal needs. In cerain circumstances a court can also create a conservatorship for a minor.

### 75. What is the purpose of a conservator?

A court creates a conservatorship to ensure that an individual who lacks the ability to exercise specific rights is provided a competent substitute decision-maker. The court gives the conservator both the power and the responsibility to make appropriate decisions on behalf of the person over whom the conservator is appointed (this person is called the "conservatee"). In making decisions for the conservatee, the conservator should attempt to ascertain what the conservatee would choose were she capable of making decisions for herself; if the conservator is not able to ascertain the conservatee's preference, the conservator must consider the best interest of the conservatee.

### 76. Where does one find the laws that govern conservatorships?

California has two general types of conservatorships: Probate conservatorships and LPS conservatorships. LPS conservatorships, established under the Lanterman-Petris-Short Act (LPS), are part of the mental health treatment system and are reserved for persons who are gravely disabled as a result of mental disorder. Both probate and LPS conservatorships involve a protective relationship created by the court. In addition, both conservatorships are broken down into conservatorships of the person and conservatorships of the estate.

In most respects, probate and LPS conservatorships are the same. Thus, the general statutes that govern probate conservatorships, found in the Probate Code beginning at section 1800, also cover LPS conservatorships. There are, however, some distinctions between probate and LPS conservatorships, differences that include additional requirements for and responsibilities of LPS conservators. The laws that outline requirements specific to LPS conservatorships are found in the Welfare and Institutions Code, beginning at section 5350.

Mental health professionals should note that California has very recently created a new form of conservatorship for individuals with Alzheimer's disease or other forms of dementia. The laws that describe this new form of conservatorship can be found in the Probate Code, beginning at section 2356.5.

### 77. What is the difference between a conservator of the person and a conservator of the estate?

Both probate and LPS conservatorships are divided into two types: conservatorship of the person and conservatorship of the estate. The court may create one type or the other, or both, depending on the needs of the proposed conservatee. When a person requires a conservatorship of the person and of the estate, the court usually appoints the same person as conservator of both.

A conservator *of the person* has responsibility for the care, custody, and control of the conservatee's person, and is therefore responsible for making decisions regarding the conservatee's basic personal needs. Basic personal needs include food, clothing, shelter, and physical health; as an example, a conservator of the person may decide where the conservatee will live (but must select the least restrictive setting that is available and necessary to meet the needs of the conservatee).

A court may appoint a conservator *of the estate* for a person who is substantially unable to manage his or her own financial resources or to resist fraud or undue influence. Specific powers (if the court so decides) may include the power to contract, to operate a business, and to buy and sell property. (Isolated incidents of negligence or improvidence do not prove "substantial inability." If they did, we might all need conservators of the estate.)

### 78. What are the differences between a probate conservator and an LPS conservator?

There are five significant differences between a probate conservator and an LPS conservator.

First and foremost, only an LPS conservator of the person is authorized to make mental health decisions. This enables an LPS conservator of the person to place a conservatee in a locked facility for purposes of psychiatric treatment. A probate conservator cannot make this decision.

Second, to establish an LPS conservatorship requires the highest standard of proof (beyond a reasonable doubt). On the other hand, a probate conservatorship requires a lower standard of proof (clear and convincing evidence). The higher standard of proof required for an LPS conservatorship is the law's way of recognizing that an LPS conservatorship represents a greater intrusion into the conservatee's right to make personal decisions than does a probate conservatorship. (For a discussion of the different standards of proof, see question 4.)

Third, a court may establish a probate conservatorship if a person is unable to provide for her basic personal needs, or is unable to manage her finances and resist fraud. An LPS conservatorship requires in addition that the inability to provide for food, clothing, or shelter result from a mental disorder or alcoholism.

Fourth, if a probate conservatorship of the person and estate already exists, the court may appoint an LPS conservator of the person, but not of the estate. In such a case, the LPS conservatorship of the person will supersede, but will not nullify, the probate conservatorship of the person. Therefore, in a situation where the two conservators disagree regarding treatment, the clinician must follow the direction of the LPS conservator.

Finally, a probate conservatorship lasts indefinitely or until a court finds that it is no longer needed. A probate court will review the conservatorship every two years. At any time an interested party, including the conservator or the conservatee, family members, the conservatee's physician, or friends, may petition (submit a written request to) the court to end a probate conservatorship. An LPS conservatorship, on the other hand, lasts for renewable one-year periods. To renew an LPS conservatorship, the conservator must petition the court for reappointment; the petition must include the opinions of two physicians or qualified psychologists that the conservatee is still gravely disabled as a result of a mental disorder. Like a probate conservatee, an LPS conservatee may challenge the conservatorship at any time.

The stricter criteria, shorter time period, and enhanced safeguards that attach to LPS conservatorships reflect the importance society places on autonomy, particularly as it relates to mental health decision-making.

### 79. Who may ask that a conservator be appointed?

Probate Code section 1820 allows any of the following to file a petition (a written request) for the appointment of a *probate* conservator: the proposed conservatee, a spouse, a relative, a friend, any state or local government agency or official, or any other interested person, except a creditor. An *LPS* conservatorship can only be recommended by the professional person in charge of an agency providing comprehensive evaluation or a facility providing intensive treatment. If the county conservatorship investigator concurs, she shall petition the court to establish an LPS conservatorship.

## DIFFERENCES BETWEEN PROBATE AND LPS CONSERVATORS

I.  Decision-making authority
    A.  LPS conservators may make **mental health decisions**, including decisions to place a conservatee on a locked psychiatric unit.
    B.  Probate conservators may not place a conservatee on a locked psychiatric unit or authorize treatment of a mental disorder.

II.  Standard of proof needed to appoint conservator
    A.  **Proof beyond a reasonable doubt** needed to appoint an LPS conservator.
    B.  **Clear and convincing evidence** needed to appoint a probate conservator.

III.  Criteria for appointing a conservator
    A.  Probate conservatorship
        1.  Inability to manage affairs *or*
        2.  Inability to provide for basic personal needs.
    B.  LPS conservatorship
        1.  Inability to provide for food, clothing, or shelter *and*
        2.  Inability **results from mental disorder or alcoholism**.

IV.  LPS conservatorship supersedes probate conservatorship
    A.  When **probate conservatorship of the person and the estate** already exists, court may appoint LPS conservator **of the person only**.
    B.  When conditions in "A" exist, LPS conservatorship will supersede, but not nullify, probate conservatorship of the person.
    C.  In cases of disagreement, clinicians should follow direction of LPS conservator.

V.  Length of time conservatorship lasts
    A.  Probate conservatorship lasts indefinitely or until court finds conservatorship no longer needed. Probate conservatorships reviewed every two years.
    B.  LPS conservatorship lasts for renewable one-year periods.

**80. What happens when an individual wants a conservator for herself?**
An individual can ask to have a conservator appointed for herself. In this case the individual is a voluntary conservatee. To create a conservatorship for a voluntary conservatee, the required standard of proof is reduced. The proposed conservatee need only establish "good cause" for

appointment to satisfy the court. If the proposed conservatee has designated, in writing, a reasonable proposed conservator, the court may appoint that nominee, unless it believes that doing so would not be in the best interest of the conservatee.

### 81. Who may serve as a conservator?

If the proposed conservatee has the capacity to form an intelligent preference, the proposed conservatee may nominate a conservator. The nomination must be in writing, and may be part of the petition if the conservatee is also the petitioner (that is, if the person is asking that a conservator be appointed for herself). The court will appoint the nominee as conservator unless it finds that the appointment of the nominee is not in the best interest of the proposed conservatee. In addition, adult family members of the proposed conservatee may nominate a conservator in the petition or at the petition hearing.

The court has the final say in who is appointed conservator. The court strives, in its appointment decision, to promote the best interest of the proposed conservatee. When a court is faced with equally qualified alternatives, section 1812 of the Probate Code provides the following order of preference for appointment as conservator: (1) the spouse of the proposed conservatee, or someone nominated by the spouse; (2) an adult child of the proposed conservatee, or someone nominated by the adult child; (3) a parent of the proposed conservatee, or the parent's nominee; (4) a sibling of the proposed conservatee, or the sibling's nominee; (5) any other person or entity eligible for appointment as a conservator. If none of these nominees are available, qualified, or willing to act as conservator, the court may appoint the public guardian to serve as conservator.

### 82. What practical steps should I take when I believe that a client needs a conservator?

The first procedural step in creating a probate conservatorship is to file a petition (a written request) in the probate court for the appointment of a conservator. The petition must be filed in the proposed conservatee's home county or in a county where it would be in the proposed conservatee's best interest to live. In addition, if the person has not filed her own petition for conservatorship, she must be given (in person) a copy of the filing 15 days prior to the hearing.

Before the hearing takes place, a court investigator will interview the proposed conservatee, unless the proposed conservatee is also the petitioner (that is, unless the person is asking that a conservator be appointed for herself). The investigator must then prepare and file a report describing the proposed conservatee's situation at least five days prior to the hearing. During the hearing, the proposed conservatee has the right to a jury trial, a court appointed attorney, and to present evidence. If, at the hearing, the court finds that the petitioner (the person asking that a conservator be appointed) has shown "by clear and convincing evidence" (see question 4) that the proposed conservatee meets the legal requirements for a conservatorship, the court will appoint a probate conservator. The appointment of the conservator will follow the order of preference outlined in the Probate Code (see question 81). Sometimes a conservatee names the individual she would like the court to appoint as conservator. These propositions are considered, but do not bind the court.

If the proposed conservatee needs psychiatric treatment or placement, an LPS conservatorship is appropriate. Most LPS conservatorships are established as part of involuntary hospitalization, which is initiated with a 72-hour hold (see question 27). Thus, if your patient is gravely disabled and in need of a conservatorship, the most practical first step is to establish a short-term involuntary hold. If the professional in charge of the facility providing involuntary treatment determines that the individual remains gravely disabled as a result of a mental disorder, she may recommend conservatorship to the county agency providing conservatorship investigations. If the investigator concurs with the recommendation, she will ask that a conservatorship be established.

### 83. What is a temporary conservator?

A court may appoint a temporary conservator while the decision whether to appoint a permanent conservator is being made. Usually, either the petitioner for the conservatorship (the person who is asking that a conservator be appointed) or the officer conducting the conservatorship investigation recommends that the court grant a temporary conservatorship. The temporary conservatorship ends when the court appoints a permanent conservator. It is almost always the case that a court creates a temporary conservatorship while it is considering a conservatorship under LPS.

A temporary *probate* conservatorship generally lasts 30 days but may be extended by the court while the decision whether to appoint a permanent conservator is being made. A temporary *LPS* conservatorship also lasts 30 days, and may be extended in only one instance: when a court holds a hearing to determine whether a permanent LPS conservator should be appointed, and the conservatee wants a jury trial on the issue. When this occurs, the court may extend the temporary LPS conservatorship until it reaches a decision, but no longer than six months.

The powers of the temporary conservator are generally the same powers granted to a permanent conservator. The court may specifically choose which powers it grants, but in no event may the powers granted to a temporary conservator be broader than those granted to a permanent conservator. An LPS temporary conservatorship can be challenged in court through a writ of habeas corpus (see question 16).

### 84. What is a limited conservator?

A limited conservator of the person or of the estate, or both, may be appointed for an adult who is developmentally disabled. A limited conservatorship may be utilized only as is necessary to promote and protect the well-being of the individual. For example, an individual with a developmental disability may have the capacity to make everyday decisions, but require a limited conservator to make major financial decisions. A limited conservatorship is designed to encourage the development of maximum self-reliance and independence of the individual. The court may order a limited conservatorship only to the extent required by the individual's proven mental and adaptive limitations. The conservatee retains all legal and civil rights, except those the court has specifically granted to the limited conservator.

Limited conservatorships reflect the legislature's intent to offer services to developmentally disabled citizens that promote independent, productive, and normal lives.

### 85. When can a conservator place a conservatee in a psychiatric hospital?

Only an LPS conservator of the person can place a conservatee in a psychiatric hospital. At the time the conservatorship is created, the court will approve the least restrictive, most appropriate placement necessary to meet treatment objectives. This placement may be a psychiatric hospital. If the court determines that a non-hospital setting is most appropriate, the conservator may still place the conservatee in a psychiatric hospital at a later time if the necessity arises. According to Welfare and Institutions Code section 5358, the conservator must have reasonable cause to believe that hospitalization is necessary before placing a conservatee on a locked unit. This belief must be based on a change in the conservatee's condition that poses an immediate and substantial danger to the conservatee or to others.

### 86. What medical treatment may a conservator authorize?

A conservatee—like every adult patient—has the right to informed consent, unless she lacks the capacity to make treatment decisions. Capacity to provide informed consent requires that a conservatee be able to understand the nature and purpose of a treatment, the risks and benefits of the treatment, and the risks and benefits of alternate treatments, including no treatment at all. Capacity to make treatment decisions also requires that the conservatee be able to communicate her decision about treatment. Note that the appointment of a conservator does *not* mean that the conservatee is unable to give informed consent to treatment; a conservatee may remain perfectly competent in this regard.

A competent probate conservatee may therefore consent to medical treatment. Except in an emergency, the consent of the probate conservator is not sufficient if a competent conservatee objects to the treatment. When a competent probate conservatee objects to treatment, the probate conservator needs a court order to authorize medical assistance. If the court determines that the probate conservatee *lacks* the capacity to give informed consent, the probate conservator has the exclusive authority to give consent to *necessary* medical treatment, whether or not the conservatee objects (Probate Code, §2354). To determine whether treatment is necessary requires the conservator to make a good faith decision based on medical advice. For example, according to *Conservatorship of Drabick*, 200 Cal. App. 3d 185 (1988), life-sustaining treatment is not necessary if it offers no reasonable possibility of returning the conservatee to reasonable quality of life and if it is not otherwise in the conservatee's best interest as determined by the conservator in good faith.

An LPS conservator, when specifically authorized by the court, may consent to both *necessary and routine* medical treatment, such as regular visits to the doctor or remedies for common ailments. If the medical treatment is not routine, or if the court has not duly authorized the LPS conservator to consent to involuntary medical treatment, the conservator must obtain a court order that permits the specific treatment. As with most medical treatment scenarios, however, an exception arises in emergencies where the conservatee faces loss of life or serious bodily injury. Conservators may *always* authorize treatment in an emergency situation. The court may also authorize an LPS conservator to require the conservatee to receive treatment specifically related to remedying or preventing the persistence of the conservatee's grave disability.

In determining whether the conservator may consent to treatment, the clinician should ask about the type of conservatorship and whether the necessary findings or granting of powers were made by the court to allow consent on the conservatee's behalf.

## 87. How can medical treatment be provided to a person who lacks the capacity to provide informed consent, but who does not have a conservator?

A clinician may legally treat without informed consent only in emergency situations. When a patient who requires treatment for an existing or continuing *nonemergent* medical condition is unable to give informed consent, a clinician who provides that treatment is potentially liable for battery. Appropriate authorization for treatment in such a circumstance may be obtained by petitioning (making a written request to) the superior court pursuant to the Probate Code, beginning at section 3200. The petition should include the nature of the medical condition, the recommended course and probable outcome of treatment, the harm to the patient if the condition remains untreated, what medical alternatives are available, and what efforts have been made to obtain informed consent.

After a hearing, or an agreement between the person who has written the request and the attorney representing the patient, the court may authorize the treatment. The court bases its authorization for treatment on the following two factors: First, the court determines whether the patient is able to give informed consent; second, the court determines how probable it is that, if left untreated, the patient's condition will become life endangering, or will result in a serious threat to the patient's physical or mental health. If the patient is not able to give consent, and the condition is or will become life threatening or will seriously endanger the patient's physical or mental health, the court may authorize the treatment even though the person is not under a probate or LPS conservatorship.

## 88. What is a guardian?

A guardian is an adult whom the court appoints to represent the interests of a minor (called a ward). Any individual whom the probate or juvenile court finds suitable may serve as a guardian. An individual is frequently found suitable simply because nothing speaks *against* that individual's appointment. A proposed guardian should be competent, have no conflict with the ward, and be able to get along reasonably well with significant persons in the ward's life.

Most guardians are family members. The value of appointing a family member or close friend as a guardian is that they may better understand the ward's needs. Family members and other interested parties are allowed to nominate guardians. Ultimately, however, the court bases its decision on what it deems to be in the child's best interest.

### 89. What is a guardian ad litem?

A guardian ad litem is a guardian for the purposes of a legal proceeding. A guardian ad litem may be appointed for any person, by the court in which the legal matter is being heard, if the court determines that representation of that person's interests would otherwise be inadequate. The court may even choose to appoint a guardian ad litem for individuals who already have a conservator or guardian.

During the course of the legal proceeding, the guardian ad litem is not considered a party, that is, a guardian ad litem is not someone, like the plaintiff or defendant, whose interests are directly at issue. Rather, she is considered the *personal representative* of a party—it is as if the guardian ad litem were standing in the party's shoes. Because she is representing a party in this manner, the guardian ad litem has the authority to make important decisions affecting the outcome of the case, such as whether to settle. Note that attorneys are not allowed to make decisions of this sort; an attorney must have a client's approval first. The power of a guardian ad litem is limited in that she cannot waive fundamental rights of the ward. A guardian ad litem cannot, for example, waive a party's right to trial by jury.

### 90. What is a durable power of attorney?

A power of attorney is a document by which one individual (called the "principal") authorizes another individual (called the "agent") to perform acts having to do with the principal's property. Examples of the sorts of things a principal may authorize an agent to do include writing checks and selling property. The principal is bound by what the agent does, in the same way the principal would be bound if she herself had performed the acts. The power of attorney will specify precisely what the agent is allowed to do on behalf of the principal. A power of attorney cannot be used to make health care decisions.

A *durable* power of attorney is a power of attorney that continues to be valid when the principal becomes incompetent, for example, because of mental illness or dementia. A durable power of attorney may commence *upon* or may remain valid *despite* the principal's incompetence. Whichever the case, the agent is authorized to act on the principal's behalf during a period of the principal's incompetence. As with a power of attorney, the principal is bound by what the agent does, in the same way as the principal would be bound if she herself had performed the acts.

### 91. What is a durable power of attorney for health care?

A durable power of attorney for health care (DPAHC) is a tool that specifically contemplates the future health care needs of an individual in the event she becomes incapacitated. If, for example, an individual knew she was at the very beginning stages of Alzheimer's disease, she could write a DPAHC to instruct a friend or member of her family (the agent) about what medical care she would like when she herself becomes unable to make decisions. Thus, a DPAHC represents a future transfer of authority from the principal (the individual) to the agent (the person chosen by the individual) to make decisions regarding the principal's health care should (or when) the principal become unable to make decisions for herself.

If an adult becomes unable to care for herself, she may be eligible for a conservatorship. A DPAHC has the advantage over a conservatorship in that it may be specifically tailored to the wishes of the principal. The reason for this advantage is that a DPAHC is written *while the principal is still competent*. While a principal may choose anyone to be an agent under DPAHC, we recommend family members, relatives, or close friends. The people who know the principal the most intimately will be able to make the sensitive health care decisions often required by a DPAHC.

### 92. Why might someone who had written a DPAHC need a conservator?

A principal (the person who has written a DPAHC) is presumed to have the capacity to revoke a DPAHC. This presumption holds *even if the principal is not competent*. Furthermore, under Civil Code section 2440, the agent may not consent to treatment over the objections of the principal, *even when the principal is incompetent*. If, therefore, a principal objects to what the agent is deciding on her behalf, the agent's only recourse to obtain treatment for the principal would be through a conservatorship or through a court order pursuant to Probate Code section 3200 (see question 87). If an individual has both a conservator and an agent under DPAHC, the agent's decision has priority over the conservator's decision.

### 93. What is a representative payee?

A representative payee is a person or an agency who accepts payment from an entitlement program on behalf of a recipient. An individual need not have a conservator or be incompetent to have a representative payee. Rather, the standard is whether having a representative payee is in the person's interest. According to the Social Security Act, a representative payee is automatically judged to be in the interest of an individual whose disability includes drug or alcohol addiction.

# 9

# CONSULTATION AND
# SUPERVISION

*From a risk management perspective, the value of a consultation
cannot be overemphasized. Every mental health professional has a
legal duty to provide care that is reasonable. If a mental health
professional's care falls below that which is reasonable, she may then
be held responsible for any damages that result from her negligence.
How do we determine whether a clinician's care is "reasonable"? By
looking to the professional community. The standard set by the community of mental health professionals will determine what care is reasonable, and any individual clinician's care will be judged against that
standard. Consultations are so valuable because they provide a link
between the individual clinician and the community. In a word, a
<u>consultation brings a clinician into the professional fold</u>.*

*Consultations are particularly helpful in difficult treatments or
when there is a transference or countertransference problem. Consultations show that the treater was working in a thoughtful manner, that she
made an effort to reach out to her professional community, and that she
was aware enough to know that a difficult aspect of the treatment—
perhaps a countertransference issue—needed to be looked at from a
perspective other than her own. A consultation is also powerful evi-*

*dence against a claim that a mental health professional was exploiting
a patient or using the transference for personal gain. Exploitation is
usually shrouded in secret; consultations provide a way of bringing a
treatment into the open, thus serving to refute a suggestion or innuendo
that the mental health professional was behaving unethically. From the
perspective of risk management, supervision, which places an entire
treatment under the scrutiny of another mental health professional,
plays much the same role as a consultation.*

## QUESTIONS DISCUSSED IN THIS CHAPTER

94. **What rules of confidentiality govern consultations?**
95. **From a professional liability perspective, what is the difference
    between a consultation and supervision?**
96. **Is a trainee required to tell a patient that the treatment is being
    supervised?**
97. **What is negligent supervision? What would be an example of
    negligent supervision?**
98. **Treaters often keep notes of their own countertransference
    fantasies, separate from the record. These are neither progress
    nor process notes; their purpose is to help the treater gauge the
    nature and intensity of her own psychic processes as they relate
    to the clinical work. Could a lawyer ever obtain them?**

## DISCUSSION

### 94. What rules of confidentiality govern consultations?

As with many areas of mental health law, there is no crystal clear guideline that governs the sharing of confidential patient information in consultations and supervisions. The unclarity stems from two realities that
occasionally conflict. The first is that information and records obtained in
the course of providing mental health services are confidential (see chapter 3); the second, that in order to provide appropriate care psychotherapists sometimes need to consult with and seek professional advice from
their colleagues. Often these realities can be molded to fit one another.
Many times, for example, therapists are able to ask for and receive enormously helpful consultations that do not require disclosing any informa-

tion that could reasonably lead to a client's identification. When a therapist is able to obtain a consultation without revealing identifying information, both the need to maintain confidentiality and the need to seek professional advice and assistance are met.

Section 5328 of the Welfare and Institutions Code does make an explicit exception to confidentiality that is relevant to consultations and supervisions. Under section 5328, a health professional may disclose client information to "providers of health care or other health care professionals or facilities for purposes of diagnosis or treatment of the patient." If the information is covered by Welfare and Institutions Code section 5328, that is, the information concerns treatment provided within the public mental health system or in a public or private psychiatric hospital (see chapter 3), the patient must consent if the treater wishes to consult with a professional who is not employed by the same facility. Note, however, that consent is necessary only when the treater wishes to reveal information that could reasonably lead to the client's identity.

It is helpful if, during your first session, you follow the Law of No Surprises by informing your client about how you handle consultations. Be sure to document that you have done so (see appendix B for a sample informed consent letter). When you get the actual consultation, follow the Parsimony Principle: Be as precise as you can about what questions you would like the consultant to answer, and then provide only the information necessary for the consultant to answer those questions.

### 95. From a professional liability perspective, what is the difference between a consultation and supervision?

The difference between a consultation and a supervision is the degree to which an individual, other than the treater, becomes involved in and responsible for a treatment. This difference in degree has significant liability implications.

A consultation consists of a treater bringing a specific question, or questions, to a consultant. A consultation is not open-ended or indefinite; the question is asked, a recommendation is made, and the treater is free to use the recommendation in whatever manner she feels will be most helpful to the treatment. The consultant assumes no responsibility for what the treater does, and makes a recommendation based only on what material the treater presents. When the consultant puts forth a recommendation, the consultant-consultee relationship ends. Because of the nature of this relationship, a consultant's liability is extremely limited. Consultants are rarely named as defendants in lawsuits.

A supervision consists of an ongoing relationship in which an entire treatment, or significant aspects of a treatment, are placed under the scrutiny of the supervisor. If the supervisee is a trainee and the supervisor has both clinical and administrative responsibility for the supervisee's work, the supervisor is nearly as responsible for the treatment as if the patient were the supervisor's own. In this sense, the supervisor is much "closer" to the patient than is the consultant. If the supervisee is a licensed clinician with experience, the supervisor's responsibility is less, yet still considerably more than that of a consultant. A supervisor will be held accountable for not actively exploring what the supervisee is doing, how the supervisee is handling the transference and countertransference, how the supervisee is addressing issues of safety, and the like. Because of their greater degree of involvement and responsibility, supervisors are more likely to be named in lawsuits than are consultants.

### 96. Is a trainee required to tell a patient that the treatment is being supervised?

Yes. Trainees must tell their patients that a treatment is being supervised.

### 97. What is negligent supervision? What would be an example of negligent supervision?

Negligent supervision is the failure to live up to the standard expected of you in the supervisory relationship. For this reason, it is important that you define the frame of the supervision at the outset. You will want to be clear about how often you and your supervisee will meet; which cases your supervisee will bring to the supervision; which aspects of those cases you will supervise; who, if anyone, will cover for you during vacations; and so forth. Once you set the frame, you will then be responsible for providing *reasonable* supervision. From a professional liability point of view, the crucial question is: Given the frame, what would a reasonable supervisor do in these circumstances?

*Andrews v. United States*, a case in federal court, provides an extreme example of negligent supervision. Sandra Andrews went into therapy with Travis Gee, a physician's assistant with experience in counseling and psychology. Gee was supervised on the case by Dr. David Frost. A short while into the therapy, Gee told Ms. Andrews that she was suffering from chronic depression and that she needed an affair. Gee added that he was available. Under the guise of a therapy, Gee convinced Ms. Andrews to have intercourse. During the time Gee was sexually involved with Ms. Andrews, one of Dr. Frost's patients complained to Frost about Gee. Specifically, this patient told Dr. Frost that Gee had engaged in sexual activity with Ms. Andrews. In response, Frost confronted Gee. After Gee denied the allegations, Frost let the matter drop. Ms. Andrews' depression became much worse and, after she revealed to her husband what had occurred between her and Gee, her marriage ended. The former Mr. and Mrs. Andrews then sued.

The federal court held that Frost's supervision of Gee had been negligent. The court reasoned that Frost had failed to investigate "properly and promptly" the allegations of sexual improprieties. Important from the court's point of view was that as a supervisor, Frost had failed to act *reasonably*. According to the court, a reasonable supervisor would have done more than simply ask Gee whether he was having sex with his patient, and then let the matter drop when Gee said "No."

Here are three more mundane examples. First, you have agreed to meet with your supervisee once per month, and you miss three months without taking the time to "check-in" with your supervisee. An untoward event happens. Your supervision could be considered negligent, because a reasonable supervisor would have made sure to communicate with the supervisee in some way about the status of the cases. Second, a supervisee talks at length about how physically attractive he finds his new patient. You do not address the erotic countertransference, nor do you attend to how the supervisee is handling the countertransference. An affair results. Your supervision could be considered negligent, because a reasonable supervisor would have made sure that the countertransference was appropriately addressed. Third, your supervisee begins to treat a patient with a long history of suicide attempts. For a period of several weeks you do not ask your supervisee about her assessment of the patient's suicidality, and the patient makes a serious suicide attempt. You could be considered negligent, because a reasonable supervisor would have made sure that the supervisee was adequately assessing the patient's suicidality. Your touchstone is what a reasonable supervisor would do under the circumstances.

**98. Treaters often keep notes of their own countertransference fantasies, separate from the record. These are neither progress nor process notes; their purpose is to help the treater gauge the nature and intensity of her own psychic processes as they relate to the clinical work. Could a lawyer ever obtain them?**

They got Bob Packwood's diary. They can get your countertransference notes.* When it comes to records or notes arising out of a treatment, the rule is: If the records exist, a lawyer can obtain them. While the records may not actually be introduced as evidence into a legal proceeding, at the very least they will be made available to a judge who will review them.

The records described in this question are the treater's personal notes. As such, they are not part of the record. The treater is not required to keep them and may dispose of them whenever she wishes *prior to receiving a subpoena*. Once the treater receives a subpoena—which will almost certainly call for "any and all" records—she is then obligated to ensure that *all* of her records remain intact until a decision is made about what material will be released. Many treaters believe that keeping a set of notes separate from the official record will insulate their notes from a subpoena. Not so. Any written materials that arise out of a treatment may be requested—and possibly obtained—by a lawyer.

* James T. Hilliard, J.D., is the author of this insightful and telling example.

# 10

# CONFIDENTIALITY, TESTIMONIAL PRIVILEGE, AND MANDATORY REPORTING

*That we have both an entire chapter and a set of questions on the subject of confidentiality emphasizes the importance of this topic to mental health professionals. As you read, recall that confidentiality involves the obligation of a mental health professional to keep patient communications within the bounds of the professional relationship. Testimonial privilege, or simply "privilege," refers to a patient's right to prevent the mental health professional from disclosing confidential information in a legal proceeding. Mandatory reporting statutes require a mental health professional to disclose confidential information in certain well-defined situations; this disclosure must take place regardless of whether the client consents.*

*The number of questions that can arise when a clinician is attempting to treat difficult or severely compromised patients is staggering; even the most routine work will inevitably raise dilemmas about when to release clinical material. The questions below are presented as much for their demonstration of the process that should govern a treater's thinking when she is faced with the possibility of disclosing confidential information, as for their content.*

# QUESTIONS DISCUSSED IN THIS CHAPTER

99. Is there a duty to break confidentiality if a patient talks about having committed a crime in the past?

100. Is there a duty to break confidentiality if a patient talks about intending to commit a crime in the future?

101. Both the Evidence Code and the *Tarasoff* statute address the disclosure of information when a patient poses a threat of violence. Are the Evidence Code and the *Tarasoff* statute saying the same thing, or is there a difference in what they tell a mental health professional to do under such a circumstance?

102. The Evidence Code talks about danger to property. Do I have a duty to break confidentiality if a patient threatens to destroy property?

103. What happens to confidentiality and testimonial privilege when a patient dies?

104. In certain circumstances following a patient's death, the executor or administrator of the estate may waive privilege; what happens when the executor of an estate wants clinical records?

105. What is a mandated reporter?

106. Does the mandatory reporting statute for child abuse require a clinician to report child abuse that is not inflicted by a caretaker? What if the abuser is another child?

107. An extremely religious set of parents forbade me to break confidentiality when their 12-year-old child talked about having been sexually touched by a member of their church's clergy. The parents were adamant that this information was to go *nowhere*, or else I would never see the child again and I would face a lawsuit for breach of confidentiality. What is the best way to handle this situation?

108. I am a psychologist. Do I have an obligation to report *whenever* I have reasonable cause to suspect that a parent is abusing a child—even if my suspicion arises from what I see at the mall?

109. If I make a report under the mandatory reporting statute for children, can the child's parent—or the alleged perpetrator— find out that I was the one who reported?

110. What should I do if a patient tells me that another treater has harmed her?

111. Do confidentiality and testimonial privilege work differently for group therapy than for individual therapy?

112. Must a clinician treat a psychological evaluation ordered by a court differently from an evaluation requested by a private client?

**113. If a patient commits a crime against a mental health professional, for example, by breaking into a therapist's office or even by assaulting a therapist, would confidentiality prohibit the therapist from bringing the matter to the police?**

# DISCUSSION

**99. Is there a duty to break confidentiality if a patient talks about having committed a crime in the past?**

California law recognizes that the psychotherapist-patient relationship requires complete trust and open communication. Without safeguards protecting the confidentiality of patient communications, many people would simply forego psychotherapy. The California Court of Appeal has said as much in reasoning that certain forms of antisocial behavior may be prevented by encouraging those in need of treatment to seek help from a mental health professional (see *Scull v. Superior Court*, 206 Cal. App. 3d 784 [1988]).

The decision regarding when confidential information will be revealed belongs to the patient. Evidence Code section 1014 states, "the patient . . . has a privilege to refuse to disclose, and to *prevent another from disclosing* [italics added], a confidential communication between patient and psychotherapist." No exception to section 1014, or to any other statute, allows a mental health professional to break confidentiality when a client talks about having committed a crime in the past. Such material should be treated in the same manner as any other material disclosed within the therapeutic context—it remains between treater and patient. Certain provisions in the law do, however, permit or require a mental health professional to disclose information about a past crime in specific, limited, and well-defined circumstances: State hospitals report to law enforcement when they have evidence of a crime committed by a confined individual who is criminally insane, incompetent to stand trial, or a mentally disordered sex offender; physicians must report certain serious crimes committed by hospitalized patients, and may report less serious crimes; and mental health professionals must report to a state agency when they have evidence of child, elder, dependent adult, or patient abuse (see chapter 3). Except in these limited circumstances, information about past crimes should be treated in the same manner as any other material disclosed within the therapeutic context—it remains confidential.

**100. Is there a duty to break confidentiality if a patient talks about intending to commit a crime in the future?**

The issue of future crimes—the contemplation of a crime—is complicated. Consider the following points in determining what to do if a patient communicates the intent to commit a crime.

First, virtually all crimes entail the possibility of harm, either to a third party or to the perpetrator. Breaking into a home or apartment, for example, can place both the inhabitants and the individual entering at great risk. Stealing a car brings with it the possibility of a police chase, which could kill or injure the individual who stole the car, a police officer, or innocent bystanders. Whenever a client talks about committing a crime in the future, the treater should assess the degree to which harm is foreseeable. If the crime is against an identifiable third party, the treater should assess whether a duty arises under the *Tarasoff* statute (see chapter 2).

Second, a question arises whenever a treater listens to a client talk about a future crime: To what extent is the treater subtlely encouraging—if only by failing to *discourage*—the client? Any action by a treater that could reasonably be viewed as encouraging or aiding a criminal could be considered actionable by the police. When such material arises during the course of a therapy, the treater should be keenly aware of what posture she adopts. A consultation could prove invaluable.

Third, Welfare and Institutions Code section 5328(r) allows a psychotherapist to disclose confidential information to potential victims and to law enforcement agencies when she reasonably believes that a patient presents a serious danger of violence, and the release of information is necessary to protect an identifiable victim. Section 5328(r) does not obligate a mental health professional to disclose this information; rather, it provides a legal mechanism whereby the therapist is able to discharge her duty pursuant to the *Tarasoff* statute. In a manner of speaking, section 5328(r) opens the door through which the therapist may walk with (the otherwise confidential) information necessary to protect the victim. Put another way, the *Tarasoff* statute gives the push (by creating a duty) and section 5328(r) opens the door (by allowing disclosure of the information). Similarly, section 1024 of the Evidence Code states, "there is no privilege . . . if the psychotherapist has reasonable cause to believe that the patient is in such mental or emotional condition as to be dangerous to himself or to the person or property of another and that disclosure of the communication is necessary to prevent the threatened danger." Note that section 1024 refers to privilege; its effect is therefore to prevent your client from keeping this information out of a legal or administrative hearing. So—if you must go to court to keep everyone safe, section 1024 ensures that your client no longer has the option of insisting you keep silent.

**101. Both the Evidence Code and the *Tarasoff* statute address the disclosure of information when a patient poses a threat of violence. Are the Evidence Code and the *Tarasoff* statute saying the same thing, or is there a difference in what they tell a mental health professional to do under such a circumstance?**

The Evidence Code indicates what evidence will be allowed in court. Because testimonial privilege keeps evidence out of court, an important role of the Evidence Code is to set forth the circumstances when testimonial privilege applies; that is, to be clear about when an individual may rely on privilege and thereby keep evidence out of a legal proceeding. By providing this clarity, the Evidence Code ensures that everyone knows what evidence is "fair play" for the legal system to consider.

Section 1024 of the Evidence Code states that what a patient communicates to a mental health professional is not privileged if the patient is a danger to himself or to someone else, and disclosure of the communication is necessary to prevent the threatened danger. Section 1024 does not require a mental health professional to disclose this information, nor does it make a mental health professional a mandated reporter (see question 105). Rather, section 1024 says, "We will no longer say that this information is protected by privilege; as a consequence, the mental health professional may discuss this material in a legal proceeding." The *Tarasoff* statute, on the other hand, compels a mental health professional to act; the *Tarasoff* statute creates a duty by virtue of which the mental health professional must *do* something.

**102. The Evidence Code talks about danger to property. Do I have a duty to break confidentiality if a patient threatens to destroy property?**

No. The purpose of the Evidence Code is to set forth the rules that govern when evidence will be allowed into a legal proceeding (see the question above). That the Evidence Code talks about danger to property does not mean that a mental health professional is required to disclose confidential information when a patient threatens to damage property; it means, rather, that a client can no longer invoke privilege in order to prevent a mental health professional from disclosing this information in a legal proceeding. The *Tarasoff* statute creates a duty to warn—an obligation for the mental health professional to *do* something—when a specific *person* is in danger; there is no similar requirement to break confidentiality when *property* is at risk.

### 103. What happens to confidentiality and testimonial privilege when a patient dies?

Numerous provisions of California law make clear that confidentiality and privilege continue after a patient has died. First, the Confidentiality of Medical Information Act (CMIA) defines a patient as "any natural person, *whether or not still living* [italics added]." Second, California Civil Code section 56.11 states that a deceased patient's medical records may be released only when the patient's beneficiary or personal representative (the executor or administrator of the patient's estate) has signed and dated a release. Third, Evidence Code section 1013 says that, after a patient has died, the patient's personal representative now holds the privilege—that is, can decide whether to release the patient's records. Each of these laws makes clear that confidentiality and testimonial privilege continue after a patient's death.

### 104. In certain circumstances following a patient's death, the executor or administrator of the estate may waive privilege; what happens when the executor of an estate wants clinical records?

A well-known psychiatrist, Martin Orne, perhaps unwittingly brought the issue of confidentiality following a patient's death to the forefront of public attention when he released audiotapes of his treatment sessions with Anne Sexton. Sexton, who won a Pulitzer Prize for her poetry following several years of therapy with Orne, had complained that she was frequently unable to remember what was said during their hours, a complaint Orne addressed by suggesting they tape-record their sessions. Following Sexton's suicide in 1974, Orne provided over 300 of these audiotapes to Diane Middlebrook, an English Professor at Stanford University and Sexton's biographer. Orne's decision to release the tapes without Sexton's written permission or express consent was met by a firestorm of controversy; the sum total of what Sexton had to say on the subject appears to have been a comment she made to Orne in 1964, when the treatment ended because Orne moved from Massachusetts (where Sexton lived) to Philadelphia. According to Orne, Sexton told him to keep the tapes to help others as he saw fit. When Orne gave the tapes to biographer Diane Middlebrook, he did so with the permission of Sexton's literary executor, who was also her daughter, Linda Grey Sexton. Despite that permission, Orne soon became the target of vehement condemnations. (The *New York Times* opined that Orne had "dishonored" his profession.)

Given that mental health professionals must not reveal confidential communications even after a patient has died, how could Orne have found his decision to release the tapes defensible?

In certain, very limited circumstances, an individual other than your patient may have the legal authority to consent to the release of your patient's records. Usually this individual is a parent or conservator; parents and conservators are entrusted with protecting the interests of a minor or someone who has been deemed unable to care for himself, and are therefore presumed to be acting in the best interest of their child or conservatee when they allow confidential treatment information to be shared with a third party. The executor of a patient's estate fills a similar role: Charged with protecting the interests of the estate, the executor may consent to the release of a deceased patient's treatment records.

Given Linda Grey Sexton's authority as executor of her mother's estate, why was Orne so severely criticized?

A distinction arises between what is legally permissible and what is ethically permissible. Whatever a mental health professional is *legally* permitted to do, the *ethical* mandate to keep patient communications confidential remains. (Keep in mind the distinction between what mental health professionals are legally permitted to do and what they are legally required to do; disclosures of information pursuant to a mandatory reporting statute or a court order are legal *requirements*.) To assess the *ethical* acceptability of releasing the records of a deceased patient when you have *legal* permission to do so from the executor of the patient's estate, ask the following four questions: (1) Will this release serve a specific and legitimate purpose? (2) Is this release the only reasonable, or clearly best, way to achieve that purpose? (3) Is this release consistent with what the patient would have wanted, insofar as those wants can be ascertained? (4) Is there a clear and substantial reason why the patient did not provide an explicit consent for this release while alive? Unless your answer to each of these four questions is "yes," our recommendation is not to release the records. The party making the request can issue a subpoena, and a judge will then determine what materials will be released (see chapter 7, Subpoenas and Court Orders). When in doubt, consult a colleague; doing so will help demonstrate that you were attempting to act in an ethically responsible manner.

Consider the following three examples. First, a patient commits suicide and her family, perhaps a bit guilty because of an estrangement, asks if they could speak to you about your patient's treatment and even look at some of your notes. The family member who makes the request is the executor of the estate and that individual, also a lawyer, cites the law that gives him the authority to consent to a release of records. In this case you would explain that you are under an ethical obligation to protect your patient's confidentiality, and so are not free to release her records or to discuss details of her treatment. While you are free to meet with the family and to discuss their feelings of sadness, loss, and even anger over the death (doing so may be enormously helpful to them), there is no "specific and legitimate" reason to release any information. The family may pursue legal means to obtain the records, in which case a judge will make a determination and indicate what you should do.

Second, an elderly patient who had been suffering from a dementia sold a valuable painting of great sentimental value shortly before her death, for a fraction of its actual worth. The executor of her estate approaches you and asks for records that might show the patient was incompetent at the time of the sale, a showing that would allow the executor to reclaim the painting for the estate and return it to the family. You, yourself, had serious questions about the patient's competence, and feel that she would want her family, with whom she was very close, to have this painting. In this case you would confirm the family member's appointment as executor of the estate; ask the executor to provide you with a written consent to release records; review the record and pick out material related to your patient's competence at the time of the sale; and release only those entries you have selected. The release in this case is ethically acceptable, because (1) it serves a specific and legitimate purpose; (2) the release is the only reasonable, or clearly best, way to achieve that purpose; (3) the release is consistent with the patient's wishes as best you can ascertain them; and (4) since the patient was incompetent, there is a clear and substantial reason why she did not provide explicit permission while alive for the release of this information.

In the third example, the executor returns for additional material after you release the records of your elderly patient, material that you do not feel is relevant to your patient's competence and that you feel could result in hurt feelings and perhaps affect the family's memory of your patient. Although you have legal permission, the release has no specific and legitimate purpose. You cite your ethical obligation to keep the material confidential and do not comply with the request.

Requests for records following the death of a patient highlight the distinction between what is legally permissible and what is ethically acceptable. The intensity of the reaction to Martin Orne's release of the therapy tapes may find at least a partial explanation in this distinction. Orne may well have stood on sound *legal* footing when he gave the therapy tapes to Diane Middlebrook. The ethical dimensions of what he did are more complicated. However legitimate a purpose the release was intended to achieve, Anne Sexton had hardly left explicit permission for Orne to provide the tapes to a biographer, and Orne certainly had the option of citing his ethical obligation of confidentiality had he chosen to do so. A judge would then have decided how the matter would be handled. Far from refusing the request, it was Orne who apprised Middlebrook of the tapes' existence and then offered them to her; subsequently he wrote an introduction to the biography and provided a photograph of himself to be included in the book. In defending his release of Anne Sexton's therapy tapes, Martin Orne remarked, "I was often more concerned about her privacy than she was." Ethics demand that mental health professionals remain concerned with their patients' privacy in perpetuity.

### 105. What is a mandated reporter?
A mandated reporter is any individual for whom a mandatory reporting statute creates a duty to report. Each mandatory reporting statute (see chapter 3) lists a series of individuals who are required to report to designated state agencies under certain circumstances. These individuals are mandated reporters. A mandated reporter's failure to make a required report may result in criminal and civil liability and/or professional disciplinary action. Bottom line: If you're required to report and do not, you can be charged with a crime, sued by someone who suffers an injury because of your failure to report, and brought before your discipline's licensing board.

### 106. Does the mandatory reporting statute for child abuse require a clinician to report child abuse that is not inflicted by a caretaker? What if the abuser is another child?
Section 11165.6 of the Penal Code defines child abuse as "a physical

injury, which is inflicted by other than accidental means on a child by another person." Any abuse perpetrated by *another person* falls within the definition and so must be reported. While the statute does not limit or specify who the other person must be before a duty to report arises, the definition of child abuse does not extend to a "mutual affray between minors." If children who are peers or classmates are fighting, it is probably not abuse and may not require a report. When the reporter has reasonable cause to suspect that a child is suffering abuse, she must contact a child protective agency immediately or as soon as practically possible. The initial report may be by telephone, but a written report must follow within 36 hours. The only exception arises when the suspected abuse is emotional or mental suffering, in which case the statute permits, rather than requires, a mental health professional to report.

If a mental health professional is unsure about whether to make a report, we recommend the following. Whenever, in your capacity as a mental health professional, you reasonably suspect child abuse, call the local child protective agency. Explain the situation and let the agency decide whether a report is necessary. If the agency decides a report is required, defer to their judgment. You will have made your report in good faith and so are protected from liability. If the agency feels that a report is unnecessary, document your call by recording the time, date, name of the individual with whom you spoke, and the facts you provided. You have then attempted to comply with the statute and may rely on the agency's judgment that no report is necessary. Remember that the individual with whom you speak will make a determination based on the facts you provide; if you are incomplete in explaining the situation—even though you may be attempting to protect your client—you will defeat the purpose of your call and so cannot rely on the advice given.

Recall (from chapter 3) that neglect is also a reportable condition under the mandatory reporting statute for children. Thus, if an older child is physically injuring a younger child, the adult caretaker may not be providing adequate supervision. In this case, you may be mandated to report because the caretaker has been neglectful.

**107. An extremely religious set of parents forbade me to break confidentiality when their 12-year-old child talked about having been sexually touched by a member of their church's clergy. The parents were adamant that this information was to go *nowhere*, or else I would never see the child again and I would face a lawsuit for breach**

**of confidentiality. What is the best way to handle this situation?**
Cases in which a disclosure of confidential information may end a therapy are especially difficult. Most poignant is that the victim—a child, and your patient—is made to suffer a second betrayal. Nevertheless, the law allows no room for discretion in this instance. The Child Abuse and Neglect Reporting Act, at section 11166 of the Penal Code, mandates that you report. You need not worry about a lawsuit because Penal Code section 11172 grants immunity to any mandated reporter who does not knowingly make a false report. In fact, if the child's parents do bring suit, the State Board of Control will reimburse you for the reasonable legal fees you incur.

The Law of No Surprises may also provide some help. If, in the first session, you review the exceptions to confidentiality with your patient and her parents, they have already been apprised of your obligation to disclose. Thus, your response might be, "We have already had this discussion—legally, my hands are tied. The law simply allows me no options other than to report." While this is certainly no guarantee that the parents will allow their child to continue in therapy, their prior understanding of your obligation to disclose may give them enough distance from the situation to consider what would be in their child's best interest.

**108. I am a psychologist. Do I have an obligation to report *whenever* I have reasonable cause to suspect that a parent is abusing a child— even if my suspicion arises from what I see at the mall?**
The mandatory reporting statutes are relevant only when you are acting *in your professional capacity*. If on a Sunday afternoon trip to the mall, the zoo, or a museum, you happen to witness what you reasonably believe to be child abuse, you are under no obligation to report. You may, of course, choose to do so; any individual acting in good faith may contact the appropriate state agency. No legal consequences will follow, however, if you do not.

To determine your obligation under the statute, ask yourself, "In what capacity have I received this information?" Put another way, the question is one of relevance—is your capacity as a mental health professional relevant to why or how you received the information? Say, for example, a reasonably reliable neighbor calls one evening and says, "I'm calling because you're the neighborhood psychologist and I want to know what to do; Sally Jones is being abused by her father." Even though Sally Jones is not your patient, you have received this information in your capacity as a psychologist and you now have an obligation to report. Or, as another example, you work at a mental health clinic and you overhear a parent threatening to scald her child with boiling water when they return home. Your professional capacity is relevant to how you received this information and so you have an obligation to report. If you were to learn of either circumstance on a walk with your family, your professional capacity would not be relevant to how or why you received the information and so you would not be a mandated reporter.

### 109. If I make a report under the mandatory reporting statute for children, can the child's parent—or the alleged perpetrator—find out that I was the one who reported?

The State wants to encourage mental health professionals to take appropriate steps to protect abused and neglected children. For this reason, section 11167 of the Penal Code requires that the identities of all persons who report under mandatory reporting statutes remain confidential. While certain exceptions do arise—the identity of the reporter may be disclosed between child protective agencies, to an attorney representing a child protective agency, to the district attorney in a criminal prosecution, or to an attorney representing the child in dependency court (see question 169)—none of the exceptions to confidentiality allow the alleged perpetrator or the patient's parents to discover who reported the incident.

### 110. What should I do if a patient tells me that another treater has harmed her?

Mental health professionals frequently ask this question, usually about a female patient who has been sexually involved with a male therapist. To answer the question, you must determine whether any mandatory reporting statute applies (see chapter 3). If, for example, your patient is under 18, you may be a mandated reporter because of your obligation to report child sexual abuse. If you are not mandated to report because of any reporting statute, you must have your client's consent before disclosing anything she tells you. You do, nevertheless, have an obligation. In this instance, Business and Professions Code section 728 requires you to provide a brochure prepared by the California Department of Consumer Affairs. This brochure explains the rights and remedies of a patient who has been sexually involved with a therapist. According to section 728, failure to provide and to discuss the brochure with your patient constitutes unprofessional conduct. (See also question 130.)

## 111. Do confidentiality and testimonial privilege work differently for group therapy than for individual therapy?

Groups complicate confidentiality in several respects. First, by definition, conducting a group means that many clients are hearing information that, if said by a single client to a therapist, would be confidential. Second, there is no statute, regulation, or code of ethics that explicitly binds "clients" to confidentiality. Third, there is no statute or regulation that extends a common testimonial privilege to the members of a group.

There are at least two possibilities when considering what legal obligation group clients may have to maintain confidentiality. First, obtaining informed consent from each participant at the beginning of the therapy may create a contractual obligation between group members to keep material confidential. If one member of a group subsequently violates confidentiality, that member could be seen as breaching another member's contractual right to confidentiality. Second, California's constitutional right to privacy could be construed as providing a way to sanction a group member who has disclosed confidential information learned in the group. In other words, if group member A, by sharing information about group member B, unduly violates B's right to privacy, B may then have a lawsuit against A.

When struggling with the issue of confidentiality, group therapists need to consider carefully whether they want to bring the long arm of the law into their work. Many group therapists prefer to discuss at the beginning of the therapy the topic of breaking the group's confidentiality, in the same manner as they discuss other possible boundary violations (e.g., arriving at group under the influence of alcohol, missing numerous sessions, speaking to group members in an abusive manner). Generally, such therapists make clear the rules of the group at the outset and explain how violations of the rules will be handled. While bringing the law into the group may have an intimidation factor, it will certainly have an effect on the group process, and the group leader should consider this effect before threatening legal sanctions.

California law does not explicitly address whether testimonial privilege applies to groups. As a consequence, it is not clear what would happen in California should a member of a group therapy receive a subpoena to testify concerning what was said during a group session. Despite the law's silence, it can be argued that information shared in group therapy is privileged. Evidence Code section 1012 states that confidential information may be communicated to others when they are present to further the interest of the patient; these communications are protected by testimonial privilege. The language of section 1012 suggests that by identifying *all* the group members as necessary to further the interest of the patient, there is a legal basis for claiming that privilege extends to all the group members. This way of thinking about group therapy and testimonial privilege makes enormous sense. The whole point of group therapy is that the *group itself* brings about therapeutic change. Because each member of the group is necessary to bring this change about, each member should fall under section 1012. As a consequence, any member should be able to invoke privilege to prevent any other member—and the group leader—from disclosing in a legal proceeding what went on in the group.

As much sense as all this makes, be aware that *California courts have not yet settled this issue.*

### 112. Must a clinician treat a psychological evaluation ordered by a court differently from an evaluation requested by a private client?

In this instance, always be clear whether your client is *the court* or *the individual with whom you are speaking.* The difference is extremely important. Section 1017 of the Evidence Code states, "there is no privilege . . . if the psychotherapist is appointed by . . . a court to examine the patient." When you have been hired by a court for the purposes of assessment or diagnosis, the court is your client. Testimonial privilege does not apply; the purpose of your work is to garner information for the legal proceeding and you will disclose what you learn. It is your ethical obligation to inform the patient, before you discuss any clinical information, that what he says will be shared with the court. If the individual begins speaking before you have had a chance to explain that what he says will be shared in court, stop him and explain the limits of confidentiality before proceeding. Section 1017 creates one exception to this rule: When a defense lawyer asks a court to appoint a psychotherapist to help determine whether an insanity defense is appropriate, the interview remains confidential and need not be disclosed. Bottom line: Psychotherapists appointed by a court order to conduct an assessment must inform the patient of the limits to confidentiality at the very outset of the interview.

If your client is the individual with whom you are speaking—that is, you are not working for the court—you are bound by confidentiality and cannot testify unless your client waives privilege. The regular rules of confidentiality and testimonial privilege apply.

**113. If a patient commits a crime against a mental health professional, for example, by breaking into a therapist's office or even by assaulting a therapist, would confidentiality prohibit the therapist from bringing the matter to the police?**

No. The commission of a crime is outside the confidential relationship. A treater may report the patient's name and facts about what occurred to the police (for example, this individual broke into my office and opened confidential files). A treater may not reveal anything about the nature, course, or content of the therapy, all of which remain confidential. The facts of the crime, and the circumstances surrounding the crime, however, are not confidential, and you do not need the client's permission to share them with the authorities.

# 11

# RECORDS AND RECORD-KEEPING

*Keeping records is an integral part of every mental health professional's work. Records provide an archive for what happened during an assessment or therapy, and are thus indispensable should care be transferred from one clinician to another. A record review is often an excellent way to help a therapy that has become "stuck" move forward. And a worthwhile consultation depends upon a reliable record. The law comes into play in a limited number of areas, for example, in a lawsuit or action before a professional board, when an accurate record of what happened is essential, or when a patient wishes to see her records and the treater does not believe such a review will be in the patient's best interests. Below are questions that address situations in which the law touches upon this area of clinical practice.*

## QUESTIONS DISCUSSED IN THIS CHAPTER

118. Under what circumstances, if any, may I deny a patient access to his records?
119. How do the requirements of the Patient's Access to Health Records Act in the Health and Safety Code fit with the confidentiality requirements of the LPS Act in the Welfare and Institutions Code?
120. What if a patient believes part of the record is inaccurate and asks to have it changed?
121. How long should I retain my records?
122. Should I retain some documentation of a treatment, even after the appropriate period of time for retaining records has passed?
123. What should I do with my records after I retire?
124. Can I withhold records from a patient who has not paid his bill?
125. What rules govern computerized records?

# DISCUSSION

### 114. Who owns a therapist's records?

The best way to answer this question is to think of the patient as owning the *contents* of the record and the therapist as owning the *physical document*. To explain, while the therapist owns the physical document, the laws of confidentiality, privilege, and mandatory reporting determine how that ownership is exercised. Thus, unless directed otherwise by statute or court order, the therapist can only do with the record what the patient authorizes.

### 115. What happens if a patient asks to see his records?

The Health and Safety Code sets forth the rules that govern the release of patient records. With few—although important—exceptions (see questions 116, 117, and 118), patients have a complete right of access. Like patients, authorized patient representatives—parents, guardians, conservators, and beneficiaries or personal representatives of deceased patients— also have a right of access to treatment records. Note that the right is to *access*; the physical records themselves belong to the provider.

Section 123110 of the Health and Safety Code states that any request to gain access to patient records must be in writing and must specify the records to be viewed or copied. Once a health care provider receives a request to inspect records, the records must be made available during regular business hours within five working days after the request is received. If the patient wants copies of all or part of the record, the health care provider must ensure that copies are transmitted within 15 days after receiving the written request. A health care provider can require copying costs of up to 25 cents per page (50 cents per page for records copied from microfilm). A provider may also include any reasonable clerical costs for locating the records and making them available.

For both clinical and risk management reasons, you should insist that you and your client review the record together. From a clinical perspective, the patient may encounter material that is unclear or troubling, and your presence will be important to address questions or concerns. From a risk management perspective, clients sometimes walk away with the record tucked under their arm. You are then deprived of your most important defense should the client make a claim against you. *A client should never be left alone with the original record.*

### 116. When a patient asks for a copy of his records, can I provide a summary of the record rather than the complete file?

Section 123130 of the Health and Safety Code allows a mental health professional to provide a summary of the record, rather than the complete file. The summary of the record must be made available to the patient within 10 working days from the date of the request. If more than 10 days is needed to prepare the summary, perhaps because the record is unusually long or because the patient was recently discharged, the patient should be informed. In any case, the summary must be delivered no later than 30 days from the patient's request.

A mental health professional is not obligated to include information in the summary that is not contained in the original record. Furthermore, a mental health professional may confer with the patient to clarify the patient's purpose and goal in obtaining the record. If the patient requests information about only certain injuries, illnesses, or episodes, it is not necessary to include information regarding other injuries, illnesses, or episodes. The summary must, however, contain certain details concerning each specified injury, illness, or episode (see H. & S. Code §123130 in appendix A). You may charge the client a reasonable fee for your actual costs and time spent preparing the summary.

### 117. Please clarify—if I am allowed to provide a summary of the record, rather than a copy of the entire record, does that mean the

**patient no longer has a right to see the entire record?**
Correct. While the Health and Safety Code is somewhat confusing on
this point, the language of section 123130 states clearly that a mental
health professional may prepare a summary rather than provide access to
the record: "If the health care provider chooses to prepare a summary of
the record *rather than* [italics added] allowing access to the entire record."
Note, however, that while a summary of the record satisfies a treater's
obligation to provide medical information to a patient under section
123130, a patient still has the right to seek access to his medical record
by going to court and asking that a judge issue an order (see question 69).

**118. Under what circumstances, if any, may I deny a patient access to
his records?**
Section 123115 of the Health and Safety Code creates the sole exception
to an adult patient's right of access to mental health records. According
to section 123115, when a mental health professional determines that
"there is a substantial risk of significant, adverse or detrimental consequences to a patient in seeing or receiving a copy of [his] mental health
records," he may refuse to allow the patient to inspect his records. In
addition, the mental health professional is not required to provide a summary or copy of the record.

A decision not to release records, however, cannot be made without
considerable thought. The legislature has made clear that every person
should have a right of access to complete medical information. To breathe
life into this right, the legislature has made several provisions. First, a
mental health professional who knowingly withholds records in violation of the statute is guilty of unprofessional conduct, and can be suspended from practice or have her license revoked. Second, a patient may
file a lawsuit to enforce his right to have access to his medical records.
The side that loses the lawsuit may be required to pay the other side's
costs, including attorneys fees. Finally, a mental health professional must
follow several steps after she has determined that allowing a patient access to his records would create a substantial risk of harm:

1. The mental health professional must make a written record that
   notes the date of the request, the reason for her refusing to allow the
   patient access to his records, and a description of the adverse
   consequences to the patient of seeing the record.
2. The mental health professional must permit another clinician,

designated by the patient, access to the records (the statute was recently amended to prohibit the other clinician from allowing the patient to see the records).

3. The mental health professional must inform the patient of her refusal to permit access to the records, and inform the patient of his right to require the mental health professional to permit another clinician to inspect the records.

4. The mental health professional must indicate in the patient's records whether the patient actually requested to have another clinician inspect the records.

When your patient is a minor, she is entitled access only to those records that concern health care for which she is authorized to consent (see question 158). When a minor has the right to see treatment records, her parents or guardian do not. Also, parents or guardians are not entitled to see a minor's record when a mental health professional determines that such access would be detrimental either to the therapist's relationship with the minor-patient, or to the minor's physical safety or psychological well-being. Unlike the decision whether to allow an adult patient access to his records, a decision not to allow a minor's parent, guardian, or representative access to the minor's records will not expose you to liability, unless your decision is made in bad faith.

*According to section 123110, "A health care provider shall not be liable to the patient or any other person for any consequences that result from disclosure of patient records as required by this chapter."*

### 119. How do the requirements of the Patient's Access to Health Records Act in the Health and Safety Code fit with the confidentiality requirements of the LPS Act in the Welfare and Institutions Code?

LPS (at section 5228 of the Welfare and Institutions Code) makes it more difficult for patients to obtain access to their records than does section 123110 of the Health and Safety Code, in two ways. First, LPS requires that when a patient designates an individual to receive records, the clinician must also consent before records may be released, and second, under LPS a therapist is not required to disclose information obtained in confidence from the patient's family. Health and Safety Code section 123110, on the other hand, gives patients almost complete right of access to records "[n]otwithstanding Section 5228 of the Welfare and Institutions Code." A mental health professional should therefore follow the Health and Safety Code when a patient requests records.

## 120. What if a patient believes part of the record is inaccurate and asks to have it changed?

A mental health record is considered a legal document. As such, you may not alter it. Altering consists of making any change to what has been written; as examples, whiting out, blacking out, and crossing out all constitute altering the record.

It sometimes happens that you or your client discover inaccuracies or mistakes in the record. While you cannot alter the record, you also do not want to perpetuate inaccurate clinical information. If you become aware of a mistake in the record, you may make an additional entry. In the entry, note the date of the mistaken information, explain that previously recorded information is inaccurate, provide the accurate information, and then date the entry according to when it is written. You may make a notation next to the entry with the mistaken information, such as "See note of September 18, 1998, for correction." Initial and date this notation. In this manner you are adding correct information to, rather than altering, the record.

It may happen that a patient brings to your attention mistaken information that has been released to a third party. (The best preventative medicine is to review the material with your patient *before* disclosure.) If material is released, perhaps in the form of a letter, and your patient wants a part of the letter corrected, you may send a second letter explaining that incorrect information was contained in the initial missive, and that the purpose of the second letter is to provide a correction.

## 121. How long should I retain my records?

Section 123145 of the Health and Safety Code provides that licensed clinics, hospitals, and other health care facilities that intend to cease operation (go out of business) must preserve records for a minimum of seven years from when a patient was discharged. If the patient is a minor, the health services provider must keep the records at least one year after the patient reaches the age of 18, but in any case not less than seven years.

California law is silent about how long other clinicians must keep their records. It is best to retain records as long as possible, for a variety of reasons: Patients sometimes wish to begin a second treatment long after finishing a first therapy, in which case records from the prior treatment can be enormously helpful; patients may need to document a claim for certain benefits such as SSI or MediCal, in which case records showing the history of a disability could prove invaluable; a treater may wish to review the child records of an adult patient, for many reasons; and patients may bring a claim against the treater, in which case records will be important to defend against an allegation of negligence or wrongdoing. That said, maintaining records can become expensive, and takes up a lot of space.

Our recommendation is to keep records as long as is reasonably possible. Keeping records for a period of 10 years following termination of treatment, and 10 years after a minor-patient has turned 21, should place you beyond the reach of any statute of limitations. If it is reasonable for you to keep the records longer, do so; if not, the records may be destroyed (see also the following question).

### 122. Should I retain some documentation of a treatment, even after the appropriate period of time for retaining records has passed?

Clinicians are not able to keep entire records forever; most of our basements are cluttered enough as it is. Hence the need to destroy records from treatments long since terminated. Nevertheless, because patients may find the records of past treatments useful, we recommend keeping a brief summary (one to three pages) of a treatment after you dispose of the record.

### 123. What should I do with my records after I retire?

Records are important after a treater retires for at least two reasons. First, patients may continue to need mental health services, in which case the treater's records may assist the transition to another clinician. Also, a treater's retirement does not bar a patient from bringing a complaint or an action in malpractice. Notes may be crucial to the treater's defense.

After a treater retires, records should be retained in a safe, accessible location, so that patients who wish to continue with another treater may obtain copies. If the treater is moving to another location, she should arrange to forward a copy of the records to patients, when clinically indicated; name another treater or responsible party to maintain the records in the event they are requested; or provide the name of another treater or responsible party who will know how to reach the treater should a patient need a copy of the records.

### 124. Can I withhold records from a patient who has not paid his bill?

No. Health and Safety Code section 123110 makes clear that a mental health professional may not withhold a patient's record or a summary of the patient's record because the patient has not paid his bill. To do so would be unprofessional conduct and could lead to the mental health professional being suspended from practice, having her license revoked, or fined.

### 125. What rules govern computerized records?
California law recognizes that large health service providers, such as clinics and health facilities, benefit by maintaining computerized records. California law also recognizes that the hazards of total reliance on an electronic medium require special safeguards. Health and Safety Code section 123149 therefore imposes additional requirements on large providers of health services who utilize *only* electronic record-keeping systems. These requirements do not apply when hard copy versions of patient records are retained.

According to section 123149, a large health care provider who relies solely on electronic record keeping systems must ensure the safety and integrity of electronic records at least to the same extent that hard-copy records are protected. Thus, the law requires an offsite backup storage system, an image mechanism that is able to copy signatures, and a mechanism to ensure that once a file is recorded the file cannot be altered. Original hard copies of patient records may be destroyed once the record has been electronically stored. If the originals are destroyed, the printout of the computerized version is considered the original.

Access to electronically stored patient records must be made available to the Division of Licensing and Certification staff upon request. Any health care provider who chooses to utilize an electronic record-keeping system must develop and implement policies and procedures that include safeguards for confidentiality. These safeguards must prevent against unauthorized access to electronically stored patient health records (e.g., authentication by electronic signature keys and systems maintenance).

# 12

## PROFESSIONAL LIABILITY

*Questions about professional liability are like fingerprints—no two are exactly alike. Change the facts, however slightly, and the answer will change as well. No wonder lawyers love the phrase "It depends."*

*The responses below are best understood as providing ways to think about problems mental health professionals often face. They are <u>not</u> intended as definitive answers or legal advice. When faced with your own dilemma, we have three recommendations: First, think carefully through your problem and consider alternative ways of responding as they present themselves; second, get a consultation; third, document your thinking and the consultation. Pay every bit as much attention to the process by which you come to your decision, and your documentation of that process, as you do to the decision itself.*

### QUESTIONS DISCUSSED IN THIS CHAPTER

of violence is considered "serious" under the *Tarasoff* statute? If not, how can I determine when I have a legal duty to act?

128. The *Tarasoff* statute creates a duty to disclose confidential information. I worry that if I make a mistake and disclose information when not appropriate, a patient could then sue me. Does the statute protect a therapist against a claim that she wrongfully disclosed confidential information?

129. Recently my car was broken into and my briefcase stolen. In the briefcase were two patient files that I had taken home to review and that identified the patients by name. Is it necessary to tell my patients what happened?

130. A colleague, also a psychotherapist, confessed to me that he had slept with a patient. He seemed quite fully to appreciate the possible consequences of becoming sexually involved with a client, but I was dumbstruck when he said he'd "do his best" to make sure it didn't happen again. While I consider this person a friend, I also want to know whether I have any legal or ethical obligation to report his behavior.

131. Should I continue to see a patient who is suing me?

132. What material should I be sure to cover during a first session?

133. Some clinicians give their clients an "informed consent" letter at a first session. Is this a good idea?

134. I serve as a med-backup for several non-MD therapists. To what extent could I be held liable for what goes on in these therapies?

135. Can you offer any guidelines as to when it is okay to accept a gift from a client, and when it is not?

136. From a professional liability standpoint, what are the implications of therapist self-disclosure?

137. I have a policy not to conduct a session with a patient who is under the influence of drugs or alcohol. Recently a client arrived at my office visibly intoxicated. When I said that we would not be having a session, he got back in his car and drove away. What should I do in this situation to minimize my exposure to liability?

138. Can I bill for a session that I have refused to hold because the patient arrived at my office under the influence of drugs or alcohol?

139. What is my liability if a patient commits suicide?

140. I'm semiretired and volunteer as a supervisor at a local mental health clinic. Given that I only do a few hours of supervision each week, need I worry about getting malpractice insurance?

141. Will my malpractice insurance pay for a lawyer to represent me before a licensing board?

142. If I receive a letter of complaint from my licensing board, may I go ahead and respond?
143. What should I do if I receive a request for records from an insurance company?
144. If I'm sued, should I hire a personal attorney, in addition to the attorney the insurance company will provide?
145. What legal and ethical steps can I take to terminate with a harassing or threatening patient?
146. I know that I am obligated to notify my insurance company if anything ever happens that might give rise to a malpractice lawsuit. Under what circumstances should I notify the company, and what is the best way to do the actual notification?
147. I've just received a managed care contract. Should I have a lawyer read it over?
148. Can a treater be held liable for not providing services that a managed care company has denied?
149. What obligations does a researcher have when, during a research interview, a subject reveals information that would require a treater to act, for example, that the subject intends to hurt herself or someone else, or that a child is being abused or neglected?
150. What are the concrete steps I can ethically and legally take to collect an unpaid fee?
151. Do you advise meeting with the family after a patient commits suicide?
152. I am a psychiatrist who works for several nursing homes. Often I prescribe a low dose of an antipsychotic medication to settle a patient. Is this an acceptable practice?
153. What should I do if a patient who is HIV positive reveals to me that he is sexually active with unsuspecting partners?

## DISCUSSION

**126. Under the *Tarasoff* statute, I have a duty to act when a patient "communicates" a serious threat of physical violence. Does such a communication have to be with words, or might I have a duty when the patient *does* something that suggests a threat of physical violence?**
In the *Tarasoff* case, the California Supreme Court was clear: When a

mental health professional must choose between public safety and client confidentiality, public safety trumps. This balance represents a public policy that holds regardless of whether your client puts a threat of violence into words. The *Tarasoff* statute—Civil Code section 43.92—uses the term "communicate." Patients communicate to us in many ways; a case could even be made that *most* patient communications are nonverbal. If your patient has communicated a serious threat of physical violence to an identifiable person—whether or not the communication takes place with spoken words—you should conclude that a duty has arisen under section 43.92. You then have an obligation under the statute to warn the potential victim and the police.

## 127. Is there any statute or case that defines when a patient's threat of violence is considered "serious" under the *Tarasoff* statute? If not, how can I determine when I have a legal duty to act?

When the California legislature first considered writing a *Tarasoff* law, it passed a statute virtually identical to Civil Code section 43.92. The sole difference—a single word—was that the proposed statute required an "actual" rather than a "serious" threat to create a duty. This bill was vetoed by the Governor because he thought the language of an "actual" threat was too narrow, and would miss too many circumstances that he felt should require a mental health professional to act. The original bill was reintroduced, with the only change that an "actual" threat was now a "serious" threat. The Governor was satisfied and signed the bill, which made the bill a law. From this history we can conclude that a "serious" threat is intended to include a greater number of situations than does an "actual" threat. Beyond this analysis, however, there is no statute or case law that defines "serious" under the *Tarasoff* statute.

In the absence of further guidance, we must consider the meaning of the word "serious" in the context of the *Tarasoff* decision itself. The Court acknowledged the value of safeguarding the confidential nature of psychotherapy. The Court then stated:

> We realize that the open and confidential character of psychotherapeutic dialogue encourages patients to express threats of violence, few of which are ever executed. Certainly a therapist should not be encouraged routinely to reveal such threats; such disclosures could seriously disrupt the patient's relationship with his therapist and with the per-

sons threatened. To the contrary, the therapist's obligations to his patient require that he not disclose a confidence unless such disclosure is
necessary to avert danger to others . . . (441)

The last phrase of this quotation is telling: A threat is serious when "disclosure is necessary to avert danger to others."

How does a therapist know which threats are "serious" under this definition? By asking what a reasonable therapist would do under similar
circumstances. Put another way, a mental health professional should ask
whether a reasonable therapist would find it necessary to disclose the
threat in order to avert the danger. A therapist need not be a fortune teller,
nor need she display extraordinary clinical skills. Rather, a therapist is
required to act as a reasonable therapist would act in a like situation. If a
therapist acts in this manner, she will not be held liable either for breaking confidentiality or for what her patient may do. Consultations are an
invaluable tool in this process—by definition, consultations "tap into"
the collective wisdom of the discipline, and thereby help to show that the
therapist was acting reasonably. Always be sure to document a consultation and your decision-making process.

**128. The *Tarasoff* statute creates a duty to disclose confidential
information. I worry that if I make a mistake and disclose information
when not appropriate, a patient could then sue me. Does the statute
protect a therapist against a claim that she wrongfully disclosed
confidential information?**
Unfortunately (and unlike *Tarasoff* statutes in other states), California's
*Tarasoff* statute does not have a "good faith" protection from liability. A
therapist is required to act according to the standards of her profession.
The question (again) is: What would a reasonable therapist do under these
circumstances? Note that the question to ask is *not* which will get you
into more trouble: failing to warn or inappropriately disclosing confidential information. Rather, therapists should ask whether a reasonable therapist would conclude that a duty has arisen under the statute. If so, then
you will be protected from liability should you disclose confidential information in the process of warning the victim and the police.

Psychotherapists should also note that section 5328(r) of the Welfare
and Institutions Code gives permission to break confidentiality when disclosure is "needed" to protect a victim. That California law both creates a
duty (Civil Code section 43.92) and gives permission (Welfare and Institutions Code section 5328(r)) to disclose confidential information for the

purpose of protecting a victim sends a powerful signal: California is intent upon protecting public safety. If a psychotherapist acts reasonably in disclosing information for the purpose of protecting a victim, she need not worry about legal liability.

**129. Recently my car was broken into and my briefcase stolen. In the briefcase were two patient files that I had taken home to review and that identified the patients by name. Is it necessary to tell my patients what happened?**

Yes. First and foremost, the therapeutic relationship is a fiduciary relationship—it is a relationship built upon trust. Few things will destroy that trust faster than hiding from a client a mistake you have made—however unwittingly or unintentionally—that could have an impact on the client's life. Clinicians in this position will sometimes use the transference implications of what has occurred as a reason for not being up front with the client; rarely, however, are the *counter*transference implications of hiding such an event given as a reason to *tell* the client about lost records. Consider that you will have a secret from your client—that something has happened, possibly to his detriment—and that you will be hiding the secret for the duration of the therapy. Moreover, whatever fears you have about telling your client will pale in comparison to what will happen if your client finds out *without* your having discussed the matter. If you lose a patient record or it is stolen, tell the client in a direct and forthright manner as soon as is reasonably practical after you have been able to confirm the loss or theft. In our experience, clients have demonstrated an enormous amount of understanding (and empathy for the clinician!) in such circumstances. Obviously, a better scenario is to keep records in a safe place that minimizes the chance they will be lost or stolen. And it always pays to think twice about whether you *really* need to take those records home before placing them in the front seat of your car.

**130. A colleague, also a psychotherapist, confessed to me that he had slept with a patient. He seemed quite fully to appreciate the possible consequences of becoming sexually involved with a client, but I was dumbstruck when he said he'd "do his best" to make sure it didn't happen again. While I consider this person a friend, I also want to know whether I have any legal or ethical obligation to report his behavior.**

In California, sex between a psychotherapist and a patient is a crime. Business and Professions Code section 729 states that sexual contact between a therapist and her patient (or former patient, if the relationship was terminated primarily for the purpose of engaging in sexual acts) is sexual exploitation—a public offense punishable by six months in jail and/or a $1000 fine. Sexual relations with a patient also constitutes unprofessional conduct and grounds for disciplinary action.

What is a mental health professional's responsibility when a colleague confesses a criminal act of unprofessional conduct that has the potential to harm a patient? In answering this question we first note that such a communication is not confidential. We are not dealing with patient confidentiality because the information came directly from the offending therapist. As a consequence, you must be guided by your professional ethics.

Specific ethical codes can be helpful. As an example, the American Psychological Association's *Ethical Principles* (1992) has two standards that speak to the resolution of a colleague's possible ethical violation: standard 8.04 and standard 8.05. Standard 8.04 states that a psychologist makes an effort to resolve informally a possible ethical violation "when appropriate," provided the resolution does not "violate any confidentiality rights that may be involved." Standard 8.05 provides that a psychologist takes additional steps when informal resolution under standard 8.04 is not possible or is unsuccessful. Additional steps may entail filing a complaint with the California or American Psychological Association ethics committees, or with the California Board of Psychology. The ethics committees of many professions have hotlines that provide guidance without asking for any identifying information; mental health professionals should feel free to call for a consultation.

If a patient, rather than your therapist-colleague, had brought the sexual relation to your attention, the information would be confidential. In that case, section 728 of the Business and Professions Code requires that you provide your patient with a brochure prepared by the Department of Consumer Affairs that sets out the rights and remedies for patients who have been sexually exploited by a previous therapist. In addition, you are required to discuss with your patient the options set out in the brochure. These options include filing a complaint with the licensing board, filing a criminal complaint, or filing a lawsuit. Without your patient's consent, however, you may not disclose the confidential information provided by your patient. (See also question 110.)

### 131. Should I continue to see a patient who is suing me?
When a patient initiates an action against you—whether by submitting

an ethics complaint or filing a lawsuit—the nature of your relationship with that patient has fundamentally changed. The frame of the therapy has shifted from words into action. While the change in your relationship will have clinical implications, the potential effects of the change extend far beyond the treatment. Your reputation, your income, and even your professional practice may be jeopardized. Your personal life cannot remain unaffected. Even the most extraordinary mental health professional would be severely challenged to control the countertransference under such circumstances, and we recommend that you not try.

First, the complaint or lawsuit will have to be discussed in the therapy; to do otherwise would constitute a major resistance for both you and your patient. Talking about a pending lawsuit or complaint will inevitably evoke an intense reaction because your patient is attacking you—not with words, but with *actions*. No treater should place herself under such a burden. Second, adding to this burden, any interpretation, recommendation, or suggestion you make to your patient immediately becomes suspect as flowing out of a countertransference reaction. You therefore have a higher standard to meet in explaining the reasons behind your work. Third, your legal bills are likely to accrue much faster than any fee your client is paying. You will thus be losing money while treating the client who is suing you. Doesn't sound like much fun to us.

You have no ethical obligation to continue treating a patient who has brought an action against you. You should arrange for an appropriate termination and ask for a consultation as the termination takes place. If you do decide to go ahead and treat a patient who has filed a complaint or lawsuit against you, it is essential that the treatment be supervised.

## 132. What material should I be sure to cover during a first session?
In the first session you should cover all the matters that speak to the "frame" of the therapy. The frame consists of those aspects of your work that create the context in which the therapy takes place. The frame therefore includes the length of sessions, your per-session fee, whether you charge for missed sessions, whether you treat client vacations as missed sessions, whether you provide legal testimony, how you handle consultations and supervisions, whether you are available on an emergency basis, whether you accept phone calls at home, how often you bill, how you handle missed payments, what rules govern confidentiality, and the like.

What's important is to convey to the client a clear sense of how you work. The Law of No Surprises is relevant: A client should never be in a position of ignorance about the frame of the therapy. What will create problems in a treatment is not so much that a client doesn't *like* your policies as that a client doesn't *know* your policies.

### 133. Some clinicians give their clients an "informed consent" letter at a first session. Is this a good idea?

An informed consent letter has a number of advantages. First, such a letter makes clear the frame of the therapy. Second, an informed consent letter provides the client with a *physical* reminder of that frame, available whenever the client wishes to look at it. Third, it can be used to fulfill the ethical and legal obligation of mental health professionals to apprise clients at the beginning of the relationship of the rules concerning confidential information. Fourth, an informed consent letter can provide an excellent reference when, into the therapy, you must disclose information for the purposes of a consultation or because a mandatory reporting statute requires you to do so: The possibility of disclosing information has already been addressed.

These advantages notwithstanding, many clinicians have very strong feelings that providing such a letter is *not* the way to begin a therapy, primarily because of what they see as the implications for the transference. Our recommendation is to think through the advantages and disadvantages of an informed consent letter for your own practice, and proceed accordingly. One alternative to a letter would be a form, which many clinics and hospitals use, given to a client before, during, or immediately following the first session. Another alternative is to convey the information orally. In considering what will work best for you, keep in mind three things. First, you will be conveying a significant amount of information, more than most people can probably absorb in one sitting, especially when they may be feeling some anxiety, as is likely at a first therapy session. Second, you are ethically and, for certain disciplines, legally obligated to convey information about exceptions to confidentiality at the beginning of the relationship. Third, problems that arise in the course of a therapy often arise because a client had not been fully informed about some aspect of the frame.

If you decide to provide your client with an informed consent letter, we suggest you make a time, no later than the second session, to discuss any questions she may have about what is in the letter. Document that you have done so. From a professional liability point of view, it makes good sense to record in your notes at least one question the client has asked. Doing so illustrates that your client read the letter, and that you took the time to clarify questions she may have had. Even if the patient does not have any questions, record that you set aside time to review the contents of the letter.

A sample informed consent letter is included in appendix B.

### 134. I serve as a med-backup for several non-MD therapists. To what extent could I be held liable for what goes on in these therapies?

First and foremost, keep in mind *the nature of your duty*. As a med-backup, your duty is to provide reasonable care in prescribing medication. You will therefore take a history, do a physical, assess your patient's mental status, monitor side effects, and so forth. You will do these things because they are called for by your profession's standard of care. Because you are not conducting a therapy, your duty does *not* extend to what care a reasonable therapist would provide. Nor does your duty extend to supervising the therapists for whom you act as med-backup. Thus, the nature of your relationship with the patient defines and limits your duty.

The situation becomes complicated when, for example, a patient tells you during a routine check for medication side effects that he is suicidal. Despite the complication, your duty remains defined by the nature of the relationship with your client. You will ask yourself what a reasonable med-backup would do in these circumstances. Your duty would be to assess the severity of the suicidal ideation, contact the patient's therapist, and make a plan with the therapist to ensure the client's safety.

### 135. Can you offer any guidelines as to when it is okay to accept a gift from a client, and when it is not?

Unfortunately, there are virtually no hard and fast rules that govern the exchange of gifts between a mental health professional and a client. Most often, the issue of gift-giving arises in an ethics complaint; once the issue is raised, the burden shifts to the treater to show what therapeutic role the gift played. If the treater can show none, the exchange will almost certainly be seen as contrary to good treatment and therefore unethical. Accepting (or giving) gifts of high monetary value (a piece of jewelry, a car) or of an intimate nature (a negligee, a card with clear sexual content) is always looked upon as unethical.

The most important principle to keep in mind is that for the vast majority of mental health professionals, words are the tools of the trade. Because the exchange of a gift is a communication, the mental health professional must ask herself what is being communicated and why the communication is not taking place in the currency of the profession, that is, with *words*. If you are faced with the dilemma of accepting, or giving, a gift, ask yourself the following three questions: First, does the gift comport with social convention? That is to say, is the gift of small or reasonable value, is the gift appropriate to a professional relationship, and does the exchange take place on an occasion that, in your patient's culture, calls for an exchange of gifts? Second, can the intrapsychic meaning of the gift be talked about in a manner appropriate to your patient's treatment? That is to say, can the communication be put into words and used to enhance or further your work, or at the very least to maintain the therapeutic alliance? Third, do you document the exchange? That is to say, do you record the fact of the exchange itself, as well as your clinical assessment of what the exchange means to the patient, and what effect it will have on the treatment? If an exchange of gifts takes place, and your response to any of these questions is "no," get a consult. You're headed for troubled waters.

Finally, what you do with the gift is important. Placing cards and letters in the file shows that you are treating them as part of the therapy. Do not place birthday cake in the file. If the gift is a perishable item, there still may be a card that can be made part of the record. If the item is expensive or of an intimate nature, the only prudent path is not to accept the gift. The burden of explaining why you accepted the gift, should you be called by an ethics board to do so, will be virtually insurmountable.

### 136. From a professional liability standpoint, what are the implications of therapist self-disclosure?

This question is somewhat complicated, insofar as *everything* a therapist does is, in some manner, self-disclosing. The cars we drive, the clothes we wear, what we choose to place on our desks, whether we wear wedding rings, how we greet our patients each day—all are enormously, and inevitably, disclosing of who we are. The question, then, can perhaps be reframed to ask what liability implications follow from a considered decision to disclose something about ourselves to a client.

Therapists from a wide range of backgrounds engage in self-disclosure for a variety of reasons. Substance abuse counselors often disclose their own histories of abuse on the theory that doing so will aid an individual's recovery; cognitive-behavioral therapists may self-disclose for the purposes of modeling effective behavior; feminist therapists have considered self-disclosure important for addressing a power difference in the therapy relationship; other therapists use self-disclosure as a manner to temper an idealizing transference or to address a patient's intense experience of shame by normalizing an experience. Psychoanalysts and psychoanalytically oriented psychotherapists have tended to engage in less self-disclosure, but recent years have shown a burgeoning literature on the role of self-disclosure in psychoanalytic work.

From a professional liability standpoint, self-disclosure can be thought about in the same manner as the exchange of a gift: It is important to clarify what role the disclosure plays in the therapy. While a carefully considered self-disclosure can have enormous clinical benefit, inappropriate disclosures about a therapist's personal life have been associated with involvements that are hugely harmful to patients, and indeed often seem to be the precursors of such involvements. If self-disclosure is an essential and ongoing aspect of your work, it would be wise to indicate as much in your treatment plans. If you self-disclose in a manner other than what you normally do, or if you choose to self-disclose when you normally would not, document the fact of the disclosure, and your assessment of how the disclosure fits into the therapy. As with gifts, if you're unwilling both to consider and document the fact of a self-disclosure and its role in the therapy, get a consultation—you're headed for trouble.

**137. I have a policy not to conduct a session with a patient who is under the influence of drugs or alcohol. Recently a client arrived at my office visibly intoxicated. When I said that we would not be having a session, he got back in his car and drove away. What should I do in this situation to minimize my exposure to liability?**

This question provides an excellent example of when *the process by which you come to a decision* and the *documentation* of that process are every bit as important as the decision itself. Our response will therefore focus on the decision-making process.

First, consider whether the *Tarasoff* statute (see chapter 2), is relevant. The statute will require you to act only if your patient has communicated a "serious threat of physical violence" toward a "reasonably identifiable victim." Although *Tarasoff* is probably not relevant to the situation you describe, pay attention to whether your patient has named any individual as the object of his anger as he walks away.

Next, consider the possibility of involuntary hospitalization. Welfare and Institutions Code section 5170 states that an individual may be involuntarily placed in a facility designated by the county for 72-hour treatment and evaluation if she is a danger to herself or others or is gravely disabled as a result of inebriation. Special facilities have been designated by the county for individuals who suffer from alcohol abuse. Unfortunately, many counties do not have these facilities; if no such facility is available, consider involuntary hospitalization under section 5150 of the Welfare and Institutions Code. Section 5150 provides that an individual may be involuntarily placed in a psychiatric hospital if she has a mental disorder and, as a result of the mental disorder, she is a danger to herself, to others, or is gravely disabled (see question 25). The complication with involuntary hospitalization under section 5150 is that mental illness—and not inebriation—provides the basis for the hospitalization. Do not, however, simply assume that the diagnosis of alcohol abuse precludes another diagnosis such as depression. A mental disorder would provide the basis for an involuntary hospitalization under section 5150.

At this point in your decision-making process, you have legal principles that are in conflict: first, the principle of respect for your patient's autonomy and privacy, which counsels confidentiality, and second, the principle of safety, which permits you to release confidential information if a patient presents a danger to self or others. We place these two conflicting principles in the context of the Law of No Surprises—to the extent that is practical and appropriate, you should discuss with your client at the beginning of the relationship the general parameters that might lead to disclosure of confidential information, and the Parsimony Principle—disclosure of information is kept to the absolute minimum needed to achieve your goal.

How is our balancing act put into practice? Begin by raising the dilemma directly with your patient, "We won't be meeting, but you're in no shape to drive. What other arrangements can we make?" Other arrangements may be for your client to sit in your waiting room with a cup of coffee, contact a friend or relative for a ride, take a bus or other public transportation, or call a cab. Each of these alternatives represents a way to work with your client that entails a minimum of intrusion. By considering and raising these possibilities, you are demonstrating to anyone who reads the record that you are approaching a difficult situation in a thoughtful, clinically appropriate manner.

If your client refuses your suggestions and insists on getting in his car, you then indicate that given the dangerousness of the situation, you may need to contact some authority. What allows you to take this next step is

that all your suggestions for a *less* intrusive intervention have
jected. If you now decide to contact the police, and indica
intoxicated individual is driving down Pacific Coast Highway
protected yourself from a claim that your disclosure was premature, ...
warranted, or more than necessary. Note that even this release of information is minimal—your "disclosure" is limited to a description of the
client's car and perhaps a license plate number. You have acted because
your client's substance abuse is creating a likelihood of serious harm and
no intervention short of disclosing this information to the police is sufficient to attenuate the danger.

*Keep in mind that every bit as important as what you eventually de-
cide to do is the process by which you make your decision and your
documentation of that process.*

### 138. Can I bill for a session that I have refused to hold because the patient arrived at my office under the influence of drugs or alcohol?

If you're asking this question when it comes time to write your bills, you're
asking too late. You may bill for the session, not bill for the session, or
reschedule the session, without concern for unwanted repercussions, *provided you made your policy clear at the beginning of your work.* Trouble
will arise not from what you decide to do, but rather from failing to have
a treatment agreement that tells your client what you will do under these
circumstances. If you intend to work with patients who struggle with substance abuse, it is wise to include your policy in an informed consent
letter (see appendix B).

### 139. What is my liability if a patient commits suicide?

No behavior can be predicted with absolute certainty. Suicide is a behavior. Suicide cannot be predicted with absolute certainty.

The task a mental health professional faces with a suicidal patient is not to
predict whether the patient will commit suicide; rather, the task is *to assess
the likelihood* that the patient will commit suicide. In assessing the likelihood that a patient will commit suicide, the clinician examines factors in the
individual's life associated with a *greater* risk of suicide, factors associated
with a *lesser* risk of suicide, and how the factors compare with one another.
Lest this analysis seem overwhelming, consider that you do the same sort of
thing each time you debate whether to carry your umbrella out the front
door. You identify factors associated with a greater risk of rain (rain is predicted; it's windy; it's raining to the west) and factors associated with a lesser

risk of rain (the sun is out; it's summer). You then balance the factors against one another and decide whether to take your umbrella.

The crucial part of a suicide assessment is identifying those factors that are relevant to the likelihood your patient will commit suicide. Examples of factors associated with a greater risk of suicide are a history of suicide attempts, the intent to commit suicide, a plan to commit suicide, readily accessible means to carry out the plan, feelings of hopelessness, a panic disorder, a delusion that suicide is a way to join a loved one who has died, social isolation, current or chronic substance abuse, a history of suicide in the family, and a belief that suicide is "fated." Examples of factors associated with a lesser risk of suicide are plans for the future, religious convictions that prohibit suicide, living with another person or persons, a sense that someone or something still endows life with meaning, and a belief that feelings of sadness, loss, or hopelessness are temporary and will pass.

In assessing the likelihood that an individual will commit suicide, you will therefore explore factors associated with greater and lesser risks of suicide, examine how the factors you have identified compare with one another, decide what to do based upon the comparison, and document the reasons behind your decision. *What protects you from liability is not that you have made the "right" decision, but that you have documented a process—the process by which you have assessed and responded to the likelihood that your patient would commit suicide. Your documentation should answer three basic questions: What did I do? Why did I do it? On what basis did I reject alternative ways of responding?*

### 140. I'm semiretired and volunteer as a supervisor at a local mental health clinic. Given that I only do a few hours of supervision each week, need I worry about getting malpractice insurance?

The need for malpractice insurance depends neither upon the number of hours you work, nor upon how much you are paid. Once you establish a professional relationship with a supervisee, you are held to a standard of care. If you fall below that standard, you can be held negligent, and thus responsible for any damages that result from your negligence.

By volunteering as you do, you are establishing a professional relationship with your supervisees. Don't be fooled—the word "professional" in this context does not refer to salary, nor to a full-time position. "Professional" refers to a relationship based upon your experience and expertise as a trained clinician. You therefore need malpractice insurance as much as any other supervisor.

### 141. Will my malpractice insurance pay for a lawyer to represent me before a licensing board?

Some malpractice carriers will insure you for up to a specified amount in legal expenses for representation before administrative agencies, such as licensing boards and professional societies. You should review your general malpractice policy to determine whether this coverage is included.

If a complaint is filed against you before a licensing board, be sure to find a lawyer who has experience before regulatory boards. The reason is that, in a great many cases, a complaint will be dismissed at the initial stage if your response is well-written.

### 142. If I receive a letter of complaint from my licensing board, may I go ahead and respond?

You need to exercise a good deal of caution when answering a letter from a licensing board. The board may ask you to produce certain materials, along with a letter responding to the allegations. Your response may require you to disclose confidential material. A complaint to a licensing board or professional association by a patient does not, in and of itself, grant the authority to discuss the patient's case or to release the patient's records. The patient must first sign a release. *If you disclose confidential information to the board without a release, you risk another complaint against you—for breach of confidentiality.*

A sample reply letter to a licensing board is contained in appendix B. It is best to send the letter by certified mail, return receipt requested, thus obtaining written confirmation that the board has received your letter. If you subsequently do receive a release from the patient, it makes good sense to contact your malpractice carrier, whose claims representative should help you draft a letter in response to the allegations. The reason contacting the carrier is a good idea is that your response to the board is subject to discovery, which means that the other side in a lawsuit can obtain your response if the case goes to trial. For this reason, what you say in the letter can be extremely important, both in the matter before the board, as well as in a future lawsuit.

### 143. What should I do if I receive a request for records from an insurance company?

Whenever a treater receives a request for records from an insurance company, the treater should discuss the request with the patient. *Do not simply rely on the fact that the insurance policy contains a clause allowing for a release of records—the request must be discussed with the patient before you do anything.* It is well within a patient's prerogative to forego insurance benefits by refusing the request.

In terms of what records to release, an insurance company is entitled to as much of the record as is necessary to determine whether the treatment is consistent with the diagnosis. This information would include, for example, diagnosis, prognosis, dates of treatment, and length of treatment sessions. An insurance company is not entitled to process notes, which should be released only when your patient gives specific permission to do so. Certain third party payors may require additional information (MediCal, for example, requires a justification of medical necessity).

### 144. If I'm sued, should I hire a personal attorney, in addition to the attorney the insurance company will provide?

A personal attorney is an attorney of your own choosing, whom you will pay out of your own pocket. There are three ways in which a personal attorney could be helpful if you are sued. First, litigation is enormously stressful. A lawsuit has the potential to invade all areas of your life, personal as well as professional, and involves people, places, and events that will feel foreign and hostile. A personal lawyer can be helpful in shepherding you through the process, explaining how things will work, and calming your anxieties. The attorney assigned by the insurance company may fill this role, but not necessarily.

The second way in which a personal attorney can be helpful is to be mindful of how your interests may diverge from the interests of the insurance company. The attorney assigned by the insurance company will pursue the company's interests; most often, but not always, these will coincide with yours. Examples of times when the insurance company's interests may differ include when the insurance company would prefer to settle and you want the case to go forward, or when the insurance company is representing more than one defendant in a single lawsuit. In the latter case, the company will want to minimize its *total* losses, which will not necessarily entail minimizing *your* losses. A personal lawyer can be helpful in watching for these and other situations where the interests of the insurance company differ from your own.

The third way in which a personal attorney can be helpful is that, unbeknownst to many clinicians, a malpractice policy may include a "consent to settle" clause. Such a clause requires the carrier to obtain your written consent before settling the case. Your own attorney can review your policy for such a clause, discuss the pros and cons of settlement if the issue arises, and deal with the carrier should there be any difference of opinion.

For these three reasons, it may well be worth the expense to hire a personal attorney as a consultant during a malpractice suit. You will want an attorney who is experienced in malpractice litigation, particularly on the defendant's side. Keep in mind that the attorney from the insurance company, not your personal attorney, is managing the case, and work to avoid any conflicts between them. That said, your own personal attorney, with whom you can "check in" as you feel the need, and who will have only your interests at heart, can be an important asset during the often long and always tumultuous experience of a lawsuit.

### 145. What legal and ethical steps can I take to terminate with a harassing or threatening patient?

When facing the need to terminate with a difficult patient, a treater should keep two points in mind. First, a therapist is not required to treat every patient. Choice about whom to treat belongs to the treater. Second, termination is *not* the same as abandonment. The second point bears elaboration.

Abandonment can be described as an inappropriate termination. Examples of abandonment occur when a treater terminates a treatment without notice, without regard for the patient's condition at the time of termination, without an adequate plan for follow-up treatment, or in order to retaliate against a patient. *A treater may not abandon a patient.*

Termination is a process that the circumstances of a treatment may demand. Termination may be appropriate because a particular therapy is no longer in a patient's best interest. Perhaps, for example, the patient is treatment resistant, has continuously missed sessions, or often comes to appointments under the influence of drugs or alcohol. Termination may also be appropriate because the patient has intruded upon the therapist's private life, has violated a professional boundary, such as by breaking into the therapist's office, or has threatened the therapist. *While a treater may not abandon a patient, a treater may terminate with a patient.*

When termination with a difficult patient is appropriate, what becomes important is the *process* by which the termination takes place. We find it helpful to break this process down into five parts, which may occur sequentially or simultaneously, depending upon the circumstances. First, discuss the difficulty with the patient and explain that, if change does not occur, termination will result. Be clear about what changes must occur, in a way that can be measured and documented. Second, if termination is or becomes the only alternative, explain to the patient why you are terminating and offer termination sessions (between one and three), unless precluded by the patient's behavior. Third, obtain a consultation to maintain your objectivity and to review whether you are proceeding appropriately. Fourth, to the extent possible, provide the patient with the names and telephone numbers of other treaters in the area. If your patient refuses the referrals, inquire why and then document both the refusal and your patient's reasons. (If your patient is in crisis, the responsibility will be yours to ensure that another treater is immediately available and to consider whether a hospitalization is appropriate. If other treaters are not immediately available, you will need to delay the termination until the crisis has abated.) Fifth, document your reasons for termination and your plan for referral. Send a letter to your patient with this information, either by registered or certified mail or by first class, depending upon what you believe is clinically indicated.

Not all terminations go smoothly. Some patients will resist, and then claim abandonment and threaten to sue or file a complaint with your licensing board. The more difficult you expect the termination to be, the more attention you should give to outside consultations and proper documentation.

A sample letter of termination is included in appendix B.

**146. I know that I am obligated to notify my insurance company if anything ever happens that might give rise to a malpractice lawsuit. Under what circumstances should I notify the company, and what is the best way to do the actual notification?**
Insurance companies require notice from treaters whenever a threat of a lawsuit arises, for several reasons. First, the insurance company will want to review the problem, decide whether something must be done, and assign the matter to an attorney for further action if called for. Second, if the insurance company decides the matter does warrant action, the company's attorney will be in touch with the treater to make sure that the treater does not make any statements that could negatively affect the lawsuit. Third, certain legal papers require a response within a defined period of time. The insurance company will want to make sure that responses are timely.

In regard to the actual notification, a treater should contact the insurance company whenever there is a reasonable basis to believe that a lawsuit is a possibility. The following circumstances would therefore warrant notification: The treater receives a summons and complaint for a lawsuit; a treater receives a letter from a lawyer representing a present or former patient that states the patient intends to bring a lawsuit; a treater receives a letter from a present or former patient or a lawyer representing a present or former patient that requests a copy of the treatment record, and something has happened in the treatment that might give rise to a complaint or lawsuit; some event occurs during the course of a treatment that a reasonable person would assume could lead to a complaint or lawsuit. Examples of such an occurrence would be a suicide, a homicide committed by a patient, or a patient complaint that the treater breached confidentiality.

There is no "right" way to notify the insurance company. The best way to begin is to call the carrier, ask to speak with a claims representative, and explain the situation. If the claims representative says that the matter is not something the company would address at present, make a note of the date, the time, and the name of the representative. If the claims representative says that the company will want to deal with the situation, send the company any documents you have received, along with a cover letter that makes note of the date and time you initially made contact with the company.

In providing information to the insurance company, you may describe the incident. *You may not send treatment records to the insurance company without a release from your patient.* Do not, however, fear that a patient may prevent you from disclosing records necessary to your defense; if the case goes to trial, you will be allowed to use whatever records necessary to defend yourself.

### 147. I've just received a managed care contract. Should I have a lawyer read it over?

When most therapists receive a managed care contract they sign it, return it to the managed care company (MCC), and file their copy away for future reference. The next time they look at the contract is to read it— usually for the first time—when a problem arises. At that point they discover that the "one-year contract" may be canceled with 60 days notice for no reason at all. This is just one of several reasons why you should never sign a managed care contract without carefully reading it through with an experienced attorney. The following are four additional examples of why it is good to be familiar with a managed care contract before you sign.

Most contracts contain some sort of *indemnification clause*. An indemnification clause requires a therapist to reimburse the MCC for losses or expenses that arise from a claim or lawsuit, if the loss or claim results from the therapist's participation in the contract. The therapist's malpractice insurance will probably not cover the cost of the reimbursement. The reason is that most malpractice insurance covers only actions in negligence, not actions based in contract, which is what an action arising from an indemnification clause will be. The wording of an indemnification clause is important, and most MCCs will work with a treater to alter the wording. The advice of an attorney as you work with the MCC is worthwhile.

Most contracts stipulate *duties that the therapist owes to the MCC and that are for the benefit of the patient*. MCCs will usually require that a therapist be available to see patients at specific times for emergencies. MCCs may also require the therapist to be available 24 hours a day, both by beeper and by "live" telephone coverage. Almost always the therapist will be required to cover for other therapists. All such contractual agreements with the MCC are for the "benefit" of the patient. If you fail to fulfill one of these requirements, and a patient comes to harm as a result of your failure, a lawsuit may ensue. It is therefore essential that you become familiar with the clinical responsibilities required by the contract.

Most contracts require a therapist *both to maintain patient confidentiality and to provide the MCC with access to and copies of all treatment records*. These two requirements often conflict, and it is important to have some resolution before beginning work under the contract. The reason a resolution is important is that your agreement with the MCC is not binding on the patient. Confidentiality belongs to your patient, who must consent before you release records to the MCC. Make this clear with the MCC before beginning to treat patients.

A therapist has *a duty to appeal a decision to deny services when the therapist believes the services are medically necessary*. When an MCC denies a service because, in the opinion of the MCC, the service is not medically necessary, a therapist has a duty to appeal the MCC's denial. Such an appeal may create an uncomfortable situation for the therapist, insofar as she will be appealing a decision of the company that is paying her. The therapist's failure to appeal, however, could lead to a claim of abandonment, especially if the therapist believes that a denied service is medically necessary. Regardless of the MCC's decision not to fund, the therapist must be careful not to stop treatment if she believes stopping would be harmful to the patient. If the therapist does decide to stop treatment, she may do so only when the patient is stabilized, and only after she has referred the patient to other treaters.

These four examples—many more could be provided—illustrate the value of having an attorney read over a managed care contract with you before you sign.

### 148. Can a treater be held liable for not providing services that a managed care company has denied?

A managed care company's (MCC) decision to deny services will not in any way protect a therapist from a claim of negligent treatment or abandonment. A therapist must provide care that is "reasonable." Care that falls below what is reasonable, regardless of an MCC's decision to deny services, may be considered negligent and may give rise to an action in malpractice.

A treater's obligation to provide reasonable care and an MCC's decisions about what treatment to fund are entirely separate. Linking the two is asking for trouble. If a treater believes that an MCC will not fund care that is reasonable, and the treater wishes to stop treatment, the termination must be handled in the same manner as any other termination (see question 145).

### 149. What obligations does a researcher have when, during a research interview, a subject reveals information that would require a treater to act, for example, that the subject intends to hurt herself or someone else, or that a child is being abused or neglected?

Once again, this question has no straightforward answer. Perhaps the best advice we could give in this situation is to follow the Law of No Surprises: When conducting research that is likely to uncover information that would create a duty to act were you a treater and your subject a patient, state explicitly how this situation will be handled in your informed consent form. Use your clinical judgment about what material your survey, interview, or questionnaire is likely to pull for. Once you've made that judgment, be up front about what you will do if such a situation arises. You may have concerns about whether your subject will be as forthcoming for your research; being up front at the outset, however, will save you much angst and spare your subject the feeling that you have betrayed a confidence that you promised you'd keep.

Consider each of the examples in the question. First, a researcher should make an effort to ensure the safety of a patient who communicates a serious threat to harm himself. This effort could take a number of forms. If, for example, the research is being conducted at a hospital, the researcher should notify the unit staff. If the research is being conducted on an outpatient basis, the researcher should notify the individual's outpatient clinician, immediately if the circumstances warrant. If the research is being conducted on an outpatient basis and the subject does not have an outpatient clinician, then a researcher should consider contacting a police officer or mental health professional with the authority to hospitalize the research subject.

Second, under *Tarasoff*, a duty arises when a "patient" communicates a serious threat of physical violence against a reasonably identifiable victim. If, however, someone gets hurt, the distinction between a "subject" and a "patient" may not hold sway over a jury, especially if the researcher is a licensed mental health professional. The prudent course would be to warn, or take some other protective measure, if a patient makes a communication that would meet the *Tarasoff* requirements. The subject may bring a complaint for breach of confidentiality, but such a complaint would be given little merit.

Third, the mandatory reporting statute for child abuse makes no mention of the relationship between the individuals involved. If the researcher is listed as a mandatory reporter, and she is acting in her professional capacity—which she will be, when conducting research—she is mandated to report whenever she "reasonably suspects."

### 150. What are the concrete steps I can ethically and legally take to collect an unpaid fee?

You have no ethical duty to treat a patient who does not pay you, and you may terminate in an appropriate manner as you initiate proceedings to collect your fee. Moreover, California law provides for disclosure sufficient to allow such proceedings to move forward. Specifically, Evidence Code section 1020 states that communications relevant to a breach of duty arising out of the psychotherapist-patient relationship by either party are not privileged. In disclosing confidential information, follow the Parsimony

Principle: Disclose only that information necessary to collect your fee.

In spite of what section 1020 allows a mental health professional to do, attempting to pursue legal means to collect a fee will likely cause you more trouble than it's worth. Your legal bills for collecting the fee will almost certainly surpass—perhaps substantially so—the fee itself, and your attempts to collect the fee may generate a countersuit or an ethics complaint, the only basis for which may be the patient's rage at what you're doing.

Our recommendation is that you bring the matter up with your client. Assess the client's ability to pay; virtually all clients will be able to pay *something*. Then determine what sort of free-care component your practice can allow. If you are able to accommodate your client's financial situation, work out a payment schedule and offer the client a reduced fee. If you are not able to accommodate your client's financial situation, arrange for an appropriate transfer of care to a low-fee clinic. Give serious thought to forgiving a debt that your client says she cannot, or refuses, to pay. In no case may you refuse to comply with a client's request for records in order to get the client to pay an unpaid bill (see question 124).

The best way to avoid this problem is to make clear to your client your policy about late or missed payments. *Payment for your services is as much a part of therapy as therapy itself; late or missed payments, if not addressed in a clear, direct manner, will inevitably be disruptive to your work.* (See the sample informed consent letter in appendix B.)

### 151. Do you advise meeting with the family after a patient commits suicide?

Meeting with a family after a patient commits suicide is like sailing between the Scylla of family grief and the Charybdis of confidentiality. Many clinicians feel an instinct to avoid any contact whatsoever with the family; most often these clinicians use confidentiality as a reason for not doing so. For the reasons explained below, we recommend that you accommodate the family's wishes in this regard.

First, meeting with the treater may be part of the family's process of grieving. In many instances, the treater is the individual who knows most about what was going on in the patient's life and merely sitting with that individual can provide comfort to many families. Second, a meeting affords the opportunity for the treater personally to express her grief to the family and to tell the family how sorry she is about their loss. Hearing the treater speak these words in their presence can be an enormous service to many families. Third, while confidentiality must be maintained, confidentiality places no constraint on the treater listening to what the family has to say about their own feelings of loss, anger, and confusion. Although a treater may not reveal what was said during sessions, she may paint with broad brushstrokes issues salient in the patient's life: "We know he had been struggling with depression for many years," "Feelings of anxiety made it difficult for him to enjoy things he had enjoyed in the past." Fourth, more from a risk management point of view, suspicions or paranoia about whether a treater is responsible for a patient's death will only be enhanced by a refusal to meet.

Our recommendation would be to inquire whether the family would like to meet with you. Your inquiry should be inviting: "Many families have found that meeting with the treater helps." You need to be clear that, while you will not be free to discuss details about your work, you are very interested in hearing what the family is experiencing. You should also feel free to tell the family that you are very sorry for their loss; such a statement is an expression of sympathy. (Take care, however, not to say that you are very sorry because your screw-up *caused* their loss; such a comment is called a "statement against interest," and may be used against you at trial.)

### 152. I am a psychiatrist who works for several nursing homes. Often I prescribe a low dose of an antipsychotic medication to settle a patient. Is this an acceptable practice?

Many psychiatrists follow this practice. When doing so, however, it is essential that you obtain informed consent from your patient. After being appropriately informed about a treatment, alternatives to the treatment, and the consequences of no treatment at all, voluntary patients have the right to refuse antipsychotic medication. Involuntary patients may also refuse antipsychotic medication—simply being an *involuntary* patient does not render a patient incompetent to make treatment decisions.

Exceptions to the right to refuse antipsychotic medication arise when the situation is a recognized statutory emergency or when the patient has been legally found incompetent to make treatment decisions. If the patient has an LPS conservator, the LPS conservator can give consent for the medication. If there is no conservator and the patient is unable to give informed consent, then you must follow the procedures for obtaining consent outlined in the Probate Code (beginning at section 3200; see question 87). What's important is that you be sure to obtain informed consent from competent patients, and to follow appropriate procedures when your patients are not competent to give consent.

### 153. What should I do if a patient who is HIV positive reveals to me that he is sexually active with unsuspecting partners?

This question (once again) raises the issue of balancing the confidentiality of patient information against the safety and protection of other individuals. California law generally protects the confidentiality of information related to HIV status and testing. Health and Safety Code section 120980 provides for civil and criminal penalties for wrongful disclosure of HIV testing results. Disclosure is permitted, however, in certain circumstances where lawmakers felt there was a compelling need to do so.

The exception carved out by Health and Safety Code section 121015 is directly applicable to this question. Section 121015 allows a physician, who has confirmed positive test results for a patient under her care, to disclose HIV status in the following circumstances: for the purpose of diagnosis, care, and treatment of persons notified, and for the purpose of interrupting the chain of transmission to the patient's spouse or to a person reasonably believed to be the patient's sexual partner. (A physician may also notify an individual who has shared a needle with an HIV positive patient. See chapter 3.) To this end, the physician may disclose HIV status to the patient's spouse, sexual partner, and county public health officer.

Notification of contacts must not include any identifying information about the individual believed to be infected. In other words, while a physician may inform the notified individual that she may have been exposed to the AIDS virus through sexual contact with an infected individual, the physician may not identify the infected person. Before disclosing any information, the physician must discuss the test results with the patient, offer educational and psychological counseling, attempt to obtain the patient's voluntary consent for notification, and tell the patient that she intends to notify the patient's contacts. Note that section 121015 is permissive rather than mandatory. A physician does not have a duty to inform; while she may do so, and is excused from liability if she follows the statute's guidelines, she will not get into trouble for failing to disclose a patient's positive HIV status.

Section 121015 is limited to physicians. It is reasonable to assume, however, that if physicians may disclose this information, then other health care providers—who may have equal or even better access to information about a patient's intentions—may do so as well. Keep in mind that it is always best to work with your patient, and you should disclose information against his will only as an absolute last resort, to be used when all else fails. Also, think through carefully whether (1) it is necessary to disclose this information to protect a third party, and (2) disclosing the information has a reasonable chance of achieving your desired goal. If you are faced with the possibility of disclosing HIV status, get a consultation from a senior colleague, an attorney who is experienced in mental health law, or both; rarely will the importance of obtaining a consultation be greater. Be sure to document your consultation.

Consider as well any other duty you may have to an unsuspecting sexual partner. If, for example, your patient has communicated that she wishes to infect a specific person, you might have a duty to warn pursuant to the *Tarasoff* statute (see chapter 2), especially in a case where the partner has reason to believe your patient is HIV negative (such as a spouse who remains unaware of her husband's IV drug use or homosexual activity). Consider also whether you might have a duty to hospitalize your client, pursuant to LPS (see question 25). A duty to hospitalize might arise if you determine that, as a result of a mental disorder, your patient's capacity to refrain from sexual activity has been significantly impaired. Ultimately your decision will depend upon the individual facts of the case.

# 13

# CHILDREN AND FAMILIES

*Perhaps no area of mental health law generates more intense feelings than that of children and families. Clinicians will not find this surprising: The bonds that tie children to their parents, parents to their children, and partners and siblings to one another are the strongest that humans experience. When the state intrudes into the life of a family—for however good a reason—that intensity can be felt by all involved. The questions below address circumstances in which family life is touched by the law.*

## QUESTIONS DISCUSSED IN THIS CHAPTER

161. I am currently treating a 15-year-old who is struggling with his sexual orientation. His parents—who are paying for the treatment—are becoming more insistent that I tell them what he is talking about in our meetings. Am I legally obligated to disclose this information?

162. What may happen to a treater if a minor says she is 18, but after several sessions the treater discovers she is not?

163. How does a court decide on custody when the parents can't agree?

164. In deciding on custody, to what extent will a judge consider a child's wishes?

165. Is sexual orientation a factor in custody determinations?

166. Is domestic violence a factor in custody determinations?

167. What happens if a noncustodial parent wishes to have a child treated?

168. Can a parent who has *not* been awarded legal custody of a child obtain the child's school or medical records?

169. When does a child become a dependent of the court?

170. What is the difference between a *dependent* of the court and a *ward* of the court?

171. What is the standard of proof required to terminate parental rights?

172. Under what circumstances can a minor be placed on trial as an adult, and so be given an adult sentence?

173. What can California criminal courts do to make testifying against an alleged perpetrator of sexual abuse easier for a child?

174. In cases involving sexual abuse, might a therapist ever be called to testify in court about what a child has said?

175. Does California recognize common law marriages?


# DISCUSSION


### 154. Up to what age can a parent admit a child to a psychiatric hospital?

Generally, a parent can hospitalize a child up to the age of majority, which is 18 years of age. The legislature and the courts, however, have recognized a significant liberty interest for children 14 years of age or over. Put another way, lawmakers and judges have felt that, even at the age of 14, a child should be accorded some privileges and protections normally accorded only to adults, in circumstances where her personal freedom is at stake. The child's liberty interest is evident in the admission procedures of both private and public mental health inpatient facilities.

Section 6002.10 of the Welfare and Institutions Code requires that *private* inpatient psychiatric facilities have specific admission procedures for minors 14 years of age or over who are neither legally emancipated (see question 157) nor dependents or wards of the court (see questions 169 and 170). The minor's admitting diagnosis must be either a mental disorder or a mental disorder together with a substance abuse disorder. (The statute recognizes that while resistance to treatment is sometimes a product of mental illness, resistance to treatment is not a mental illness in and of itself, nor by itself does resistance to treatment imply the presence of a mental illness that would justify hospitalization.) If a minor 14 years or older disagrees with the decision to hospitalize, she may request an independent clinical review within 10 days of her admission. The child may be assisted by a patients' rights advocate (see question 17). The independent clinical review must be conducted by a neutral psychiatrist who determines whether further inpatient treatment is likely to benefit the minor, and whether placement in the facility represents the least restrictive, most appropriate setting.

With respect to *public* mental health facilities, the California Supreme Court held in *In re Roger S.,* 19 Cal. 3d 921 (1977), that a parent may not waive the right of a minor 14 years of age or older to "procedural due process in determining whether the minor is mentally ill or disordered, and whether, if the minor is not gravely disabled or dangerous to himself or others as a result of mental illness or disorder, the admission sought is likely to benefit him." The bottom line (in plain English): While a parent can place a child in a public psychiatric hospital if he is likely to benefit from the admission, a minor 14 years or older is entitled to certain safeguards in order to protect against possible arbitrary placement. These safeguards include a right to a *pre*admission hearing by a neutral decision-maker, an opportunity to appear in person and present evidence at the hearing, and the opportunity to cross-examine adverse witnesses (e.g., people who disagree with the minor's wish to stay out of the hospital). The minor is also entitled to an attorney, in order to assure that she can effectively present her case. A minor may waive these protections and agree to placement in the hospital without a hearing. Such a waiver must be voluntary, "intelligent" (the result of a rational decision), and based upon consultation with an attorney.

Note that these safeguards apply when the minor is 14 years of age or older. Parents can unilaterally place children below the age of 14 in a public or private psychiatric hospital, if the treaters agree that the child is likely to benefit from the hospitalization.

### 155. What should I do if I recommend that a child be hospitalized and the parents refuse to follow my recommendation?

First, you should review the reasons behind your recommendation, ideally with a consultant. If, following the review, you continue to believe that failure to hospitalize places the child at risk of serious harm, you should attempt to persuade the parents to accept your recommendation. If the parents, in turn, continue to refuse the hospitalization, you should determine whether you have an obligation to report the situation to a child protective agency. If the child is likely to suffer serious harm from lack of hospitalization, the child protective agency has the authority to step in and assess the situation. (See also the following question.)

### 156. Can a child be placed in a psychiatric hospital without a parent's consent, or treated with antipsychotic medication against the child's wishes?

A treater generally requires parental consent before she may hospitalize a child. A treater may, however, proceed without the parents' consent if the child meets the statutory requirements for involuntary hospitalization or treatment. Welfare and Institutions Code section 5585.50 states that when any minor, as a result of a mental disorder, is a danger to herself, a danger to others, or is gravely disabled, *and authorization for voluntary treatment is unavailable,* a designated professional may take the minor into custody. Grave disability for a minor is defined as the inability "to use the elements of life which are essential to health, safety, and development, including food, clothing, and shelter, even though provided to the minor by others" (Welf. & Inst. Code §5585.25). The designated professional will then place the minor in a facility designated by the county and approved by the State Department of Mental Health as a facility for 72-hour treatment and evaluation of minors. If the child continues to meet involuntary hospitalization criteria after 72 hours, she can be held for additional periods of involuntary treatment under LPS (see chapter 5, Involuntary Hospitalization and Treatment).

Whether a mature minor (see questions 157 and 158) can be given antipsychotic medication against her will is an open legal question—the matter is not yet settled. Before an adult may be given antipsychotic medications against her will, a court must first determine that the adult lacks the capacity to make treatment decisions (see question 38). Most counties do *not* require this sort of capacity hearing before a minor (even though unwilling) may be administered antipsychotic medication. The reasoning is that because a child lacks the capacity to make treatment decisions regarding inpatient psychiatric hospitalization, a child lacks the capacity to make treatment decisions regarding antipsychotic medication as well. A few counties do require a capacity hearing before a mature minor may be medicated against her will. Requiring a capacity hearing is based upon the reasoning found in *Riese v. St. Mary's Hospital*, 209 Cal. App. 1303 (1987) (see question 38), and a general recognition that mature minors have privacy interests similar to those of adults (see question 159, regarding minor consent to abortion).

### 157. What makes a minor "emancipated"?

By definition, minors—individuals under the age of 18—are subject to another's care. Courts can release a minor from the care of a parent or guardian through a process called "emancipation." The idea is that certain minors are mature enough to take on adult responsibilities and therefore should be accorded adult rights. According to Family Code sections 7120 and 7122, a court may emancipate a minor when it finds that emancipation would not be contrary to the minor's best interest, and that all four of the following conditions are met:

1. The minor is at least 14 years of age.
2. She willingly lives separate and apart from her parents or legal guardian, with their consent or acquiescence.
3. She is managing her own financial affairs.
4. Her income is not derived from criminal activity.

Minors who have entered into a valid marriage or who are on active duty with any of the armed forces of the United States are also considered emancipated. In each of these cases, the legislature has decided that a minor's life circumstances indicate that he or she is sufficiently mature to assume responsibilities—and therefore rights—normally accorded to adults.

### 158. Can a minor consent to treatment?

Minors are generally not able to consent to treatment. A parent or guardian, the individual charged with the minor's care and upbringing, makes treatment and a host of other decisions for the minor. That said, important exceptions to this general rule arise in three broad categories of circumstances: first, when the minor is emancipated and is thus considered capable of making her own treatment decisions; second, when requiring parental consent would discourage the minor from getting care or treatment, and the treatment is necessary to prevent serious physical or psychological harm; and third, when a court determines that a minor is sufficiently mature to make a specific treatment decision.

Section 7050 of the Family Code states that minors who have been emancipated may consent to treatment without parental consent or knowledge. This exception to the general rule that the consent of a parent or guardian is necessary makes perfect sense—emancipated minors are no longer under the care of a parent or guardian. Similarly, Family Code section 6922 allows minors age 15 years or older, who have not been emancipated, to consent to medical care if they are living separate and apart from their parents or guardian and are managing their own financial affairs—regardless of the source of their income. In addition, section 6924 of the Family Code provides that a minor 12 years of age or over whom a treater believes is mature enough to participate intelligently in outpatient treatment may consent to treatment if she would present a danger of serious physical or mental harm without treatment, or if she is a victim of incest or child abuse. The exceptions found in sections 6922, 6924, and 7050 of the Family Code are based on an assessment that the minor is sufficiently mature to make a decision about what treatment is in her best interest.

A minor may also consent to treatment in situations where requiring parental consent might discourage the minor from receiving necessary care and treatment. Section 6929 of the Family Code, for example, states that a minor 12 years of age or older can consent to "medical care and counseling related to the diagnosis and treatment of a drug or alcohol related problem" (this exception does not include replacement narcotic abuse treatment). Minors 12 years or older are also able to consent to treatment for communicable and sexually transmitted diseases (Fam. Code §6926) and for treatment of conditions caused by rape (Fam. Code §6927). Minors of any age are able to consent to treatment of conditions caused by sexual assault (Fam. Code §6928).

Finally, minors who are 16 years of age and older—and are thus nearing the age of majority—can petition (submit a written request to) the

# MINORS AND CONSENT TO TREATMENT

I. A minor is generally **not able to consent** to treatment.
   A. A minor is an individual **under 18 years** of age.
   B. A parent with legal custody, or a guardian, may consent to treatment for a minor.

II. Exceptions that permit a minor to consent to treatment:
   A. **Emancipated** minors (Fam. Code §7050)
      1. A court finds that emancipation is in **the minor's best interest** and **all four** of following conditions are met:
         a. The minor is at least 14 years of age *and*
         b. The minor willingly lives apart from parents or guardian, with their consent or acquiescence *and*
         c. The minor is managing her own financial affairs *and*
         d. The minor's income is not derived from criminal activity *or*
      2. The minor has entered into a valid marriage *or*
      3. The minor is on active duty in the armed forces of the United States.
   B. A minor **15 years of age** or older may consent to **medical treatment** if she is (Fam. Code §6922)
      1. Living apart from a parent or guardian *and*
      2. Managing her own affairs.
   C. A minor who is **12 years of age** or older may consent to **outpatient mental health treatment** if (Fam. Code §6924)
      1. The treater believes the minor is mature enough to consent to treatment *and*
      2. The minor would present a danger of severe physical or mental harm without treatment *or*
      3. The minor is a victim of incest or child abuse.
   D. A minor may consent in certain situations where requiring parental consent **might discourage** the minor from receiving **necessary care and treatment**.
      1. A minor **12 years of age** or older may consent to treatment of a **drug or alcohol** related problem (Fam. Code §6929).
      2. A minor **12 years of age** or older may consent to treatment for a **communicable and sexually transmitted disease** (Fam. Code §6926).
      3. A minor **12 years of age** or older may consent to treatment for conditions caused by **rape** (Fam. Code §6927).
      4. A minor **of any age** may consent to treatment for conditions caused by **sexual assault** (Fam. Code §6928).
   E. A minor who is **16 years of age** or older can **petition a court** for consent to treatment when no parent or guardian is available (Fam. Code §6911).

court for consent when no parent or guardian is available. This exception recognizes a reality of today's society: Certain individuals, by the time they reach 16, are living apart from their caretakers and are, for all intents and purposes, self-sufficient. Because the law wants these minors to receive necessary care and medical treatment, it allows them to go before a court and ask permission to consent to treatment.

The law balances opposing values in allowing minors to consent to treatment. While the law generally deems minors not competent to consent to treatment, certain minors are especially mature. When we believe that a minor is mature, for example, because she lives apart from her parents and governs her own finances, we allow that minor to make her own treatment decisions. Similarly, despite the presumption that minors are incompetent to make treatment decisions, they are unlikely to tell parents about drug use or sexually transmitted diseases, and so may not get treatment if their parents must know. Because the law wants to encourage minors to get treatment in these circumstances, it makes a second set of exceptions to the general rule. Finally, a third exception arises in recognition of the reality that many adolescents are raising themselves without parent support or even involvement; these individuals should be able to obtain necessary care and treatment for themselves, and may therefore ask a court for permission to do so.

### 159. Can a minor consent to an abortion?
Section 6925 of the Family Code allows a minor to consent to medical treatment related to the prevention or treatment of pregnancy.

Prior to a recent California Supreme Court decision, California law prohibited a minor from receiving an abortion without authorization from a parent, except in two circumstances: when a medical emergency required immediate medical action, or when the juvenile court had issued an order allowing the abortion. In *Academy of Pediatrics v. Lungren*, 16 Cal. 4th 307 (1997), however, the California Supreme Court struck down this law. The Court found that there was no sufficiently good reason to require that a parent or a court consent to the minor's having an abortion; the Court therefore concluded that requiring permission from a parent or a court was unconstitutional. Minors may now provide informed consent to an abortion without parental consent. Note that the physician must still determine whether the minor has the capacity to give informed consent (see question 86). If the minor lacks the capacity to give informed consent, she may ask a judge to authorize the abortion.

## 160. What rules of confidentiality govern the treatment of minors?

The rules of confidentiality that govern the treatment of minors are similar to the rules that govern the treatment of adults: Treaters are bound by confidentiality and testimonial privilege. Information about a minor's treatment may generally be shared with the minor's parent or guardian, who has legal responsibility for the child. LPS (see question 24) also gives parents the right to designate individuals to whom the minor patient's records may be disclosed. Health and Safety Code section 123110 provides that a minor is entitled to gain access only to records that pertain to health care to which she is lawfully authorized to consent. Thus, only when a minor can legally consent to treatment does the minor have the right to obtain for herself records from that treatment. Conversely, according to Health and Safety Code section 123115, the parent or guardian does not have access to patient records that arise from treatment when the minor herself is able to consent to that treatment (see question 158). Section 123115 also gives mental health professionals the authority to refuse to disclose the records of a minor patient to a parent or guardian, if the treater determines either that disclosure would have a detrimental effect on the therapeutic relationship, or that disclosure would have a detrimental effect on the minor's physical safety or psychological well-being. The statute protects the professional from liability for her good faith decision to provide or withhold the records of a minor.

Note that several minor consent statutes permit or require notification and/or inclusion in treatment of the parent or guardian (see question 161). While most of these statutes allow the treater discretion about whether to notify parents, one law, Family Code section 6929, is mandatory. Section 6929 states that when parents seek drug or alcohol treatment for their child, the treating physician *must* disclose medical information, even if the minor objects to the disclosure.

Finally, it should be noted that Evidence Code section 1027 creates an exception to psychotherapist-patient privilege (see chapter 3, Privacy, Confidentiality, and Testimonial Privilege). Section 1027 says there is no privilege when the patient is under the age of 16, the psychotherapist has reasonable cause to believe that the patient has been the victim of a crime, and the disclosure of the communication is in the child's best interest. The exception is consistent with other areas of the law that permit disclosure of information necessary to protect the health and well-being of a child.

**161. I am currently treating a 15-year-old who is struggling with his sexual orientation. His parents—who are paying for the treatment— are becoming more insistent that I tell them what he is talking about in our meetings. Am I legally obligated to disclose this information?**
California law has a strong policy of including a minor's parent or guardian in the treatment. Our recommendation is that mental health professionals attempt to consult with, obtain information from, and make part of the treatment the parents, guardians, or families of the minors and adolescents with whom they treat. That said, clinical reasons sometimes demand that a minor or adolescent be treated on an individual basis, with minimal involvement or contact with a parent or guardian. The scenario you describe may very well be an example of when less contact is clinically indicated.

One statute requires a treater to disclose medical information about a minor's treatment; when the minor is treated for substance abuse (see question 160). This statute aside, there is a large discretionary element in the other statutes that encourage parental involvement or that indicate mental health professionals should inform the parent or guardian of certain elements of the treatment. In deciding whether to include, notify, or inform a parent or guardian, a clinician is allowed to exercise her professional judgment. As an example, a treater might determine that discussing a child's struggle over his sexual identity could irreparably harm the child's relationship with his parent, could unduly disrupt the treatment relationship, or could be otherwise detrimental to the child's psychological well-being. The treater might decide that, for clinical reasons, she will not provide this information to the parent, even if the parent were to ask for it. As the age of a minor-patient increases, a treater should give greater deference to the minor's wish to keep what is discussed within the bounds of the therapy.

If a parent insists that you discuss the treatment, or that you provide your records for review, and you believe that such disclosures are clinically *contra*indicated, reply that you are not able to do so and explain why. A statement that the treatment's success depends on keeping certain information within the bounds of the therapy will suffice. Given the strong presumption in favor of involving a parent or guardian in the treatment, a mental health professional should always document her decision-making process when she decides not to disclose clinical material to a parent or guardian. The parent or guardian is then free to ask a court to order that your records be made available; at that point, you would have an opportunity to tell a judge your reasons for not sharing the information. The judge will decide what should happen.

### 162. What may happen to a treater if a minor says she is 18, but after several sessions the treater discovers she is not?

If you rely in good faith on a minor's word that she is 18 or over or that she meets one of the criteria allowing minors to consent to treatment (see question 158), and you act reasonably in attempting to confirm her age, it is unlikely you will find yourself in trouble. But be careful: You must make a *reasonable* effort to confirm an individual's age. If your patient says she is 18, but looks 15, you cannot simply rely on what she tells you. Make it your standard practice to ask for confirming documentation, such as a school record or driver's license, whenever you have questions about age. Be sure to document that you have done so.

### 163. How does a court decide on custody when the parents can't agree?

In California, the principal focus when making custody decisions is the "best interest" of the child. A court must decide both who will have *physical* custody of the child (i.e., with whom the child will reside) and who will have *legal* custody of the child (i.e., who will make decisions that concern the child's physical and mental health, education, and moral and religious development). (See also question 167.) Section 3011 of the Family Code provides a list of factors a court must consider when making its decision. Such factors include the health, safety, and welfare of the child; the nature of contact with both parents; any history of a parent perpetrating physical abuse; and any parent's habitual abuse of alcohol or other drugs. (Note that if, during a custody proceeding, the court is presented with evidence regarding a parent's physical or emotional abuse, or substance abuse, it must corroborate the evidence with information from reliable outside sources.) While section 3011 does provide the court with specific guidance in making custody determinations, it leaves broad discretion with the court to consider any relevant information. In the case of *In re Marriage of Burgess*, 32 Cal. App. 4th 1786 (1995), the Court of Appeal described the determination of custody as necessarily "Solomon like" in nature—but more than subjective judgment. A custody determination is not simply what the judge thinks is in the child's best interest. Rather, a custody determination represents a balance of factors that are relevant to the child's best interest.

One final note: While California law presumes that joint legal custody is the most appropriate custody arrangement following a divorce, the actual custody decision is always subject to the overarching concern of the child's best interest.

### 164. In deciding on custody, to what extent will a judge consider a child's wishes?

The rule of thumb follows common sense—as the child gets older, her preferences matter more. Section 3042 of the Family Code states that a judge shall consider and give due weight to the wishes of the child, if she is of sufficient age and reasoning capacity to form an intelligent custody preference. If the child is actually called as a witness to indicate her preference, the judge should take steps to make testifying easier. Such steps include protecting the child from undue harassment or embarrassment, restricting the unnecessary repetition of questions, and ensuring that the questions are in a form appropriate to the age of the witness. If the child's best interests preclude her from being called as a witness in the proceeding, the court may obtain information regarding the child's preferences through alternative means, such as meeting with the child in the judge's chambers or accepting written testimony.

### 165. Is sexual orientation a factor in custody determinations?

Trial courts are given wide latitude within which they may exercise their discretion in determining what custody arrangement is in a child's best interest. In *Nadler v. Superior Court of Sacramento County*, 255 Cal. App. 2nd 523 (1967), the Court of Appeal examined the issue of whether the sexual orientation of a parent should be dispositive on the question of custody. The lower court held that a mother's homosexuality, in and of itself, was sufficient to deny her custody. The Court of Appeal held that the trial court "failed in its duty to exercise the very discretion with which it is vested by holding as a matter of law that petitioner was an unfit mother on the basis that she is homosexual." That is, the Court of Appeal was telling the trial court to hear the case all over again, and this time to focus on the child's best interest; the court's instruction told the trial court to consider a parent's sexual orientation as one—and only one—of many factors in this determination. The Court of Appeal did not give the trial court any direction concerning *how* to evaluate a parent's homosexuality; it said simply that a parent's homosexuality was one among a host of factors to be considered.

### 166. Is domestic violence a factor in custody determinations?

Family Code section 3011 states that, in determining the best interest of the child, the court may consider any history of abuse by a parent, or by any person seeking custody, against any child, spouse, or partner. Before a court considers allegations of abuse, it may choose to require substantial independent corroboration of the abuse. Clearly, the legislature is concerned about false allegations of domestic violence in the context of custody determinations.

In Family Code section 3020, the California legislature stated, "the perpetration of child abuse or domestic violence in a household where a child resides is detrimental to the child." The legislature further declared that despite the public policy in favor of encouraging divorced parents to continue contact, and to share the rights and responsibilities of rearing their child, it is the health, safety, and welfare of the child and the safety of all family members that are paramount in determining custody. Thus, California takes domestic violence seriously. California courts may take a corroborated history of domestic violence into consideration in deciding which parent will receive custody of a child.

### 167. What happens if a noncustodial parent wishes to have a child treated?

If the situation is an emergency, no consent is necessary. You may go ahead and treat the child, regardless of who brought her to you.

If the situation is not an emergency, you must distinguish between legal custody and physical custody. Physical custody refers to living arrangements; physical custody indicates with which parent a child resides. Legal custody, on the other hand, refers to a parent's right and responsibility to make decisions that concern a child's physical and mental health, education, and moral and religious development. The distinction between types of custody is frequently irrelevant, since courts often award joint legal and physical custody. When, however, a court elects not to award joint legal and physical custody, the distinction between physical and legal custody becomes important.

Only a parent with legal custody may consent to a child's treatment. That said, there is no duty to inquire about custody when a parent brings a child to you, and no requirement that you obtain the consent of both parents before you begin to treat. If, however, you have reason to believe that the parent who has brought the child to you does not have legal custody, it is important that you clarify the situation. The reason it is important to clarify the situation is that, if you continue to treat the child despite a reasonable doubt about custody, you may be treating the child *without legal consent.* If you are a physician, treating a child without consent may constitute battery, because you are touching the child without permission. Treating a child without consent may also constitute malpractice. And if anything untoward happens in the treatment, you have no defense—you shouldn't have been treating the child in the first place. So, when in doubt, *clarify.*

### 168. Can a parent who has not been awarded legal custody of a child obtain the child's school or medical records?

Yes. Section 3025 of the Family Code states that "access to records and information pertaining to a minor child, including, but not limited to, medical, dental, and school records, shall not be denied to a parent because that parent is not the child's custodial parent." Thus, a parent may obtain school or medical records even though she does not have legal custody.

### 169. When does a child become a dependent of the court?

A child can become a dependent of the court for a number of reasons, each of which is relevant to the abuse or neglect of the child by her assigned caretakers. Being made a dependent of the court is tantamount to saying that the court will now take over responsibility for the child's care. In determining whether to make a child a dependent of the court, a court considers the safety and the physical and mental well-being of the child. Welfare and Institutions Code section 300 gives jurisdiction of dependency cases to the juvenile court. The juvenile court may name a child a dependent of the court when, in her current situation, she is being physically, sexually, or emotionally abused; when she is being neglected or exploited; or when she is at risk of being abused, neglected, or exploited.

The idea behind section 300 is that under extreme circumstances, society must step into the life of a family in order to protect a child. Section 300 states the circumstances that, in California, warrant such intervention. Section 300 does not mean to suggest that the legislature wishes to prescribe specific parenting methods; rather, this list is meant to define the boundary between acceptable and unacceptable ways of raising a child. Furthermore, the focus of the dependency laws is on both protecting the safety and well-being of the child as well as on preserving the family. California law intends that the family and the child receive a full array of social and health services to protect the child's safety, to prevent abuse from occurring again, and to preserve the integrity of the family.

### 170. What is the difference between a *dependent* of the court and a *ward* of the court?

The circumstances warranting dependency share the common theme that a minor has been abused or neglected, or risks being abused or neglected, by a parent or guardian. A *ward* of the court, on the other hand, is a minor whose behavior merits the court's attention. Thus, in making a child a ward of the court, the law focuses on the minor's behavior, rather than on the behavior of the parent or guardian.

Welfare and Institutions Code sections 601 and 602 list the types of behavior that a juvenile court requires to name a child a ward of the court. Section 601 states that any minor who is beyond parental control, violates curfew, is truant four or more times, refuses to follow reasonable school rules, or violates any law or ordinance may be placed under the jurisdiction of the juvenile court. The juvenile court may then decide that the minor is a ward of the court. Section 602 applies to minors who violate criminal laws. Under section 602, the minor is not formally charged with the crime as an adult would be. Rather than criminally prosecuting the child, section 602 allows the court to consider making the child a ward of the court.

### 171. What is the standard of proof required to terminate parental rights?

Termination of parental rights, the very final step of the dependency process, severs all legal ties between a parent and a child. The United States Supreme Court recognized the profound implications of such an action by the state: termination of parental rights impinges on the fundamental right of family integrity. Because a fundamental right is affected, the Supreme Court held in *Santosky v. Kramer*, 455 U.S. 745 (1982) that the standard of proof required to terminate parental rights is *clear and convincing evidence* (see question 4). Note that the clear and convincing standard is not our strictest standard of proof—*beyond a reasonable doubt* is the highest standard of proof in our legal system. Thus, the clear and convincing standard is a compromise: Because the Court gives great weight to a parent's right to raise a child, the Court "raises the proof hurdle" (see question 5) before those rights may be taken away. At the same time, however, the Court does not want to make it too difficult to remove a child from an unsafe environment. The clear and convincing standard recognizes the possible conflict between a desire to protect the rights of a parent, and the desire to protect the safety of a child.

In 1993, The California Supreme Court rejected the clear and convincing standard. The Court approved the lesser standard of *preponderance of the evidence*, the lowest standard of proof in our judicial system (see question 4). In *Cynthia D. v. Superior Court*, 5 Cal. 4th 242 (1993), the Court examined the process by which parental rights are terminated. The Court reasoned that termination of parental rights is the conclusion of a long and complicated process. According to the California Supreme Court, at the time parental rights are being terminated it has *already* been shown by clear and convincing evidence that the child is a dependent of the court—that is, that the child was abused, neglected, exploited, or at risk of such treatment. To require a standard higher than preponderance of the evidence at this much later stage, reasoned the Court, would be harmful to the child. The California Supreme Court distinguished the California proceeding from the proceeding considered by the U. S. Supreme Court by the number of *previous* findings of fault in the California scheme, and by the seriousness of the resulting danger to the minor should an appropriate decision to terminate parental rights be even further delayed.

### 172. Under what circumstances can a minor be placed on trial as an adult, and so be given an adult sentence?

Placing a minor on trial as an adult is an alternative to making the minor a ward of the court. When a minor age 16 or over commits a crime, the prosecuting attorney may petition (submit a written request to) the juvenile court for a hearing to determine whether the minor should remain in the juvenile court system. If the crime is a serious felony (e.g., armed robbery), there is a *presumption* that the minor no longer belongs in the juvenile court; at the hearing, it is the court's job to decide whether the minor is amenable to the care, treatment, and training programs available in the juvenile justice system. Welfare and Institutions Code section 707 says that, in making its decision, a court should consider the following five factors:

- the degree of criminal sophistication
- whether the minor can be rehabilitated before he is an adult
- previous history of delinquency

- success of previous rehabilitation
- seriousness of the alleged offense

If, after considering these five factors, the court decides that the minor no longer belongs in juvenile court, charges can be filed in criminal court and the minor will be brought to trial as an adult.

Minors 14 and 15 years of age can also be found unfit to remain in the juvenile court if they are charged with committing a serious felony. Such a minor is presumed unfit to remain in juvenile court if the charge is murder. (Note, however, that these presumptions are not binding; the judge has the authority to decide whether the minor will remain in juvenile court or be transferred to criminal court.)

*A cautionary note: This is a highly politicized area of law that is evolving rapidly.*

### 173. What can California criminal courts do to make testifying against an alleged perpetrator of sexual abuse easier for a child?

Any reasonable person would want to make testifying less stressful, burdensome, and traumatic for a child. Attempts to protect a child witness may, however, conflict with certain clauses of the State and Federal Constitution that provide criminal defendants basic rights at trial. The United States Constitution, for example, provides that a criminal defendant has the right to information that could help prove his innocence, as well as the right to confront face-to-face those who accuse him of a crime. These rights are balanced against the interests of victims and witnesses, who deserve sympathy, support, and justice. Courts have recognized that when the victim testifying is a child, special supports may be needed.

In *People v. Sharp*, 29 Cal. App. 4th 1772 (1994), the California Court of Appeal was asked whether the defendant's Constitutional rights were violated when the prosecutor positioned herself so that one of the defendant's alleged victims—a child—did not actually have to look at the defendant while the child testified about what the defendant had done to her. The Court of Appeal held that, in a sexual molestation prosecution, a trial court may allow something less than *literal* face-to-face confrontation between an adult defendant and the child victim. The less than face-to-face testimony is allowed only when the court finds that testifying directly in front of the defendant would cause the child emotional trauma. Such emotional stress, the court reasoned, might impair the child's ability to communicate, and thereby render her testimony unreliable. Although less than a face-to-face confrontation with the defendant is legally permissible, the defense must still be allowed to cross-examine the child.

Evidence Code section 1228 includes another accommodation to child witnesses by allowing evidence other than direct testimony to be admitted. Normally, the admission of such evidence would be a violation of the rule against hearsay (see question 174). As an example, when a minor under the age of 12 makes a statement describing sexual abuse to a law enforcement officer or to an employee of the county welfare department, a special provision applies to how the statement may be used. If the child's statement was made *prior* to a confession by the alleged abuser, the statement may be used in court to establish the elements of the crime, so that the defendant's confession can be introduced as evidence. In this example, the child would not have to take the stand and testify. Under usual circumstances, the individual would have to testify regardless of the defendant's confession.

The court may also close a proceeding to the public when a child testifies about a sex offense. To close a proceeding for this reason, the court has to find that testimony before the general public would likely cause the child serious psychological harm, and that there are no alternative ways of protecting the child.

Additionally, in certain circumstances set forth in Penal Code section 1347, the testimony of a minor 10 years of age or younger concerning a sexual offense may be transmitted to the court via closed-circuit television. In such cases, the child is examined and cross-examined contemporaneously and live, completely outside the presence of the judge, jury, defendant, and attorneys. For the court to allow testimony by closed-circuit television, the minor must recite the facts of the alleged sexual offense and tell of its impact on her. The court will make certain rules about the equipment to be used; the equipment must accurately communicate to the courtroom the image and demeanor of child. In addition, the equipment must be two-way, unless the court finds by clear and convincing evidence that testifying by two-way television would be psychologically harmful to the child. A final protection available to a child witness is the videotaping of the child's testimony at the preliminary hearing. A preliminary hearing is a less formal proceeding that takes place before the actual trial. The child's testimony from the preliminary hearing can then be used at trial, in place of live testimony, provided the judge finds that the child would suffer emotional trauma if required to testify at the actual trial.

These provisions reflect the compelling state interest of protecting a child victim of sexual assault, when the child victim's testimony is needed to bring a perpetrator to justice. The state's interest in protecting a child witness, however, must always be placed in the context of a criminal defendant's fundamental right to confront his accuser. As a consequence, procedures designated for child witnesses are intended to be used selectively, when the facts and circumstances in the individual case present compelling evidence of their necessity, most often because the usual way of taking testimony would be emotionally harmful to the child. The court's discretion to use any of these methods to protect a child witness requires a delicate balance of the child's rights, the rights of the defendant, and the integrity of the judicial process.

## 174. In cases involving sexual abuse, might a therapist ever be called to testify in court about what a child has said?

Courts generally do not allow a witness to testify in court about what someone *else* has said. Such statements—made outside a courtroom and reported by someone who happened to hear them—are hearsay. The law doesn't like hearsay because it is often not reliable and there is usually better evidence available. Occasionally, however, courts will allow hearsay evidence. Courts allow hearsay evidence when there is a special reason to believe that it is reliable and there is no better evidence available to help the court make its decision.

Statements made by a child to a therapist would be hearsay and inadmissible unless they fell within an exception to the hearsay rule. Several exceptions to the hearsay rule have been successfully used to introduce a child's out-of-court statement about abuse, for example, when a child has made a statement immediately following the abuse (the "fresh complaint" exception), when the child has made a statement in response to the shock or trauma of the abuse (the "excited utterance" exception), or when the child has made a statement about the abuse for the purpose of medical diagnosis or treatment. Each of these exceptions is allowed because in each circumstance the child is likely to be telling the truth, and there may be no better evidence available to help the court make its decision.

Finally, the California Supreme Court created another exception to the rule against hearsay in *In re Malinda S.*, 51 Cal. 3d 368 (1990). Under appropriate circumstances, held the Court, a social worker's report may be introduced into a legal proceeding. Such reports may contain statements made by the child that would otherwise be considered hearsay, and the author of the report may be allowed or required to testify in court about the contents of the report. In 1997, the California Supreme Court further extended *Malinda S.* by holding in *In re Cindy L.* (17 Cal. 4th 15 [1997]) that hearsay statements by a child who is incompetent to testify in court may nevertheless be admitted into evidence by a judicially created exception to the hearsay rule.

### 175. Does California recognize common law marriages?

No. Section 300 of the Family Code defines marriage as "a personal relation arising out of a *civil contract* [italics added] between a man and a woman, to which the consent of the parties capable of making that contract is necessary." Section 300 is thus clear that consent *alone* does not constitute marriage. In addition to consent, the parties must obtain a marriage license and the union must be solemnized in order to be recognized by the state. Solemnization requires that the parties declare before a judicial officer (or a religious representative) and witnesses that they take each other as husband and wife.

Although California does not recognize common law marriage, the California Supreme Court has held that a promise to perform certain services, such as homemaking services, may give rise to obligations under contract law. In *Marvin v. Marvin,* 18 Cal. 3d 660 (1976) (a case involving the actor Lee Marvin), the Court held that some nonmarital relationships may implicate the same rights and responsibilities as do civil marriages. Under contract law, explained the Court, an unmarried adult couple is free to agree to share property and income, or to pay support if the relationship dissolves. The Court went on to state that even in the absence of an *express* contract (a contract that the parties explicitly agree to), the law should explore the conduct of the parties, whose actions or reasonable expectations might indicate an *implied* contract. This type of quasi-marital relationship is sometimes called a "Marvin agreement." As a consequence, California courts may hold implicit agreements or understandings—if made in the context of a relationship that closely resembles a common law marriage—legally binding. Ongoing financial support based upon such an agreement has been dubbed "palimony."

# Afterword

*The Essentials of California Mental Health Law* has two important points. If we've made them, we'll consider our book a success. First, laws are not made in a vacuum. Behind each law there is a value or principle the law seeks to advance. Sometimes the value is straightforward. Communications between a patient and her therapist are confidential because we want to promote the mental health of our citizenry and because we respect an individual's right to decide with whom she will share sensitive and perhaps intimate information about her life. At other times the law must balance important goals against one another. While confidentiality is important, for example, confidentiality yields to matters of public safety. When you read a statute, regulation, or case, try to see what value the law seeks to promote or which values the law is balancing against one another. The law will make infinite more sense if you are able to find the spirit behind its letter.

The second point follows from the first: When faced with a dilemma that has legal implications, the process by which you decide becomes as important as the decision itself. Don't begin by asking, "What specific statute or regulation do I need to follow?" Begin by asking, "What's at stake here? What values are at issue, and how can I act consistent with those values?" When uncertain, seek a consultation with an attorney experienced in mental health law. Carefully consider the consultant's recommendations. The process you bring to bear on your decision-making will be your greatest protection against legal troubles.

# Appendix A

## *Central Elements of California Laws Governing Confidentiality, Testimonial Privilege, and Mandatory Reporting*

# CONFIDENTIALITY

## CIVIL CODE
## CONFIDENTIALITY OF MEDICAL INFORMATION ACT

*§56.10. AUTHORIZATION; NECESSITY; EXCEPTIONS*
(a) No provider of health care shall disclose medical information regarding a patient of the provider without first obtaining an authorization, except as provided in subdivision (b) or (c).

(b) A provider of health care shall disclose medical information if the disclosure is compelled by any of the following:

(1) By a court pursuant to an order of that court.

(2) By a board, commission, or administrative agency for purposes of adjudication pursuant to its lawful authority.

(3) By a party to a proceeding before a court or administrative agency pursuant to a subpoena, subpoena duces tecum . . . or any provision authorizing discovery in a proceeding before a court or administrative agency.

(4) By a board, commission, or administrative agency pursuant to an investigative subpoena . . .

(5) By an arbitrator or arbitration panel, when arbitration is lawfully requested by either party, pursuant to a subpoena duces tecum . . .

(6) By a search warrant lawfully issued to a governmental law enforcement agency . . .

(c) A provider of health care may disclose medical information as follows:

(1) The information may be disclosed to providers of health care or other health care professionals or facilities for purposes of diagnosis or treatment of the patient. This includes, in an emergency situation, the communication of patient information by radio transmission between

emergency medical personnel at the scene of an emergency, or in an emergency medical transport vehicle, and emergency medical personnel at a health facility . . .

(2) The information may be disclosed to an insurer, employer, health care service plan, hospital service plan, employee benefit plan, governmental authority, or any other person or entity responsible for paying for health care services rendered to the patient, to the extent necessary to allow responsibility for payment to be determined and payment to be made . . .

(3) The information may be disclosed to any person or entity that provides billing, claims management, medical data processing, or other administrative services for providers or for any of the persons or entities specified in paragraph (2) . . .

(4) The information may be disclosed to organized committees and agents of professional societies or of medical staffs of licensed hospitals, or to licensed health care service plans, or to professional standards review organizations, or to utilization and quality control peer review organizations as established by Congress in Public Law 97-248 in 1982, or to persons or organizations insuring, responsible for, or defending professional liability which a provider may incur, if the committees, agents, plans, organizations, or persons are engaged in reviewing the competence or qualifications of health care professionals or in reviewing health care services with respect to medical necessity, level of care, quality of care, or justification of charges . . .

(7) The information may be disclosed to public agencies, clinical investigators, health care research organizations, and accredited public or private nonprofit educational or health care institutions for bona fide research purposes. However, no information so disclosed shall be further disclosed by the recipient in any way which would permit identification of the patient.

(8) A provider of health care that has created medical information as a result of employment-related health care services to an employee conducted at the specific prior written request and expense of the employer may disclose to the employee's employer that part of the information which:

(A) Is relevant in a law suit, arbitration, grievance, or other claim or challenge to which the employer and the employee are parties and in which the patient has placed in issue his or her medical history, mental or physical condition, or treatment, provided it may only be used or disclosed in connection with that proceeding.

(B) Describes functional limitations of the patient that may entitle the patient to leave from work for medical reasons or limit the patient's fitness to perform his or her present employment, provided that no statement of medical cause is included in the information disclosed.

(9) Unless the provider is notified in writing of an agreement by the sponsor, insurer, or administrator to the contrary, the information may be disclosed to a sponsor, insurer, or administrator of a group or individual insured or uninsured plan or policy which the patient seeks coverage by or benefits from, if the information was created by the provider of health care as the result of services conducted at the specific prior written request and expense of the sponsor, insurer, or administrator for the purpose of evaluating the application for coverage or benefits.

(10) The information may be disclosed to a group practice prepayment health care service plan by providers which contract with the plan and may be transferred among providers which contract with the plan, for the purpose of administering the plan . . .

(12) The information relevant to the patient's condition and care and treatment provided may be disclosed to a probate court investigator engaged in determining the need for an initial conservatorship or continuation of an existent conservatorship, if the patient is unable to give informed consent, or to a probate court investigator, probation officer, or domestic relations investigator engaged in determining the need for an initial guardianship or continuation of an existent guardianship . . .

(14) When the disclosure is otherwise specifically authorized by law . . .

# HEALTH AND SAFETY CODE

*§12105. LIABILITY FOR DISCLOSURE OF AIDS TEST RESULTS; CONFIDENTIALITY OF IDENTITY OF PERSON TESTED AND PERSONS CONTACTED*

(a) Nothwithstanding [any other law], no physician and surgeon who has the results of a confirmed positive test to detect infection by the probable causative agent of acquired immune deficiency syndrome of a patient under his or her care shall be held criminally or civilly liable for disclosing to a person reasonably believed to be the spouse, or to a person reasonably believed to be a sexual partner or a person with whom the patient has shared the use of hypodermic needles, or to the county health officer, that the patient has tested positive on a test to detect infection by the probably causative agent of acquired immune deficiency syndrome, except that no physician and surgeon shall disclose any identifying information about the individual believed to be infected.

(b) No physician and surgeon shall disclose the information described in subdivision (a) unless he or she has first discussed the test results with the patient and has offered the patient appropriate educational and psychological counseling, that shall include information on the risks of transmitting the human immunodeficiency virus to other people and methods of avoiding those risks, and has attempted to obtain the patient's voluntary consent for notification of his or her contacts. The physician and surgeon shall notify the patient of his or her intent to notify the patient's contacts prior to any notification. When the information is disclosed to a person reasonably believed to be a spouse, or to a person reasonably believed to be a sexual partner, or a person with whom the patient has shared the use of hypodermic needles, the physician and surgeon shall refer that person for appropriate care and follow-up. This section shall not apply to disclosures made other than for the purpose of diagnosis, care and treatment of persons notified pursuant to this section, or for the purpose of interrupting the chain of transmission.

(c) This section is permissive on the part of the attending physician . . . No physician has a duty to notify any person of the fact that a patient is reasonably believed to be infected by the probable causative agent of acquired immune deficiency syndrome . . .

# HEALTH AND SAFETY CODE
## PATIENT ACCESS TO HEALTH RECORDS

*§123110. INSPECTION OF RECORDS; COPYING OF RECORDS; VIOLATIONS*

(a) Notwithstanding Section 5328 of the Welfare and Institutions Code . . . any adult patient of a health care provider, any minor patient authorized by law to consent to medical treatment, and any patient representative shall be entitled to inspect patient records upon presenting to the health care provider a written request for those records and upon payment of reasonable clerical costs incurred in locating and making the records available. However, a patient who is a minor shall be entitled to inspect patient records pertaining only to health care of a type for which the minor is lawfully authorized to consent. A health care provider shall permit this inspection during business hours within five working days after receipt of the written request. The inspection shall be conducted by the patient or the patient's representative requesting the inspection, who may be accompanied by one other person of his or her choosing . . .

(e) This chapter shall not be construed to render a health care provider liable for the quality of his or her records or the copies provided in excess of existing law and regulations with respect to the quality of medical records. A health care provider shall not be liable to the patient or any other person for any consequences that result from the disclosure of patient records as required by this chapter . . .

(f) [Health care providers who willfully violate laws found in the Health and Safety Code regarding disclosure or records pursuant to a patient's request are subject to fines or a finding of unprofessional conduct.] The state agency, board, or commission that issued the health care provider's professional or institutional license shall consider a violation as grounds for disciplinary action with respect to the licensure, including suspension or revocation of the license or certificate.

(g) This section shall be construed as prohibiting a health care provider from withholding patient records or summaries of patient records because of an unpaid bill for health care services. Any health care provider who willfully withholds patient records or summaries of patient records because of an unpaid bill for health care services shall be subject to the sanctions specified in subdivision (f).

*§123115. REPRESENTATIVES OF MINORS; RISKS OF ADVERSE CONSEQUENCES TO PATIENT IN INSPECTING RECORDS*
(a) The representative of a minor shall not be entitled to inspect or obtain copies of the minor patient's records in either of the following circumstances:

(1) With respect to which the minor has a right of inspection under Section 123110.

(2) Where the health care provider determines that access to the patient records requested by the representative would have a detrimental effect on the provider's professional relationship with the minor patient or the minor's physical safety or psychological well-being. The decision of the health care provider as to whether or not a minor's records are available for inspection under this section shall not attach any liability to the provider, unless the decision is found to be in bad faith.

(b) When a health care provider determines there is substantial risk of significant adverse or detrimental consequences to a patient in seeing or receiving a copy of mental health records requested by the patient, the provider may decline to permit inspection or provide copies of the records to the patient, subject to the following conditions:

(1) The health care provider shall make a written record, to be included with the mental health records requested, noting the date of the request and explaining the health care provider's reason for refusing to permit inspection or provide copies of the records, including a description of specific adverse or detrimental consequences to the patient that the provider anticipates would occur if inspection or copying were permitted.

(2) The health care provider shall permit inspection by, or provide copies of the mental health records to, a licensed physician and surgeon, licensed psychologist, licensed marriage, family, and child counselor, or licensed clinical social worker designated by request of the patient. The [health care provider] to whom the records are provided for inspection or copying shall not permit inspection or copying by the patient.

(3) The health care provider shall inform the patient of the provider's refusal to permit him or her to inspect or obtain copies of the requested records, and inform the patient of the right to require the provider to permit inspection by, or provide copies to, [one of the named health care providers who is] designated by written authorization of the patient.

(4) The health care provider shall indicate in the mental health records of the patient whether the request was made under paragraph (2).

*§123130. PREPARATION OF SUMMARY OF RECORD; CONFERENCE WITH PATIENT*
(a) A health care provider may prepare a summary of the record, according to the requirements of this section, for inspection and copying by a patient. If the health care provider chooses to prepare a summary of the record rather than allowing access to the entire record, he or she shall make the summary of the record available to the patient within 10 working days from the date of the patient's request. However, if more time is needed because the record is of extraordinary length or because the patient was discharged from a licensed health facility within the last 10 days, the health care provider shall notify the patient of this fact and the date that the summary will be completed, but in no case shall more than 30 days elapse between the request by the patient and the delivery of the

summary. In preparing the summary of the record the health care provider shall not be obligated to include information that is not contained in the original record.

(b) A health care provider may confer with the patient in an attempt to clarify the patient's purpose and goal in obtaining his or her record. If as a consequence the patient requests information about only certain injuries, illnesses, or episodes, this subdivision shall not require the provider to prepare the summary required by this subdivision for other than the injuries, illnesses, or episodes so requested by the patient. The summary shall contain for each injury, illness, or episode any information included in the record relative to the following:

(1) Chief complaint or complaints including pertinent history.

(2) Findings from consultations and referrals to other health care providers.

(3) Diagnosis, where determined.

(4) Treatment plan and regimen including medications prescribed.

(5) Progress of the treatment.

(6) Prognosis including significant continuing problems or conditions.

(7) Pertinent reports of diagnostic procedures and tests and all discharge summaries.

(8) Objective findings from the most recent physical examination . . .

(d) The summary shall contain a list of all current medications prescribed, including dosage, and any sensitivities or allergies required by law . . .

(f) The health care provider may charge no more than a reasonable fee based on actual time and cost for the preparation of the summary . . . It is the intent of the Legislature that summaries of the records be made available at the lowest possible cost to the patient.

# CIVIL CODE
# INFORMATION PRACTICES ACT OF 1977

*§1798.24. PERSONAL INFORMATION*

No agency may disclose any personal information in a manner that would link the information disclosed to the individual to whom it pertains unless the disclosure of the information is:

(a) To the individual to whom the information pertains.

(b) With the prior written voluntary consent of the individual to whom the record pertains, but only if such consent has been obtained not more than 30 days before the disclosure, or in the time limit agreed to by the individual in the written consent.

(c) To the duly appointed guardian or conservator of the individual or a person representing the individual provided that it can be proven with reasonable certainty through the possession of agency forms, documents or correspondence that such person is the authorized representative of the individual to whom the information pertains . . .

(k) To any person pursuant to a subpoena, court order, or other compulsory legal process if, before the disclosure, the agency reasonably attempts to notify the individual to whom the record pertains, and if the notification is not prohibited by law.

(l) To any person pursuant to a search warrant . . .

(n) For the sole purpose of verifying and paying government health care service claims made pursuant to Division 9 (commencing with Section 10000) of the Welfare and Institutions Code.

(o) To a law enforcement or regulatory agency when required for an investigation of unlawful activity or for licensing, certification, or regulatory purposes, unless the disclosure is otherwise prohibited by law . . .

(t) To the University of California or a nonprofit educational institution conducting scientific research, provided the request for information includes assurances of the need for personal information, procedures for protecting the confidentiality of the information and assurances that the personal identity of the subject shall not be further disclosed in individually identifiable form . . .

# WELFARE AND INSTITUTIONS CODE
## SERVICES FOR THE DEVELOPMENTALLY DISABLED

*§4514. CONFIDENTIAL INFORMATION AND RECORDS; DISCLOSURE; CONSENT*

All information and records obtained in the course of providing intake, assessment, and services under [applicable law] to persons with developmental disabilities shall be confidential. Information and records obtained in the course of providing similar services to either voluntary or involuntary recipients prior to 1969 shall also be confidential. Information and records shall be disclosed only in any of the following cases:

(a) In communications between qualified professional persons, whether employed by a regional center or state developmental center, or not, in the provision of intake, assessment, and services or appropriate referrals. The consent of the person with a developmental disability, or his or her guardian or conservator, shall be obtained before information or records may be disclosed by regional center or state developmental center personnel to a professional not employed by the regional center or state developmental center, or a program not vendored by a regional center or state developmental center.

(b) When the person with a developmental disability, who has the capacity to give informed consent, designates individuals to whom information or records may be released, except that nothing in this article shall be construed to compel a physician, psychologist, social worker, marriage, family, and child counselor, nurse, attorney, or other professional to reveal information which has been given to him or her in confidence by a family member of the person unless a valid release has been executed by that family member.

(c) To the extent necessary for a claim, or for a claim or application to be made on behalf of a person with a developmental disability for aid, insurance, government benefit, or medical assistance to which he or she may be entitled.

(d) If the person with a developmental disability is a minor, ward, or conservatee, and his or her parent, guardian, conservator, or limited conservator with access to confidential records, designates, in writing, persons to whom records or information may be disclosed, except that nothing in this article shall be construed to compel a physician, psychologist, social worker, marriage, family, and child counselor, nurse, attorney, or other professional to reveal information which has been given to him or her in confidence by a family member of the person unless a valid release has been executed by that family member.

(e) For research, provided that the Director of Developmental Services designates by regulation rules for the conduct of research and requires the research to be first reviewed by the appropriate institutional review board or boards. These rules shall include, but need not be limited to, the requirement that all researchers shall sign an oath of confidentiality as follows:

As a condition of doing research concerning persons with developmental disabilities who have received services from _____ (fill in the facility, agency or person), I, _____, agree to obtain the prior informed consent of persons who have received services to the maximum degree possible as determined by the appropriate institutional review board or boards for protection of human subjects reviewing my research, or the person's parent, guardian, or conservator, and I further agree not to divulge any information obtained in the course of the research to unauthorized persons, and not to publish or otherwise make public any information regarding persons who have received services so those persons who received services are identifiable. I recognize that the unauthorized release of confidential information may make me subject to a civil action under provisions of the Welfare and Institutions Code.

(f) To the courts, as necessary to the administration of justice.

(g) To governmental law enforcement agencies as needed for the protection of federal and state elective constitutional officers and their families.

(h) To the Senate Rules Committee or the Assembly Rules Committee for the purposes of legislative investigation authorized by the committee.

(i) To the courts and designated parties as part of a regional center report or assessment in compliance with a statutory or regulatory requirement . . .

(j) To the attorney for the person with a developmental disability in any and all proceedings upon presentation of a release of information signed by the person, except that when the person lacks the capacity to give informed consent, the regional center or state developmental center director or designee, upon satisfying himself or herself of the identity of the attorney, and of the fact that the attorney represents the person, shall release all information and records relating to the person except that nothing in this article shall be construed to compel a physician, psychologist, social worker, marriage, family, and child counselor, nurse, attorney, or other professional to reveal information which has been given to him or her in confidence by a family member of the person unless a valid release has been executed by that family member.

(k) Upon written consent by a person with a developmental disability previously or presently receiving services from a regional center or state developmental center, the director of the regional center or state developmental center, or his or her designee, may release any information, except information which has been given in confidence by members of the family of the person with developmental disabilities, requested by a probation officer charged with the evaluation of the person after his or her conviction of a crime if the regional center or state developmental center director or designee determines that the information is relevant to the evaluation . . .

(l) Between persons who are trained and qualified to serve on "multidisciplinary personnel" teams pursuant to [applicable law] . . .

(n) To authorized licensing personnel who are employed by, or who are authorized representatives of, the State Department of Health Services, and who are licensed or registered health professionals, and to authorized legal staff or special investigators who are peace officers who are employed by, or who are authorized representatives of, the State Department of Social Services, as necessary to the performance of their duties to inspect, license, and investigate health facilities and community care facilities, and to ensure that the standards of care and services provided in such facilities are adequate and appropriate and to ascertain compliance with the rules and regulations to which the facility is subject.

(o) To any board which licenses and certifies professionals in the fields of mental health and developmental disabilities pursuant to state law, when the Director of Developmental Services has reasonable cause to believe that there has occurred a violation of any provision of law subject to the jurisdiction of a board and the records are relevant to the violation. The information shall be sealed after a decision is reached in the matter of the suspected violation, and shall not subsequently be released except in accordance with this subdivision. Confidential information in the possession of the board shall not contain the name of the person with a developmental disability.

(p) To governmental law enforcement agencies by the director of a regional center or state developmental center, or his or her designee, when (1) the person with a developmental disability has been reported lost or missing; or (2) there is probable cause to believe that a person with a developmental disability has committed, or has been the victim of [a serious crime] . . . This subdivision shall be limited solely to information directly relating to the factual circumstances of the commission of the enumerated offenses and shall not include any information relating to the mental state of the patient or the circumstances of his or her treatment unless relevant to the crime involved . . .

(q) To the Youth Authority and Adult Correctional Agency or any component thereof, as necessary to the administration of justice.

(r) To an agency mandated to investigate a report of abuse filed pursuant to [applicable law] for the purposes of either a mandated or voluntary report or when those agencies request information in the course of conducting their investigation.

(s) When a person with developmental disabilities, or the parent, guardian, or conservator of a person with developmental disabilities who lacks capacity to consent, fails to grant or deny a request by a regional center or state developmental center to release information or records relating to the person with developmental disabilities within a reasonable period of time, the director of the regional or developmental center, or his or her designee, may release information or records on behalf of that person [when necessary to protect the person's health, safety, or welfare, or under other circumstances specified by this law].

# WELFARE AND INSTITUTIONS CODE
# LANTERMAN-PETRIS-SHORT ACT

*§5328. CONFIDENTIAL INFORMATION AND RECORDS; DISCLOSURE; CONSENT*
All information and records obtained in the course of providing services under [applicable law] to either voluntary or involuntary recipients of services shall be confidential. Information and records obtained in the course of providing similar services to either voluntary or involuntary recipients prior to 1969 shall also be confidential. Information and records shall be disclosed only in any of the following cases:
(a) In communications between qualified professional persons in the provision of services or appropriate referrals, or in the course of conservatorship proceedings. The consent of the patient, or his or her guardian or conservator shall be obtained before information or records may be disclosed by a professional person employed by a facility to a professional person not employed by the facility who does not have the medical or psychological responsibility for the patient's care.
(b) When the patient, with the approval of the physician, licensed psychologist, or social worker with a master's degree in social work, who is in charge of the patient, designates persons to whom information or records may be released, except that nothing in this article shall be construed to compel a physician, psychologist, social worker, nurse, attorney, or other professional person to reveal information which has been given to him or her in confidence by members of a patient's family.
(c) To the extent necessary for a recipient to make a claim, or for a claim to be made on behalf of a recipient for aid, insurance, or medical assistance to which he or she may be entitled.
(d) If the recipient of services is a minor, ward, or conservatee, and his or

her parent, guardian, guardian ad litem, or conservator designates, in writing, persons to whom records or information may be disclosed, except that nothing in this article shall be construed to compel a physician, psychologist, social worker, nurse, attorney, or other professional person to reveal information which has been given to him or her in confidence by members of a patient's family.

(e) For research, provided that the Director of Mental Health or the Director of Developmental Services designates by regulation, rules for the conduct of research and requires the research to be first reviewed by the appropriate institutional review board or boards. The rules shall include, but need not be limited to, the requirement that all researchers shall sign an oath of confidentiality as follows:

> As a condition of doing research concerning persons who have received services from _____ (fill in the facility, agency or person), I, _____, agree to obtain the prior informed consent of such persons who have received services to the maximum degree possible as determined by the appropriate institutional review board or boards for protection of human subjects reviewing my research, and I further agree not to divulge any information obtained in the course of such research to unauthorized persons, and not to publish or otherwise make public any information regarding persons who have received services such that the person who received services is identifiable. I recognize that the unauthorized release of confidential information may make me subject to a civil action under provisions of the Welfare and Institutions Code.

(f) To the courts, as necessary to the administration of justice.

(g) To governmental law enforcement agencies as needed for the protection of federal and state elective constitutional officers and their families.

(h) To the Senate Rules Committee or the Assembly Rules Committee for the purposes of legislative investigation authorized by the committee.

(i) If the recipient of services who applies for life or disability insurance designates in writing the insurer to which records or information may be disclosed.

(j) To the attorney for the patient in any and all proceedings upon presentation of a release of information signed by the patient, except that when the patient is unable to sign the release, the staff of the facility, upon satisfying itself of the identity of the attorney, and of the fact that the attorney does represent the interests of the patient, may release all information and records relating to the patient except that nothing in this article shall be construed to compel a physician, psychologist, social worker, nurse, attorney, or other professional person to reveal information which has been given to him or her in confidence by members of a patient's family.

(k) Upon written agreement by a person previously confined in or otherwise treated by a facility, the professional person in charge of the facility or his or her designee may release any information, except information which has been given in confidence by members of the person's family, requested by a probation officer charged with the evaluation of the person after his or her conviction of a crime if the professional person in charge of the facility determines that the information is relevant to the evaluation . . .

(l) Between persons who are trained and qualified to serve on "multidisciplinary personnel" teams pursuant to [applicable law] . . . The information and records sought to be disclosed shall be relevant to the prevention, identification, management, or treatment of an abused child . . .

(m) To county patients' rights advocates who have been given knowing voluntary authorization by a client or a guardian ad litem. The client or guardian ad litem, whoever entered into the agreement, may revoke the authorization at any time, either in writing or by oral declaration to an approved advocate . . .

(r) When the patient, in the opinion of his or her psychotherapist, presents a serious danger of violence to a reasonably foreseeable victim or victims, then any of the information or records specified in this section may be released to that person or persons and to law enforcement agencies as the psychotherapist determines is needed for the protection of that person or persons . . .

*§5328.01. CONFIDENTIAL INFORMATION AND RECORDS; DISCLOSURE TO LAW ENFORCEMENT AGENCIES; CONSENT; COURT ORDERS*
Notwithstanding Section 5328, all information and records made confidential under the first paragraph of Section 5328 shall also be disclosed to governmental law enforcement agencies investigating evidence of a crime where the records relate to a patient who is confined or has been confined as a mentally disordered sex offender or pursuant to [appli-

cable law] and the records are in the possession or under the control of any state hospital serving the mentally disabled, as follows:

(a) In accordance with the written consent of the patient; or

(b) If authorized by an appropriate order of a court of competent jurisdiction in the county where the records are located compelling a party to produce in court specified records and specifically describing the records being sought, when the order is granted after an application showing probable cause therefor. In assessing probable cause, the court shall do all of the following:

(1) Weigh the public interest and the need for disclosure against the injury to the patient, to the physicianpatient relationship, and to the treatment services.

(2) Determine that there is a reasonable likelihood that the records in question will disclose material information or evidence of substantial value in connection with the investigation or prosecution.

(3) Determine that the crime involves the causing of, or direct threatening of, the loss of life or serious bodily injury . . .

(5) If a court grants an order permitting disclosure of such records, the court shall issue all orders necessary to protect, to the maximum extent possible, the patient's privacy and the privacy and confidentiality of the physicianpatient relationship . . .

### §5328.1. INFORMATION TO PATIENT'S FAMILY; PATIENT AUTHORIZATION; LIABILITY FOR DAMAGES

(a) Upon request of a member of the family of a patient, or other person designated by the patient, a public or private treatment facility shall give the family member or the designee notification of the patient's diagnosis, the prognosis, the medications prescribed, the side effects of medications prescribed, if any, and the progress of the patient, if, after notification of the patient that this information is requested, the patient authorizes its disclosure. If, when initially informed of the request for notification, the patient is unable to authorize the release of such information, notation of the attempt shall be made into the patient's treatment record, and daily efforts shall be made to secure the patient's consent or refusal of authorization. However, if a request for information is made by the spouse, parent, child, or sibling of the patient and the patient is unable to authorize the release of such information, the requester shall be given notification of the patient's presence in the facility, except to the extent prohibited by federal law.

(b) Upon the admission of any mental health patient to a 24-hour public or private health facility licensed pursuant to Section 1250 of the Health and Safety Code, the facility shall make reasonable attempts to notify the patient's next of kin or any other person designated by the patient, of the patient's admission, unless the patient requests that this information not be provided. The facility shall make reasonable attempts to notify the patient's next of kin or any other person designated by the patient, of the patient's release, transfer, serious illness, injury, or death only upon request of the family member, unless the patient requests that this information not be provided. The patient shall be advised by the facility that he or she has the right to request that this information not be provided.

(c) No public or private entity or public or private employee shall be liable for damages caused or alleged to be caused by the release of information or the omission to release information pursuant to this section . . .

### §5328.4. CRIMES AGAINST PERSON BY OR UPON PATIENT; RELEASE OF INFORMATION

The physician in charge of the patient, or the professional person in charge of the facility or his or her designee, when he or she has probable cause to believe that a patient while hospitalized has committed, or has been the victim of [a serious crime] or escape from a hospital by a mentally disordered sex offender as provided [by applicable law] . . . shall release information about the patient to governmental law enforcement agencies.

The physician in charge of the patient, or the professional person in charge of the facility or his or her designee, when he or she has probable cause to believe that a patient, while hospitalized has committed, or has been the victim of assault or battery may release information about the patient to governmental law enforcement agencies.

This section shall be limited solely to information directly relating to the factual circumstances of the commission of the enumerated offenses and shall not include any information relating to the mental state of the patient or the circumstances of his or her voluntary or involuntary admission, commitment, or treatment . . .

### §5328.7. CONSENT FORMS; RECORD OF FORMS USED; COPY FOR PATIENT

Signed consent forms by a patient for release of any information to which such patient is required to consent under [applicable law] shall be obtained for each separate use with the use specified, the information to be released, the name of the agency or individual to whom information will be released indicated on the form and the name of the responsible individual who has authorization to release information specified. Any use of this form shall be noted in the patient file. Patients who sign consent forms shall be given a copy of the consent form signed.

# TESTIMONIAL PRIVILEGE

## EVIDENCE CODE

*§912. WAIVER OF PRIVILEGE*
(a) Except as otherwise provided in this section, the right of any person to claim a privilege provided by Section 954 (lawyer-client privilege), 980 (privilege for confidential marital communications), 994 (physician-patient privilege), 1014 (psychotherapist-patient privilege), 1033 (privilege of penitent), 1034 (privilege of clergyman), or 1035.8 (sexual assault victim-counselor privilege) is waived with respect to a communication protected by such privilege if any holder of the privilege, without coercion, has disclosed a significant part of the communication or has consented to such disclosure made by anyone. Consent to disclosure is manifested by any statement or other conduct of the holder of the privilege indicating consent to the disclosure, including failure to claim the privilege in any proceeding in which the holder has the legal standing and opportunity to claim the privilege.

*§917. PRESUMPTION THAT CERTAIN COMMUNICATIONS ARE CONFIDENTIAL*
Whenever a privilege is claimed on the ground that the matter sought to be disclosed is a communication made in confidence in the course of the lawyer-client, physician-patient, psychotherapist-patient, clergyman-penitent, or husband-wife relationship, the communication is presumed to have been made in confidence and the opponent of the claim of privilege has the burden of proof to establish that the communication was not confidential.

*§1010. DEFINITION OF PSYCHOTHERAPIST*
As used in this article, "psychotherapist" means:

(a) A person authorized, or reasonably believed by the patient to be authorized, to practice medicine in any state or nation who devotes, or is reasonably believed by the patient to devote, a substantial portion of his or her time to the practice of psychiatry.

(b) A person licensed as a psychologist . . .

(c) A person licensed as a clinical social worker . . . when he or she is engaged in applied psychotherapy of a nonmedical nature.

(d) A person who is serving as a school psychologist and holds a credential authorizing that service issued by the state.

(e) A person licensed as a marriage, family, and child counselor . . .

(f) A person registered as a psychological assistant who is under the supervision of a licensed psychologist or board certified psychologist . . . or a person registered as a marriage, family, and child counselor intern who is under the supervision of a licensed marriage, family, and child counselor, a licensed clinical social worker, a licensed psychologist, or a licensed physician certified in psychiatry . . .

(g) A person registered as an associate clinical social worker who is under the supervision of a licensed clinical social worker, a licensed psychologist, or a board certified psychiatrist . . .

(h) A person exempt from the Psychology Licensing Law . . . who is under the supervision of a licensed psychologist or a board certified psychiatrist.

(i) A psychological intern . . . who is under the supervision of a licensed psychologist or board certified psychiatrist.

(j) A trainee . . . who is fulfilling his or her supervised practicum . . . and is supervised by a licensed psychologist, board certified psychiatrist, a licensed clinical social worker, or a licensed marriage, family, and child counselor.

(k) A person licensed as a registered nurse . . . who possesses a master's degree in psychiatric mental health nursing.

(l) A person rendering mental health treatment or counseling services as authorized pursuant to Section 6924 of the Family Code.

### §1012. CONFIDENTIAL COMMUNICATION BETWEEN PATIENT AND PSYCHOTHERAPIST

As used in this article, "confidential communication between patient and psychotherapist" means information, including information obtained by an examination of the patient, transmitted between a patient and his psychotherapist in the course of that relationship and in confidence by a means which, so far as the patient is aware, discloses the information to no third persons other than those who are present to further the interest of the patient in the consultation, or those to whom disclosure is reasonably necessary for the transmission of the information or the accomplishment of the purpose for which the psychotherapist is consulted, and includes a diagnosis made and the advice given by the psychotherapist in the course of that relationship.

### §1013. HOLDER OF THE PRIVILEGE
As used in this article, "holder of the privilege" means:
(a) The patient when he has no guardian or conservator.
(b) A guardian or conservator of the patient when the patient has a guardian or conservator.
(c) The personal representative of the patient if the patient is dead.

### §1014. PSYCHOTHERAPIST-PATIENT PRIVILEGE
Application to individuals and entities subject to Section 912 and except as otherwise provided in this article, the patient, whether or not a party, has a privilege to refuse to disclose, and to prevent another from disclosing, a confidential communication between patient and psychotherapist if the privilege is claimed by:
(a) The holder of the privilege.
(b) A person who is authorized to claim the privilege by the holder of the privilege.
(c) The person who was the psychotherapist at the time of the confidential communication, but such person may not claim the privilege if there is no holder of the privilege in existence or if he or she is otherwise instructed by a person authorized to permit disclosure . . . The word "persons" as used in this subdivision includes partnerships, corporations, limited liability companies, associations and other groups and entities.

### §1016. EXCEPTION: PATIENT-LITIGANT EXCEPTION
There is no privilege under this article as to a communication relevant to an issue concerning the mental or emotional condition of the patient if such issue has been tendered by:
(a) The patient;
(b) Any party claiming through or under the patient;
(c) Any party claiming as a beneficiary of the patient through a contract to which the patient is or was a party; or

(d) The plaintiff in an action brought under [applicable law] for damages for the injury or death of the patient.

## §1017. EXCEPTION: PSYCHOTHERAPIST APPOINTED BY COURT OR BOARD OF PRISON TERMS

(a) There is no privilege under this article if the psychotherapist is appointed by order of a court to examine the patient, but this exception does not apply where the psychotherapist is appointed by order of the court upon the request of the lawyer for the defendant in a criminal proceeding in order to provide the lawyer with information needed so that he or she may advise the defendant whether to enter or withdraw a plea based on insanity or to present a defense based on his or her mental or emotional condition.

(b) There is no privilege under this article if the psychotherapist is appointed by the Board of Prison Terms to examine a patient pursuant to [applicable law].

## §1018. EXCEPTION: CRIME OR TORT

There is no privilege under this article if the services of the psychotherapist were sought or obtained to enable or aid anyone to commit or plan to commit a crime or a tort or to escape detection or apprehension after the commission of a crime or a tort.

## §1019. EXCEPTION: PARTIES CLAIMING THROUGH DECEASED PATIENT

There is no privilege under this article as to a communication relevant to an issue between parties all of whom claim through a deceased patient . . .

## §1020. EXCEPTION: BREACH OF DUTY ARISING OUT OF PSYCHOTHERAPIST-PATIENT RELATIONSHIP

There is no privilege under this article as to a communication relevant to an issue of breach, by the psychotherapist or by the patient, of a duty arising out of the psychotherapist-patient relationship.

## §1021. EXCEPTION: INTENTION OF DECEASED PATIENT CONCERNING WRITING AFFECTING PROPERTY INTEREST

There is no privilege under this article as to a communication relevant to an issue concerning the intention of a patient, now deceased, with respect to a deed of conveyance, will, or other writing, executed by the patient, purporting to affect an interest in property.

*§1022. EXCEPTION: VALIDITY OF WRITING AFFECTING PROPERTY*
*INTEREST*
There is no privilege under this article as to a communication relevant to
an issue concerning the validity of a deed of conveyance, will, or other
writing, executed by a patient, now deceased, purporting to affect an
interest in property.

*§1023. EXCEPTION: PROCEEDING TO DETERMINE SANITY OF*
*CRIMINAL DEFENDANT*
There is no privilege under this article in a proceeding under [applicable
law] initiated at the request of the defendant in a criminal action to determine his sanity.

*§1024. EXCEPTION: PATIENT DANGEROUS TO HIMSELF OR OTHERS*
There is no privilege under this article if the psychotherapist has reasonable cause to believe that the patient is in such mental or emotional condition as to be dangerous to himself or to the person or property of another
and that disclosure of the communication is necessary to prevent the
threatened danger.

*§1025. EXCEPTION: PROCEEDING TO ESTABLISH COMPETENCE*
There is no privilege under this article in a proceeding brought by or on
behalf of the patient to establish his competence.

*§1027. EXCEPTION: CHILD UNDER 16 VICTIM OF CRIME*
There is no privilege under this article if all of the following circumstances
exist:
(a) The patient is a child under the age of 16.
(b) The psychotherapist has reasonable cause to believe that the patient
has been the victim of a crime and that disclosure of the communication
is in the best interest of the child.

# MANDATORY REPORTING

## PATIENTS

## PENAL CODE

*§11161.8. INJURIES OR CONDITION RESULTING FROM NEGLECT OR ABUSE; REPORTS*
Every person, firm, or corporation conducting any hospital in the state, or the managing agent thereof, or the person managing or in charge of such hospital, or in charge of any ward or part of such hospital, who receives a patient transferred from a health facility, as defined [by applicable law] or from a community care facility, as defined [by applicable law], who exhibits a physical injury or condition which, in the opinion of the admitting physician, reasonably appears to be the result of neglect or abuse, shall report such fact by telephone and in writing, within 36 hours, to both the local police authority having jurisdiction and the county health department.

Any registered nurse, licensed vocational nurse, or licensed clinical social worker employed at such hospital may also make a report under this section, if, in the opinion of such person, a patient exhibits a physical injury or condition which reasonably appears to be the result of neglect or abuse.

Every physician and surgeon who has under his charge or care any such patient who exhibits a physical injury or condition which reasonably appears to be the result of neglect or abuse shall make such report.

The report shall state the character and extent of the physical injury or condition.

No employee shall be discharged, suspended, disciplined, or harassed for making a report pursuant to this section.

No person shall incur any civil or criminal liability as a result of making any report authorized by this section.

# CHILDREN

# PENAL CODE

### §11165.6. CHILD ABUSE

As used in this article, "child abuse" means a physical injury which is inflicted by other than accidental means on a child by another person. "Child abuse" also means the sexual abuse of a child or any act or omission proscribed by Section 273a (willful cruelty or unjustifiable punishment of a child) or 273d (unlawful corporal punishment or injury). "Child abuse" also means the neglect of a child or abuse in outofhome care . . . "Child abuse" does not mean a mutual affray between minors. "Child abuse" does not include an injury caused by reasonable and necessary force used by a peace officer acting within the course and scope of his or her employment as a peace officer.

### §11166. REPORT; DUTY; TIME

(a) Except as provided in subdivision (b), any child care custodian, health practitioner, employee of a child protective agency, child visitation monitor, firefighter, animal control officer, or humane society officer who has knowledge of or observes a child, in his or her professional capacity or within the scope of his or her employment, whom he or she knows or reasonably suspects has been the victim of child abuse, shall report the known or suspected instance of child abuse to a child protective agency immediately or as soon as practically possible by telephone and shall prepare and send a written report thereof within 36 hours of receiving the information concerning the incident. A child protective agency shall be notified and a report shall be prepared and sent even if the child has expired, regardless of whether or not the possible abuse was a factor contributing to the death, and even if suspected child abuse was discovered during an autopsy. For the purposes of this article, "reasonable suspicion" means that it is objectively reasonable for a person to entertain a suspicion, based upon facts that could cause a reasonable person in a like position, drawing, when appropriate, on his or her training and experience, to suspect child abuse. For the purpose of this article, the pregnancy of a minor does not, in and of itself, constitute a basis of reasonable suspicion of sexual abuse.

(b) Any child care custodian, health practitioner, employee of a child protective agency, child visitation monitor, firefighter, animal control officer, or humane society officer who has knowledge of or who reasonably suspects that mental suffering has been inflicted upon a child or that his or her emotional well-being is endangered in any other way, may report the known or suspected instance of child abuse to a child protective agency.

(c)(1) Except as provided in paragraph (2) and subdivision (d), any clergy member who has knowledge of or observes a child, in his or her professional capacity or within the scope of his or her duties, whom he or she knows or reasonably suspects has been the victim of child abuse, shall report the known or suspected instance of child abuse to a child protective agency immediately or as soon as practically possible by telephone and shall prepare and send a written report thereof within 36 hours of receiving the information concerning the incident. A child protective agency shall be notified and a report shall be prepared and sent even if the child has expired, regardless of whether or not the possible abuse was a factor contributing to the death.

(2) A clergy member who acquires knowledge or reasonable suspicion of child abuse during a penitential communication is not subject to paragraph (1). For the purposes of this subdivision, "penitential communication" means a communication, intended to be in confidence, including, but not limited to, a sacramental confession, made to a clergy member who, in the course of the discipline or practice of his or her church, denomination, or organization, is authorized or accustomed to hear those communications, and under the discipline, tenets, customs, or practices of his or her church, denomination, or organization, has a duty to keep those communications secret.

(3) Nothing in this subdivision shall be construed to modify or limit a clergy member's duty to report known or suspected child abuse when he or she is acting in the capacity of a child care custodian, health practitioner, employee of a child protective agency, child visitation monitor, firefighter, animal control officer, humane society officer, or commercial film print processor.

(d) Any member of the clergy who has knowledge of or who reasonably suspects that mental suffering has been inflicted upon a child or that his or her emotional well-being is endangered in any other way may report the known or suspected instance of child abuse to a child protective agency.

(e) Any commercial film and photographic print processor who has knowledge of or observes, within the scope of his or her professional capacity or employment, any film, photograph, videotape, negative, or slide depicting a child under the age of 16 years engaged in an act of sexual conduct, shall report the instance of suspected child abuse to the law enforcement agency having jurisdiction over the case immediately, or as soon as practically possible, by telephone, and shall prepare and send a written report of it with a copy of the film, photograph, videotape, negative, or slide attached within 36 hours of receiving the information concerning the incident . . .

(f) Any other person who has knowledge of or observes a child whom he or she knows or reasonably suspects has been a victim of child abuse may report the known or suspected instance of child abuse to a child protective agency . . .

(h) The reporting duties under this section are individual, and no supervisor or administrator may impede or inhibit the reporting duties, and no person making a report shall be subject to any sanction for making the report. However, internal procedures to facilitate reporting and apprise supervisors and administrators of reports may be established provided that they are not inconsistent with this article.

The internal procedures shall not require any employee required to make reports pursuant to this article to disclose his or her identity to the employer . . .

### §11167. REPORT; CONTENTS; CONFIDENTIALITY OF IDENTITY OF PERSONS REPORTING

(a) A telephone report of a known or suspected instance of child abuse shall include the name of the person making the report, the name of the child, the present location of the child, the nature and extent of the injury, and any other information, including information that led that person to suspect child abuse, requested by the child protective agency.

(b) Information relevant to the incident of child abuse may also be given to an investigator from a child protective agency who is investigating the known or suspected case of child abuse.

(c) Information relevant to the incident of child abuse may be given to the licensing agency when it is investigating a known or suspected case of child abuse, including the investigation report, and other pertinent materials.

(d) The identity of all persons who report under this article shall be confidential and disclosed only between child protective agencies, or to counsel representing a child protective agency, or to the district attorney in a criminal prosecution or [to other specified attorneys or agencies for the purpose of investigating reports of child abuse] . . .

(e) Persons who may report pursuant to subdivision (f) of Section 11166 are not required to include their names.

## §11172. IMMUNITY FROM LIABILITY; LIABILITY FOR FALSE REPORTS; ATTORNEYS' FEES; FAILURE TO REPORT; OFFENSE

(a) No child care custodian, health practitioner, firefighter, clergy member, animal control officer, humane society officer, employee of a child protective agency, child visitation monitor, or commercial film and photographic print processor who reports a known or suspected instance of child abuse shall be civilly or criminally liable for any report required or authorized by this article. Any other person reporting a known or suspected instance of child abuse shall not incur civil or criminal liability as a result of any report authorized by this article unless it can be proven that a false report was made and the person knew that the report was false or was made with reckless disregard of the truth or falsity of the report, and any person who makes a report of child abuse known to be false or with reckless disregard of the truth or falsity of the report is liable for any damages caused . . .

(c) The Legislature finds that even though it has provided immunity from liability to persons required to report child abuse, that immunity does not eliminate the possibility that actions may be brought against those persons based upon required reports of child abuse. In order to further limit the financial hardship that those persons may incur as a result of fulfilling their legal responsibilities, it is necessary that they not be unfairly burdened by legal fees incurred in defending those actions. Therefore, a child care custodian, health practitioner, firefighter, clergy member, animal control officer, humane society officer, employee of a child protective agency, child visitation monitor, or commercial film and photographic print processor may present a claim to the State Board of Control for reasonable attorneys' fees incurred in any action against that person on the basis of making a report required or authorized by this article if the court has dismissed the action upon a demurrer or motion for summary judgment made by that person, or if he or she prevails in the action. The State Board of Control shall allow that claim if the requirements of this subdivision are met, and the claim shall be paid from an appropriation to be made for that purpose. Attorneys' fees awarded pursuant to this section shall not exceed an hourly rate greater than the rate charged by the Attorney General of the State of California at the time the award is made and shall not exceed an aggregate amount of fifty thousand dollars ($50,000) . . .

(e) Any person who fails to report an instance of child abuse which he or she knows to exist, or reasonably should know to exist, as required by this article, is guilty of a misdemeanor, punishable by confinement in a county jail for a term not to exceed six months, by a fine of not more than one thousand dollars ($1,000), or by both that imprisonment and fine.

# ELDER AND DEPENDENT ADULTS

# WELFARE AND INSTITUTIONS CODE

*§15610.07. ABUSE OF AN ELDER OR A DEPENDENT ADULT*
"Abuse of an elder or a dependent adult" means physical abuse, neglect, fiduciary abuse, abandonment, isolation, abduction, or other treatment with resulting physical harm or pain or mental suffering, or the deprivation by a care custodian of goods or services that are necessary to avoid physical harm or mental suffering.

*§15610.23. DEPENDENT ADULT*
(a) "Dependent adult" means any person residing in this state, between the ages of 18 and 64 years, who has physical or mental limitations that restrict his or her ability to carry out normal activities or to protect his or her rights including, but not limited to, persons who have physical or developmental disabilities or whose physical or mental abilities have diminished because of age.

(b) "Dependent adult" includes any person between the ages of 18 and 64 who is admitted as an inpatient to a 24-hour health facility, as defined in section 15610.25. "Developmentally disabled person" means a person with a developmental disability specified by or as described in subdivision (a) of Section 4512.

*§15610.53. MENTAL SUFFERING*
"Mental suffering" means fear, agitation, confusion, severe depression,

or other forms of serious emotional distress that is brought about by threats, harassment, or other forms of intimidating behavior.

### §15610.65. REASONABLE SUSPICION

"Reasonable suspicion" means an objectively reasonable suspicion that a person would entertain, based upon facts that could cause a reasonable person in a like position, drawing when appropriate upon his or her training and experience, to suspect abuse.

### §15630. MANDATED REPORTERS; KNOWN OR SUSPECTED ABUSE; TELEPHONE REPORTS; FAILURE TO REPORT; PENALTY

(a) Any elder or dependent adult care custodian, health practitioner, or employee of a county adult protective services agency or a local law enforcement agency is a mandated reporter.

(b) Any mandated reporter, who, in his or her professional capacity, or within the scope of his or her employment, has observed an incident that reasonably appears to be physical abuse, observed a physical injury where the nature of the injury, its location on the body, or the repetition of the injury clearly indicates that physical abuse has occurred or is told by an elder or dependent adult that he or she has experienced behavior constituting physical abuse shall report the known or suspected instance of abuse by telephone immediately or as soon as possible, and by written report sent within two working days, as follows:

(1) If the abuse has occurred in a long-term care facility, except a state mental health hospital or a state developmental center, the report shall be made to the local ombudsman or the local law enforcement agency.

(2) If the suspected or alleged abuse occurred in a state mental health hospital or a state developmental center, the report shall be made to designated investigators of the State Department of Mental Health or the State Department of Developmental Services or to the local law enforcement agency.

(3) If the abuse has occurred any place other than one described in paragraph (1), the report shall be made to the adult protective services agency or the local law enforcement agency.

(c) (1) Any mandated reporter who has knowledge of, or reasonably suspects that, types of elder or dependent adult abuse for which reports are not mandated have been inflicted upon an elder or dependent adult or that his or her emotional well-being is endangered in any other way, may report the known or suspected instance of abuse.

(2) If the suspected or alleged abuse occurred in a long-term care facility other than a state mental health hospital or a state developmental center, the report may be made to the long-term care ombudsman program.

(3) If the suspected or alleged abuse occurred in a state mental health hospital or a state developmental center, the report may be made to the designated investigator of the State Department of Mental Health or the State Department of Developmental Services, or to a local law enforcement agency or to the local ombudsman.

(4) If the suspected or alleged abuse occurred anywhere else, the report may be made to the county adult protective services agency.

(5) If the conduct involves criminal activity not covered in subdivision (b), it may be immediately reported to the appropriate law enforcement agency . . .

(e) A telephone report of a known or suspected instance of elder or dependent adult abuse shall include the name of the person making the report, the name and age of the elder or dependent adult, the present location of the elder or dependent adult, the names and addresses of family members or any other person responsible for the elder or dependent adult's care, if known, the nature and extent of the elder or dependent adult's condition, the date of the incident, and any other information, including information that led that person to suspect elder or dependent adult abuse requested by the agency receiving the report.

(f) The reporting duties under this section are individual, and no supervisor or administrator shall impede or inhibit the reporting duties, and no person making the report shall be subject to any sanction for making the report . . .

(h) Failure to report physical abuse of an elder or dependent adult, in violation of this section, is a misdemeanor, punishable by not more than six months in the county jail or by a fine of not more than one thousand dollars ($1,000), or by both that fine and imprisonment.

*§15631. NONMANDATED REPORTERS; KNOWN OR SUSPECTED ABUSE*
(a) Any person who is not a mandated reporter under Section 15630, who knows, or reasonably suspects, that an elder or a dependent adult has been the victim of abuse may report that abuse to a long-term care ombudsman program or local law enforcement agency when the abuse is alleged to have occurred in a long-term care facility.

(b) Any person who is not a mandated reporter under Section 15630, who knows, or reasonably suspects, that an elder or a dependent adult has been the victim of abuse in any place other than a long-term care facility may report the abuse to the county adult protective services agency or local law enforcement agency.

*§15632. PHYSICIAN-PATIENT PRIVILEGE; PSYCHOTHERAPIST-PATIENT PRIVILEGE*
(a) In any court proceeding or administrative hearing, neither the physician-patient privilege nor the psychotherapist-patient privilege applies to the specific information reported pursuant to this chapter . . .

*§15658. WRITTEN ABUSE REPORT FORMS; CONTENTS; TIMING*
 (a) (1) The written abuse reports required for the reporting of abuse, as defined in this chapter, shall be submitted on forms adopted by the State Department of Social Services . . .

(2) The forms required by this section shall contain the following items:

(A) The name, address, telephone number, and occupation of the person reporting.

(B) The name and address of the victim.

(C) The date, time, and place of the incident.

(D) Other details, including the reporter's observations and beliefs concerning the incident.

(E) Any statement relating to the incident made by the victim.

(F) The name of any individuals believed to have knowledge of the incident.

(G) The name of the individuals believed to be responsible for the incident and their connection to the victim . . .


# DISORDERS CHARACTERIZED BY LAPSES OF CONSCIOUSNESS

# HEALTH AND SAFETY CODE

*§103900. REPORTS FOR USE OF STATE DEPARTMENTS; DEFINITIONS; GUIDELINES; LIABILITY*
(a) Every physician and surgeon shall report immediately to the local health officer in writing, the name, date of birth, and address of every patient at least 14 years of age or older whom the physician and surgeon

has diagnosed as having a case of a disorder characterized by lapses of consciousness. However, if a physician and surgeon reasonably and in good faith believes that the reporting of a patient will serve the public interest, he or she may report a patient's condition even if it may not be required under the department's definition of disorders characterized by lapses of consciousness pursuant to subdivision (d).

(b) The local health officer shall report in writing to the Department of Motor Vehicles the name, age, and address, of every person reported to it as a case of a disorder characterized by lapses of consciousness.

(c) These reports shall be for the information of the Department of Motor Vehicles in enforcing the Vehicle Code, and shall be kept confidential and used solely for the purpose of determining the eligibility of any person to operate a motor vehicle on the highways of this state . . .

(f) A physician and surgeon who reports a patient diagnosed as a case of a disorder characterized by lapses of consciousness pursuant to this section shall not be civilly or criminally liable to any patient for making any report required or authorized by this section.

# Appendix B

## *SAMPLE FORMS AND LETTERS*

Subpoena
Reply to a Licensing Board Letter of Complaint
Informed Consent Letter for a Psychodynamic Psychotherapy
Letter Terminating a Therapy Relationship

# Subpoena

*On the following page is an example of a subpoena.\* The subpoena has a somewhat intimidating quality; most probably because it is intended to intimidate. Remember, though, that a subpoena is a demand for your appearance. Once you have appeared, you have fulfilled your obligation. A subpoena does not allow you to release records or to discuss confidential information, and doing either without a court order or client consent—notwithstanding that you have received a subpoena—will expose you to liability for having breached your client's confidentiality.*

\* Reprinted with permission from *West's California Judicial Forms.*

Joe Smith, Esq. (213) 111-1111
324 Elm Blvd.
Los Angeles, CA 90014

Attorney for Bob Jones

Los Angeles Superior Court
111 N. Hill Street
Los Angeles, CA 90012

Plaintiff/Petitioner: Bob Jones

Defendant/Respondent: William Hubbs

**CIVIL SUBPOENA**                                    Case Number:
 X  **Duces Tecum**                                    A001111111

THE PEOPLE OF THE STATE OF CALIFORNIA, TO:   Dr. Richard Coyle

1. **You are ordered to appear as a witness** in this action at the date, time,
and place shown below **unless** you make a special agreement with the
person named in item 3:

| a. Date: | June 21, 1998 | Time: 11:00 AM |
| b. Address: | 324 Elm Blvd. | |
| | Los Angeles, CA 90014 | |

2. AND YOU ARE ordered to appear in person and to produce the records
described in the accompanying affidavit. The **personal attendance** of the
custodian or other qualified witness and the production of the original
records is **required** by this subpoena.
3. **IF YOU HAVE ANY QUESTIONS ABOUT THE TIME OR DATE FOR
YOU TO APPEAR, OR IF YOU WANT TO BE CERTAIN THAT YOUR PRES-
ENCE IS REQUIRED, CONTACT THE FOLLOWING PERSON BEFORE
THE DATE ON WHICH YOU ARE TO APPEAR:**
     a. Name: Joe Smith       b. Telephone number: (213) 111-1111
4. Witness Fees: You are entitled to witness fees and mileage actually
travelled both ways, as provided by law, if you request them at the time of

service. You may request them before your scheduled appearance from the person named in item 3.

> DISOBEDIENCE OF THIS SUBPOENA MAY BE PUNISHED AS CON-
> TEMPT BY THIS COURT. YOU WILL ALSO BE LIABLE FOR THE SUM
> OF FIVE HUNDRED DOLLARS AND ALL DAMAGES RESULTING
> FROM YOUR FAILURE TO OBEY.

Date issued: June 10, 1998

JAMES H. DEMPSEY

_____

(Signature of person issuing subpoena)

_____

(Title)

# REPLY TO A LICENSING BOARD LETTER OF COMPLAINT

*Your initial response to a licensing board should be a request that the individual who made the complaint provide a release of information. Without a release, providing a substantive response—a response that discloses confidential information—could lay the basis for another claim against you, for breach of confidentiality.*

*Once you receive a release and are prepared to respond to the complaint itself, be sure to consult with your malpractice carrier. Your response to the complaint is "discoverable," which means that if the matter goes to court, the other side's lawyer will have the opportunity to read your letter and possibly use it to your disadvantage. Also, a well-written response is likely to end the matter. For these reasons, it is wise to consult with your carrier as you draft your letter.*

Ms. Curtiss
Board of Psychology
1422 Howe Avenue
Sacramento, CA 95825-3200

April 19, 1998
RE: Complaint #PHD-97-1347

Dear Ms. Curtiss,

I have received your letter of April 14, 1998, that contained a complaint from Mr. Mark Foster. It is my understanding of patient-therapist confidentiality that I am required to have a consent from the patient before I may release any information concerning a treatment.* If you would forward a copy of Mr. Foster's consent giving me permission to discuss this matter with your Board, as well as to share his record with you, I will provide a response to the complaint.

I will assume that the allotted time for my response will not begin to run until I have received Mr. Foster's consent to release information.

Thank you for your understanding in this matter.

Sincerely,

Dr. Saks

---

*The consent to release information should include *all* treaters involved in the patient's care. Thus, an additional paragraph might read:

> I note from my records that I consulted with Dr. Wizner and Dr. Parrish during the course of Mr. Foster's treatment. Because it will be necessary for my response to include their input about Mr. Foster's treatment, I would ask that Mr. Foster also provide consent for Drs. Wizner and Parrish to release information. Mr. Foster's consent for Drs. Wizner and Parrish to release information may be sent to me directly, or to Dr. Wizner and Dr. Parrish at the addresses below.

# Informed Consent Letter for a Psychodynamic Psychotherapy

*Below is an example of an informed consent letter; this particular letter involves a psychodynamic psychotherapy, as the second paragraph explains. Clinicians have <u>very</u> different responses to the idea of using such a letter. While some clinicians find letters helpful in making the frame of a psychotherapy clear at the outset, other clinicians would not even consider using written material to start off a therapeutic relationship, mostly because of what they see as detrimental implications for the transference.*

*Most important is that, at the beginning of your work, enough information is conveyed for your prospective client to make a reasoned judgment about whether to begin a therapy with you. Whether this information is conveyed in a letter, a form, or orally, is not as important as that your client understand the nature of what you do, as well as the essential elements of the frame. Note, however, that the letter contains a significant amount of information, probably more than can be absorbed in a single sitting, especially since most clients are somewhat anxious at a first session. From this perspective, a written explanation of how you work affords a client the opportunity to review what you've said in a more relaxed setting.*

*As this letter makes clear, important aspects of the therapy—such as what gets talked about, how often sessions are held, and how long the therapy lasts—are left to be decided as the psychotherapy progresses. In this sense, the letter does not constitute informed consent; rather, it informs the client about nonnegotiable aspects of your work, and encourages discussion of other important aspects of the treatment. An informed consent letter is therefore best understood as the beginning, rather than the end, of the process of obtaining informed consent.*

May 15, 1998

Dear Mr. Edwards,

I provide a letter when I first meet with someone interested in beginning therapy, to explain important aspects of how I work. I encourage you to read it before we meet next, so that you have the chance to ask any questions you have either about my way of working or about psychotherapy in general. Please feel free to bring the letter to our session.

The work I do is best described as psychodynamically-oriented psychotherapy.* Sessions consist of my listening to what a client has to say and then responding with a comment or question. Sometimes I simply remain silent, in order not to interfere with what a client is thinking or feeling. It is natural and expected for very strong feelings to arise during the course of a psychotherapy; coming to understand such feelings is an important part of the work. While not all psychotherapies meet a client's expectations, and a client's symptoms may become more pronounced during the course of therapy, many psychotherapies do help with painful feelings, difficult memories, or problems in relating to others. Clients should always feel free during the course of a session to discuss their experience of how the psychotherapy is going.

I hold 45-minute sessions, in my office, at 38383 Ventura Boulevard in Studio City. The frequency of sessions and the length of the psychotherapy are aspects of the work that the client and I decide together. Generally, a psychotherapy will continue until the client and I decide our work is complete. It is important to begin sessions on time; my schedule requires that I end sessions promptly, which means that a client who arrives late for an appointment will not have a full 45-minute session.

Messages for me can be left with my answering service (734-1300) at any time. Although I check my answering service several times each day, I cannot be sure of receiving a message immediately, so that arrangements must be in place should an emergency arise. In an emergency clients may go to the emergency room of any hospital, or call 911. The

* Some clinicians may want to provide information about their training and background (e.g., Ph.D. or M.D.).

time to use an emergency room or "911" is when physical safety is at
risk.*

My fee is $110 per session. I bill once per month, on the final ses-
sion of the month. I ask that the bill be paid by the final session of the
following month. If more than two months worth of unpaid payments
accumulate, it is necessary to discuss and agree upon a payment plan
before the psychotherapy can continue.

Clients who use insurance are responsible for co-payments. I encourage clients to read their insurance policies with care; many policies place significant limitations on mental health benefits and it is
important to know what these are. It is also important to know that
using mental health benefits may have implications for future insurance coverage. I ask that clients please let me know if it would be
helpful to discuss such implications; I am happy to do so.

I do not charge for sessions that are missed because of an emergency or ill health when I have at least 24 hours notice. I do charge for
sessions missed with less than 24 hours notice.† Because insurance
companies do not cover missed sessions, clients who miss sessions
without 24 hours notice are responsible for the full session fee. I ask
that clients give at least one week notice of their vacation.

I take approximately four weeks vacation each year. When I am
away, another clinician will provide coverage. I will share with the
covering clinician any important issues the client and I agree the covering clinician should know about, in case the client needs to contact
that person in my absence. The clinician covering for me can be reached
through my answering service.

I have both a legal and an ethical duty to ensure that what a client
and I talk about remains confidential. In addition, both law and ethics
require that I discuss circumstances in which aspects of the work may
not be kept confidential. First, if I have reason to believe that a child,
an elderly person, or a dependent adult is being abused, neglected, or
financially exploited, I am legally obligated to disclose this information to a state agency. Laws that are referred to as "mandatory reporting
statutes" leave me no room for discretion; I must convey my concerns
to the appropriate authorities. Second, I am obligated to break confi-

---

* Therapists who have contracts with managed care companies will need to make sure that
nothing in an informed consent letter is inconsistent with their contract. Thus, therapists
should be sure to read provisions of the contract which concern availability during emergencies, coverage during vacations, billing, and the like.

† Clinicians who work with individuals struggling with substance abuse may want to explain their policy should a client show up for an appointment under the influence. It seems
perfectly appropriate from a legal, ethical, and clinical point of view to treat this circumstance as a missed session.

dentiality when doing so is necessary to protect an individual's physical safety. Finally, certain legal proceedings would require that information be disclosed. If, for example, a client's mental status, emotional condition, or capacity to care for a child is introduced into a legal proceeding, I may be required to turn records over to a court or to testify. Should a client initiate a legal proceeding that places at issue any aspect of the psychotherapy, the likelihood that confidential information will be disclosed is significantly increased. For clients who would find it helpful, I can provide a copy of the actual laws and regulations governing confidentiality. Should the necessity of releasing confidential information arise, I make every reasonable effort to discuss this matter with the client first; it is my preference to make any such disclosures together with the client, in my office.

I consult with other mental health professionals when I judge that doing so would be helpful to the psychotherapy. When speaking with other professionals I make every reasonable effort to disguise identifying information about a client. Any professional with whom I speak is, like me, bound by confidentiality.

I am not an expert in matters involving the law, and do not conduct evaluations ordered by a court. If a client is involved in or intends to commence a legal proceeding in which any aspect of his or her mental or emotional functioning will be examined, it is essential that this matter be discussed as soon as possible.

I am sometimes asked to provide documentation when clients belong to an HMO or are using their  insurance. If I receive such a request, it is my policy not to release material until the client and I have discussed the matter.

Finally, it is important to know that other therapies are available. Clients should feel free to explore other therapies if they find this therapy not as helpful as they would like; I can provide referrals to therapists whose way of working is different than my own.

When we next meet I will leave time for you to ask questions you may have about anything in this letter, or about psychotherapy in general.*

I look forward to our next session,

Dr. Elyn Seagal

---

* Some clinicians may want to mention the law concerning access to records; whether to do so will, of course, entail a good deal of thinking about the clinical implications of raising this issue. (For a description of the California law, see question 115.)

*While this letter covers a great deal of material, two points should be emphasized. First, the letter, in and of itself, does not constitute informed consent. Rather, the letter begins a <u>process</u> of discussing with your client the nature, purpose, and intended outcome of the psychotherapy. Second, in regard to a letter, what's most important is not the substance of your policies concerning billing, missed sessions, emergencies, and the like, but rather <u>that you make your policies clear to your client</u>. Adopt whatever policies make most clinical sense to you— but be sure to make those policies clear as you begin your work.*

# LETTER TERMINATING A THERAPY RELATIONSHIP

*In a letter of termination, be sure to state clearly the reasons for termination, your assessment that the treatment is no longer viable, a plan for termination sessions, any conditions that would precipitate a deviation from the plan for termination sessions, a plan for referring the patient to other treaters, and ways in which the patient may obtain treatment on an emergency basis.*

*Below is an example of a termination letter written by a therapist who has been harassed by a patient. By including each of the elements listed above, the therapist has protected herself from a claim that she abandoned the patient.*

January 26, 1998

Dear Mr. Sheridan,

I am writing this letter to confirm our understanding that our work together will stop as of Monday, February 17. I realize that we discussed the reasons for stopping treatment when we met this afternoon for your weekly session, but I wanted also to write them down in case you had any questions or wanted to review what had been said.

In our first session, we went over how our work together would proceed. My letter of September 17, 1995, in which I outlined our treatment agreement, said that messages could be left with my answering service outside of our regularly scheduled meetings. We also discussed ways to handle emergencies: by going to an emergency room or calling 911.

This past Fall, beginning in September, you began to call me at night, sometimes as late as 11 p.m. I reminded you that you could leave messages with my answering service outside of our regularly scheduled appointments, and that I did not accept calls at home. You said that you understood and would not call me at home again. In late November, and then around the holidays, I received numerous calls from you. When we met for the first time this year, on January 5, I told you that you must stop calling me at home. While you said that you understood our agreement, and assured me that you would not call me at home again, during the week of January 19 you called me at home no less than 15 times. One call came at 3 a.m. On Friday, January 23, you stopped your car and came to my front door. To the person who answered the door you appeared upset and angry that I was not available to see you. You left only when that person threatened to call the police. I am sorry that you are either unable or unwilling to abide by the agreements we established during our initial sessions.

It has become clear to me that we will no longer be able to work together. For this reason, our work will stop in three weeks. Our regularly scheduled times will be available for termination sessions; these will be on February 2, February 9, and February 16. Our work will stop immediately should you again come to my house or disturb my family.

I am enclosing the names of five clinicians and their phone numbers. I have spoken with the first two, Dr. Ronald Smith and Dr. Judith Barney. Both have said that they have times available in their schedules. In addition, you may seek treatment at the mental health center near where you live. I would encourage you to begin contacting possible treaters immediately. I will speak with a treater of your choosing and then send your records to that individual as soon as you sign a release for me to do so. Also, as we have discussed numerous times, and as I explained in my September 1995 letter to you, emergency treatment is available at any hospital emergency room or by calling 911.

If you have any questions, please bring this letter with you to our February 2 session so that we may discuss them.

I will see you on February 2, and hope that our session can focus on how to make this transition go as smoothly as possible for you.

Sincerely,

Dr. Elyn Seagal

# BIBLIOGRAPHY

American Psychiatric Association. (1994). *Diagnostic and statistical manual of mental disorders* (4th ed.). Washington, DC: Author.

American Psychiatric Association. (1995). *The principles of medical ethics, with annotations especially applicable to psychiatry.* Washington, DC: Author.

American Psychological Association. (1992, December). Ethical principles of psychologists and code of conduct. *American Psychologist,* 1597-1611.

American Psychological Association Ethics Committee. (1992, December). Rules and procedures. *American Psychologist,* 1612-1628.

Appelbaum, P. S., & Gutheil, T. G. (1991). *Clinical handbook of psychiatry and the law* (2nd ed.). Baltimore: Williams & Wilkins.

Appelbaum, P. S., Lidz, C. W., & Meisel, A. (1987). *Informed consent: Legal theory and clinical practice.* New York: Oxford University.

Appelbaum, P. S., & Roth, L. H. (1981). Clinical issues in the assessment of competency. *American Journal of Psychiatry, 138,* 1462-1467.

Berkowitz, S. (1979-1996). Legal briefing [column]. *Massachusetts Psychological Association Quarterly.*

Bray, J. H., Shepherd, J. N., & Hays, J. R. (1985). Legal and ethical issues in informed consent to psychotherapy. *The American Journal of Family Therapy, 13,* 50-60.

Caudill, O. B., & Pope, K. S. (1995). *Law and mental health professionals: California.* Washington, DC: American Psychological Association.

Clark, D. C., & Fawcett, J. (1992). An empirically based model of suicide risk assessment for patients with affective disorder. In D. Jacobs, *Suicide and clinical practice* (pp. 55-73). Washington, DC: American Psychiatric Press.

Clark, D. C., & Fawcett, J. (1992). Review of empirical risk factors for evaluation of the suicidal patient. In B. Bongar, *Suicide: Guidelines for assessment, management, and treatment* (pp. 16-48). New York: Oxford University.

Gabbard, G., & Lester, E. (1996). *Boundaries and boundary violations.* New York: Basic.

Grisso, T. (1986). *Evaluating competencies: Forensic assessment and instruments.* New York: Plenum.

Handelsman, M. M., & Galvin, M. D. (1988). Facilitating informed consent for outpatient psychotherapy: A suggested written format. *Professional Psychology: Research and Practice 19,* 223-225.

Handelsman, M. M., Kemper, M. B., Kesson-Craig, P., McLain, J., & Johnsrud, C. (1986). Use, content, and readability of written informed consent forms for treatment. *Professional Psychology: Research and Practice, 17,* 514-518.

Katz, J. (1984). *The silent world of doctor and patient.* New York: Free.

Keith-Speigel, P., & Koocher, G. P. (1985). *Ethics in psychology. Professional standards and cases.* New York: Random House.

McBeth, J. E., Wheeler, A. M., Sither, J. W., & Onek, J. N. (1994). *Legal and risk management issues in the practice of psychiatry.* Washington, DC: Psychiatrists' Purchasing Group.

Millstein, B., Rubenstein, L., & Cyr, R. (1991, March). The Americans with Disabilities Act: A breathtaking promise for people with mental disabilities. *Clearinghouse Review,* 1240-1249.

Nolan, J. R., Nolan-Haley, J. M., Connolly, M. J., Hicks, S. C., & Albrandi, M. N. (1990). *Black's law dictionary: Definition of the terms and phrases of American and English jurisprudence, ancient and modern* (6th ed). St. Paul: West.

*Physicians' desk reference.* (1997). Montvale, NJ: Medical Economics.

Rozovsky, F. A. (1990). *Consent to treatment* (2nd ed.). Boston: Little, Brown.

Soler, M. I., Shotton, A. C., Bell, J. R., Jameson, E. J., Shauffer, C. B., Warboys, L. M., & Dale, M. J. (1998). *Representing the child client.* New York: Matthew Bender.

Tribe, L. H. (1988). *American constitutional law* (2nd ed.). Mineola, NY: Foundation.

West Group. (1998). *West's California judicial forms* (Vol. I, January ed.). San Francisco: Author.

Winslade, W. J., & Ross, J. W. (1983). *The insanity plea.* New York: Charles Scribner's Sons.

Woodward, B., Duckworth, K. S., & Gutheil, T. G. (1983). Pharmaco-therapist-psychotherapist collaboration. In J. M. Oldham, M. B., Riba, & A. Tasman, *American Psychiatric Press review of psychiatry* (pp. 631-649). Washington, DC: American Psychiatric Press.

# INDEX

## INDEX OF CONSTITUTIONAL PROVISIONS

## INDEX OF CASES

## INDEX OF STATUTES

# BY CODE

# INDEX OF REGULATIONS

# INDEX OF SUBJECTS